ENTERPRISE ASSET MANAGEMENT

ENTERPRISE ASSET MANAGEMENT

CONFIGURING AND ADMINISTERING SAP R/3 PLANT MAINTENANCE

Ian McMullan

iUniverse, Inc.
New York Lincoln Shanghai

Enterprise Asset Management
Configuring and Administering SAP R/3 Plant Maintenance

All Rights Reserved © 2004 by Ian McMullan

No part of this book may be reproduced or transmitted in any form or by any means, graphic, electronic, or mechanical, including photocopying, recording, taping, or by any information storage retrieval system, without the written permission of the publisher.

iUniverse, Inc.

For information address:
iUniverse, Inc.
2021 Pine Lake Road, Suite 100
Lincoln, NE 68512
www.iuniverse.com

ISBN: 0-595-32575-0

Printed in the United States of America

The configuration and instructions contained herein have been included for their instructional value. Neither the author nor the publisher offer any warranties or representations in respect of their fitness for a particular purpose, and neither the author nor the publisher accept any liability for loss or damage arising from their use.

"SAP" and mySAP.com are trademarks of SAPAktiengesellschaft, Systems, Applications and Products in Data Processing, Neurottstrasse16, 69190 Walldorf, Germany. The publisher gratefully acknowledges SAP's kind permission to use its trademark in this publication. SAP AG is not the publisher of this book and is not responsible for it under any aspect of press law.

SAP, the SAP logo, mySAP, SAP R/3, SAP R/2, SAP B2B, SAP BW, SAP CRM, EarlyWatch, SAP ArchiveLink, SAPGUI, SAP Business Workflow, SAP Business Engineer, SAP Business Navigator, SAP inter-enterprise solutions, SAP (Word), SAP APO, AcceleratedSAP, Accelerated Solutions, Accelerated HR, Accelerated HiTech, Accelerated Consumer Products, ABAP, ABAP/4, ALE/WEB, BAPI, Business Framework, BW Explorer, EnjoySAP, mySAP.com, mySAP.com e-business platform, mySAP Enterprise Portals, RIVA, SAPPHIRE, TeamSAP, Webflow and NetWeaver are trademarks or registered trademarks of SAP AG in Germany and in many other countries. All other products mentioned are trademarks or registered trademarks of their respective companies.

All screen images, partial screen images, icons, and other graphics contained herein are copyright SAP AG.

About This Book

The focus of this book is to provide the reader with a good understanding of the configuration required to implement SAP R/3 Plant Maintenance, as well as how that configuration affects the day to day use of the system.

Configuration will be explored step by step through the Implementation Guide (IMG). An overview of master data, the work order process, preventive maintenance, and reporting will be provided.

After reviewing other SAP-related documents, a common criticism is that the configuration of the R/3 system is not discussed adequately, if at all. In response to that criticism, this book spends more time discussing the configuration of the R/3 Plant Maintenance module than in discussing the actual day-to-day use of the module.

Some topics associated with the R/3 Plant Maintenance module that could not adequately be covered include Customer Service (formerly Service Management), Classification, Cross Application Time Sheet (CATS), Document Management, Work Clearance Management (WCM), and Archiving. None of those topics are specific to the Plant Maintenance module and, although some of the Customer Service functionality relies on Plant Maintenance configuration, Customer Service also relies on Sales and Distribution (SD) functionality. SAP training specific to Customer Service is recommended in order to obtain a complete understanding of the Customer Service "module." See *Appendix A: Topics Not Covered* for further information regarding the functionality that could not be explored further in this book.

About the Author

Ian McMullan is an SAP certified Plant Maintenance consultant. He lives with his family in Calgary, Alberta, Canada and has been working with SAP R/3, specializing in the Plant Maintenance module, since 1994.

Mr. McMullan welcomes the opportunity to share this accumulation of knowledge with the SAP community.

Acknowledgements

The author would like to thank the following individuals for their part in the accumulation of knowledge that contributed to this book.

Steve Brinkworth	Bernie Lawlor
Lloyd Campbell	Allan Marshall
Tom Carpenter	Jim Marter
Dave Daugherty	Nancy McConeghy
Mike Davis	Jim McNamee
Carina Eckard	Mark Mize
Ranjit Ghosh	Scott Rowlands
Jim Harnage	Anuj Saxena
Ian Heathcote	Bob Schneider
Albert Israel	Tom Swiston
Julie Jones	Keith Terry
Mitch Kastein	Ron Uptergrove
Janet Kearney	Mark Vann
Danny Kieller	Tony Waadevig
Garry Lang	Gord Wenger
Paul Petro	Al Williams
Darren Rothenburger	Terri Wimberly

There are others I would like to thank, but who are too numerous to mention by name.

Since it is impossible for one person to know everything, even if the topic is as narrow as one module of one software system, it is very likely that I have overlooked some functionality, misinterpreted the intention of a function, or was not aware of the ways in which a function could be used.

I would appreciate receiving any corrections, additions, or other comments in regards to the content of this book at book@skira.com. Those whose contributions are used will be acknowledged in any future editions of this work.

It is said that you can learn something from everyone. I have attempted to learn something from each person with whom I have worked and hope to share some of that knowledge here.

Special thanks to Janet Kearney, whose talents have made this book easier to read and understand.

Further Reading

SAP R/3 Plant Maintenance: Making It Work for Your Business, Britta Stengl & Reinhard Ematinger, (ISBN 0-201-67532-3)

Maintenance Planning and Scheduling Handbook, Richard D. Palmer

SAP Authorization System, IBM Business Consulting Services GmbH

Contents

Exploring SAP and Plant Maintenance 1
   Plant Maintenance Background 2
   SAP Background 2
   Plant Maintenance in an R/3 Environment 3
      Re-engineering *3*
      SAP R/3 Instances and Clients *4*
   Concepts and Terminology of R/3 Plant Maintenance 8
      Configuration Data, Master Data, and Transactional Data *8*
   Preparing the System 8
      Cost Centers and Cost Elements *8*
      Bills of Material *9*
      Work Centers *9*

Configuring SAP R/3 Plant Maintenance 11
   The Implementation Guide (IMG) 12
      Transports and Change Requests *15*
      Back to the Implementation Guide—Plant Maintenance Configuration .. *21*
      Security: Authorizations and Roles *22*
      Engineering Change Management *25*
      Number Ranges *25*
   Plant Maintenance-Specific Configuration 30
      Master Data in Plant Maintenance and Customer Service *30*
         Basic Settings 30
         Permits 32
         Make System Settings for Measuring Points and Measurement Documents 34
         Field Selection 35
         Technical Objects—General Data 41

Defining Technical Objects 44
   The Object Hierarchy *44*
      Functional Location, Equipment, Bill of Material 45
      Hierarchical Data Transfer (Inheritance) 46
      Functional Locations 47
      Reference Functional Locations 48
      Equipment 49
      Assets 49
      Bills of Material 50
      Measuring Points 52
   Back to the Implementation Guide (IMG) *53*
      Functional Locations 53
      Equipment 59
      Settings for Fleet Management 66
      Object Links 68
      Serial Number Management 70
      Bills of Material 72
Preventive Maintenance 76
   Preventive Maintenance Overview *76*
   Maintenance Task Lists *77*
   Maintenance Strategies *77*
   Maintenance Items *78*
   Maintenance Plans *78*
      Creating and Maintaining Maintenance Plans 78
      Starting a Maintenance Plan (Scheduling) 79
      Maintaining Maintenance Calls 81
   Back to the Implementation Guide (IMG)—Maintenance Plans *82*
      Basic Settings 82
      Maintenance Plans 83
      Work Centers 85
      Task Lists 90

Production Resources/Tools 94
  Service Contracts 96
The Work Order Cycle 96
  Notifications 97
  Catalogs 98
  Work Orders 99
  Back to the Implementation Guide (IMG)—Maintenance and Service
  Processing *100*
    Basic Settings 100
    Maintenance and Service Notifications 107
    Notification Creation 109
    Notification Content 114
    Notification Processing 119
    Object Information 124
    Condition Indicator 127
    List Editing 128
    Set Workflow for Maintenance Notifications 129
    Set Workflow for Service Notifications 129
  Maintenance and Service Orders *129*
    Functions and Settings for Order Types 129
    Maintenance Activity Type 139
    Costing Data for Maintenance and Service Orders 140
    General Data 148
    User Status for Orders 152
    Scheduling 153
    Production Resource/Tool Assignments 156
    Print Control 157
    Object Information 159
    List Editing 163
    Completion Confirmations 163

Information Systems for Plant Maintenance and Customer Service 172
   The Plant Maintenance Information System (PMIS) *172*
      Customer-Specific Key Figures 173
   System Enhancements and Data Transfer *174*
   Updating the PMIS *179*
End of Configuration 179

Administering SAP R/3 Plant Maintenance 181
Master Data 182
   Functional Locations *183*
      Reference Functional Locations 186
   Equipment *186*
      Object Links 189
   Materials *190*
   Bills of Material *191*
   Work Centers *191*
      Basic Data Tab 193
      Default Values Tab 193
      Capacities Tab 194
      Capacity Header Screen 194
      Scheduling Tab 196
      Costing Tab 196
The Work Order Process 197
   Notification Creation 199
   Work Order Creation 200
   Work Order Release 203
   Work is Performed 203
   Materials are Used 205
   Operations are Completed 206
   Findings (Catalog Entries) are Recorded in the Notification 206
   Work Order is Technically Completed 207
   Work Order is Settled 208
   Work Order is Closed 209

> *Refurbishment Work Orders* *209*
> The Preventive Maintenance Process 210
> > Task List Creation 211
> > Maintenance Plan Creation 212
> > Maintenance Plan Scheduling 218
> > *An Additional Note on Maintenance Strategies* *219*
> > *Performance-based Maintenance* *221*
> > *Work Order (and/or Notification) Creation* *221*
> Reporting 223
> > *List Editing* *223*
> > *The Plant Maintenance Information System (PMIS)* *225*
> > *The Early Warning System* *226*

Additional Resources **231**

Appendix A: Topics Not Covered **233**
> Classification 233
> CATS (Cross Application Time Sheet) 233
> Document Management 233
> Archiving 234
> Customer Service (Formerly Service Management) 234
> Work Clearance Management (WCM) 235

Appendix B: PM Transaction Codes **237**

Index **239**

CHAPTER 1
EXPLORING SAP AND PLANT MAINTENANCE

In this chapter

- Plant Maintenance Background and Concepts
- SAP Background
- Plant Maintenance in an SAP R/3 Environment

Plant Maintenance Background

Plant maintenance is an often-overlooked department of a plant or company where substantial savings and even earnings can be gained. When maintenance is managed properly, materials and labor can be used less in order to achieve cost savings, or more materials and labor can even be used in order to prevent costly breakdowns of equipment, possibly affecting production.

Some of the maintenance philosophies that can help attain such efficiency and cost savings include Preventive Maintenance (PM), Total Productive Maintenance (TPM), and Reliability Centered Maintenance (RCM). Maintenance philosophies will not be discussed to any depth in this book, since they are adequately covered elsewhere. However, an appropriate maintenance philosophy coupled with a computerized maintenance management system (CMMS) such as SAP R/3 Plant Maintenance can attain significant cost savings and a more reliable production or process environment.

SAP Background

SAP was founded in Germany in 1972 and is now one of the world's largest software companies. Its first product was a "real time" accounting system, a departure from the batch-oriented systems of the time. Transactions could be processed immediately ("real time") instead of hours later (batch).

In 1982, the second generation SAP product, R/2, was released for the mainframe computer market. R/2 expanded on the accounting functionality and integrated several other modules, or business functions.

In 1992, SAP released R/3, an ambitious offering that promised to help companies reengineer business processes and integrate those same business processes, all in a client/server environment. Reengineering, integration, and client/server architecture in one package proved irresistible to a great many companies striving for efficiency gains. While the current client/server Enterprise Resource Planning (ERP) product name is R/3, many people refer to the product as well as the company as SAP.

Recently, SAP introduced mySAP.com, an environment that normally includes R/3 as well as functionality originally intended to support an internet-based sales environment. More recently, use of the ".com" suffix has been discontinued and the environment is now referred to as the "mySAP Business

Suite," which includes the R/3 functionality as well as some additional functionality such as SAP NetWeaver and mySAP Mobile Business.

More information about SAP's history and products can be found in many other books and articles.

While certainly not perfect, SAP R/3 Plant Maintenance is robust, its integration with other R/3 modules is excellent, and is suitable for the vast majority of implementations with some configuration.

Plant Maintenance in an R/3 Environment
Re-engineering

In order to avoid implementing a new software system that simply supports existing business processes, in effect spending vast sums of money and getting little improvement in return, the re-engineering of business processes is often performed in conjunction with an ERP (Enterprise Resource Planning) implementation. Without digressing into a formal discussion of re-engineering, which already has many books dedicated to the subject, some of the relevant terminology will be discussed here.

A proper re-engineering project can add a significant amount of time to a project, since it involves discovering and documenting existing business processes ("As-is" processes), discussing and formulating ideal business processes ("To-be" processes), deciding how the SAP R/3 system can best support the to-be processes and where it cannot (Gap or Fit/Gap Analysis). Depending on the size of a particular company, the number of business processes that exists, the scope of functionality to be implemented and other factors, a great many months may be spent on re-engineering business processes. In some cases, substantial gains can be made through a re-engineering of business processes.

Once a gap analysis has been completed, decisions must be made regarding whether to change the R/3 system in order to meet the business process requirements or adjust the business process requirements to meet the system's constraints. In some cases, compromises must be made. It is also important during these decisions to consider that making some changes to the R/3 system (or any system, for that matter) may affect upgrades to the system as they are released. Re-introducing and testing modifications after each upgrade can be a time consuming and costly practice and so modifications (outside of configuration and other SAP-approved methods) to the R/3 system are strongly discouraged. It may be possible to accommodate requirements in other ways, however. If the R/3 system will not meet the business process requirements of a particular company, even after configuration, those requirements should be discussed with experienced consultants.

At the other end of the spectrum, especially in the case of Plant Maintenance, where a relatively small company has only one plant, may be just starting up, and has no business processes in place, it may be possible to dispense with much of the re-engineering process. To do so, a company must be willing to accept SAP's business processes as "best business practices," a requirement for a truly rapid implementation.

To assist with a rapid implementation, SAP has developed Accelerated SAP (ASAP), more recently referred to as ValueSAP, a methodology available to many consulting firms and customers in order to better accommodate a rapid implementation.

A determination, in co-operation with other implementation team members and management, should be made of the level of business process re-engineering, if any, required for any particular implementation.

SAP R/3 Instances and Clients

An SAP R/3 implementation is usually performed with more than one R/3 "system." As with any software and database, the environments where configuration is performed and where new programs are written and tested should not be the same environment where the system is used on a day-to-day basis. SAP accommodates the need for these separate environments with *instances* and *clients*.

An *instance* is typically named for the type of environment it supports, it often has a three-character name, and its data is contained in a separate database from other instances. An instance named DEV, for example, would indicate that development work would be performed on this instance. An instance named PRD, for another example, would indicate that this instance is used for "production," or day-to-day use, and programming, configuration, and testing should not be performed in this instance. Once configuration settings are satisfactory in a particular instance, they will be *transported* to another instance. Transporting will be discussed later. There are typically three or more instances defined. The purposes of each instance include (but are certainly not limited to) development & testing, quality assurance, and production.

A *client*, in SAP terms, indicates a "subsystem" within an instance, and is indicated by a number, usually three digits. A PRD (productive) instance will likely have only one client (that is usable). That instance and client combination may be referred to as PRD100, for example. Other instances may contain a number of clients, particularly if some development, configuration, program development, testing, or training must be done without affecting or being affected by other work currently being performed.

It is common to see a DEV instance with clients such as 100, 200, 300, and so on defined. In such a case, DEV100 may be the instance/client that is considered the "clean" source for the configuration that will be used in the production instance & client, perhaps PRD100. DEV200 might be used for configuration testing. While much configuration is client-specific (if it is configured in DEV200, for example, it only affects DEV200), some configuration is cross-client or not client specific (if it is configured in DEV200, it affects every client in the DEV instance—100, 200, 300, and so on). Usually, the system will provide a warning that a configuration step is cross-client.

Programming (ABAP programming and so on) is usually cross-client. If a programmer activates a program in DEV300, for example, it will affect DEV100, DEV200, DEV300, and so on. It is for this reason, in part, that during some SAP R/3 implementations, a separate instance may be reserved for program testing.

Keep in mind that the R/3 system is integrated. While it is beneficial to perform some configuration and testing for one module in isolation from other modules' configuration to avoid affecting each other while testing, configuration for the modules must be tested together at some point.

Testing module configuration is often performed first as *unit testing*, to ensure that the module's functionality operates as expected. For unit testing, scripts (lists of steps to be performed) are created beforehand, containing step-by-step instructions for the processes to be tested along with the data to be used for the testing and the expected results. The actual results are recorded beside the expected results, comparisons are made, and differences and issues are then resolved. Unit testing is an iterative process and, as adjustments are made to configuration and/or data, the tests are repeated until the results are satisfactory.

Once unit testing has successfully been completed for all of the modules, *integration testing* can be performed. Again, scripts are created beforehand, but some cooperation is required by representatives of each module. The scripts must include each step to be performed according to a process that is not restricted to a specific module. From a Plant Maintenance perspective, a work order process script could include steps to be performed by Plant Maintenance (creating the notification & work order), Controlling (the cost centers, activity types, and settlement to be used), Materials Management (the materials to be used, their costs and quantities), and any other module required to perform the process. Expected results are noted on the script, which is often created in a Microsoft Excel spreadsheet, and compared to actual results recorded by the testers.

An integration script is often tested by several people, and is passed from person to person to complete each step or group of steps, somewhat resembling the actual process that would take place. For integration testing, it is also a good idea to have security in place (roles, authorizations, etc.) and assigned to each person/team as it would be in an actual "live" environment. During the testing, discrepancies in the security can be determined as well as discrepancies in the process itself.

As with unit testing, integration testing is an iterative process and must be repeated, making adjustments as required after each test, until all testers/groups/teams are satisfied that the processes are working as expected. A representative of each team should sign each integration test script to verify that it has tested acceptably from the perspective of that module.

Transporting configuration settings in the Implementation Guide (IMG) from one instance to another should only be performed from the same client number every time, in order to provide some control, consistency, and data integrity. An example might be to experiment with different configuration settings in DEV400 (development instance, client 400), and then perform the satisfactory configuration settings in DEV100 (development instance, client 100) for transport to QAS100 (quality assurance instance, client 100). There, further testing, particularly integration testing with other modules, may take place. Once satisfied, the configuration settings will then be transported to PRD100 (production instance, client 100). There may be more instances defined for a particular implementation and there will certainly be more clients defined. Transporting into the production instance may be performed from the development instance or the quality assurance instance, depending on how the instances and controls have been set up for a particular implementation.

Any configuration performed in a given instance cannot affect another instance (DEV, QAS, PRD, etc.) without transporting, but some configuration, as mentioned previously, performed in a given client (010, 100, 200 etc.) may affect other clients within the same instance. In addition to the terms discussed previously, *client-specific* and *cross-client*, configuration that does not affect a different client may also be referred to as *client-dependent* and configuration that does affect other clients in the same instance is regarded as *client-independent*, often a source of confusion.

Client-dependent (also sometimes called "*client-specific*") configuration data will only be defined, changed, and deleted in the client where the definition, change, or deletion was performed. The configuration will not be changed in any other client.

Client-independent (also sometimes called "*cross-client*") configuration data will be defined, changed, or deleted in ALL clients in the same instance, regardless of which client the definition, change, or deletion was performed. The R/3 system will usually provide a warning that client-independent data is about to be changed.

In any case, there should be one "clean" instance/client that will be the source for any configuration to be transported to the production (productive) SAP R/3 environment. In the previous example, that instance/client was DEV100. Only configuration that has been tested acceptably elsewhere should be performed in that client, and no data should exist in that client. Of course, there may be some minor exceptions to the "no data" rule, but there should not be any transactional data in that client. A valid exception to the rule is when specific master data must be already created in order to use it as a default setting during configuration.

If master data, and especially transactional data, has been entered into the "clean" instance/client, it can make it difficult to change or delete configuration items that are no longer required at a later date. If transactional data has been entered, it can make it even more difficult, if not impossible, to eventually change or delete configuration items that are no longer required.

Work with the basis team members, who are normally responsible for the definition and maintenance of the SAP R/3 instances and clients, to ensure that the environment is used as it is intended.

Concepts and Terminology of R/3 Plant Maintenance

Configuration Data, Master Data, and Transactional Data

In the SAP R/3 system, there are three basic types of data. *Configuration data* is usually defined in the Implementation Guide (IMG), and consists of data such as plants, object types, units of measure, and so on. This data, once configured, is rarely changed but if changes are required, they are most often performed in another SAP instance (system) and, when tested appropriately, are "transported" to the SAP R/3 production environment. Configuration data is often used to provide valid values in *matchcode* searches (pull-down/drop-down menus).

Master data, which is entered and changed on an ongoing basis, but not usually frequently, is mostly used to define equipment, bills of materials, and so on. For example, once a piece of equipment has been defined, it is unlikely to change very often.

The other basic type of data is *transactional data*, which consists of information entered into the system on a day-to-day basis, such as work orders. While master data is largely static and does not change often, transactional data is provided and/or changes often. After a work order is created, for example, various changes may be made to the work order, such as planned labor and materials.

Configuration data, master data, and transactional data are also discussed in the Administration Section, on page 143.

It would be beneficial to consider the expected volume of transactional data into the system in order to plan for sufficient storage space for the data. In addition, plan for the length of time for which to retain data in the system, after which time the data should be archived and deleted from the system in order to control storage requirements and improve system response.

Preparing the System

Cost Centers and Cost Elements

If the cost of maintenance is of even the slightest interest, cost centers and cost elements must be defined from the CO (Controlling) module. Costs incurred by work orders may be settled to cost centers. Cost centers are also used to determine the rate at which people are charged to work orders. Work with accounting/controlling personnel to determine the cost centers that may have been defined or that may need to be defined as well as levels at which to accumulate maintenance costs.

Bills of Material

Before bills of material can be defined for any module, the materials that make up the bill of materials must first be defined, typically from the MM (Materials Management) module. Work with those responsible for the maintenance of material records to define materials required for BOM use.

If material costs are of interest, ensure that any materials required are defined as valuated materials. It is not necessary to define materials required for Plant Maintenance use as Spare Parts. All materials used for Plant Maintenance are regarded as Spare Parts. Use another appropriate material type for materials required for Plant Maintenance use.

Any materials that may be refurbished or machined can be defined with a split valuation. This will allow the individual materials to be withdrawn from inventory/stores, refurbished or machined, and returned to stores with a different value. Inventory levels are maintained, but stock value changes to reflect the possibly reduced value of the materials. There is a refurbishment work order in the Plant Maintenance module to accommodate this function, which will be discussed later.

Although the Plant Maintenance module can use bills of material defined for the use of other modules, it is a better policy to develop bills of material strictly for Plant Maintenance use. Changes to bills of material can then be made without a lengthy analysis of the effect of the changes.

Work Centers

Plant Maintenance Work Centers are based on the same functionality as Production Planning Work Centers in the R/3 system. That is, an entity with a finite capacity for work can be defined as a *Work Center*, whether it is a person or a machine.

There are many fields on several screens available to define a work center. The behavior of the screens for Plant Maintenance use can be controlled somewhat in the configuration of the Plant Maintenance module.

For more information regarding Plant Maintenance work centers, refer to the section on work centers on page 85.

Chapter 2
Configuring SAP R/3 Plant Maintenance

In this chapter

- Transports and Change Requests
- Plant Maintenance Configurations
- Other Necessary Configurations

Long before anyone can use the R/3 system on a daily basis, the system must be configured and populated with master data. During configuration, decisions are made that will affect how the system will be used and data is provided that will guide those who will use the system.

While it is possible to configure the Plant Maintenance module in as little as two or three months [1], some configuration of other modules, such as FI, CO, and MM will already be in place or be configured with the PM module. In addition, a rapid configuration will require the acceptance of default master data that has been provided by SAP. It is not recommended to attempt a rapid implementation without experienced guidance. Time spent on each decision will extend the implementation, sometimes significantly. An experienced consultant, for example, should be able to explain where it is necessary to spend time on decisions, some of which will affect the use of the system months or even years from now. At least some configuration is required in order to achieve some benefit from the use of the system.

The following chapters will provide some guidance for configuring the Plant Maintenance module, but cannot replace an experienced person who can assist with tailoring the configuration for a particular industry or company.

The Implementation Guide (IMG)

The SAP R/3 Implementation Guide, often referred to as the IMG, is where the R/3 system is configured for the requirements of a company. There are two possible "levels" of the IMG:

SAP Reference IMG

The SAP Reference IMG provides all of the possible configuration steps provided by SAP, regardless of whether they are required or desired.

---

[1] *The Plant Maintenance module could, in fact, be configured in two to three days, but without regard to any requirements or integration with other modules, and by accepting many of the default settings provided by SAP, whether suitable or not.*

Project IMG

One or more Project IMGs can be created as subsets of the Reference IMG. It is sometimes preferable to minimize the number of Project IMGs in order to centralize management and documentation of the projects. However, as discussed later, it may be preferable to create separate Project IMGs to provide a more thorough checklist for each configuration team.

Enterprise IMG

The Enterprise IMG, which provided an intermediate reduction of the IMG, was removed as of SAP R/3 version 4.6.

While it is possible to configure the system through the SAP Reference IMG, it is not advisable to do so during an implementation project, since a Project IMG allows for some project management, documentation, and control over the configuration process. Once the initial implementation project has been completed, minor changes are better suited to the SAP Reference IMG.

It may be beneficial to create a separate project for a Plant Maintenance implementation in the project area of the Implementation Guide (IMG). Having the R/3 system generate a project specifically for PM will provide a thorough checklist of all of the configuration points that affect Plant Maintenance, including configuration steps outside of the Plant Maintenance section of the IMG. Some of the resulting steps may be configured already, may be configured by another module's configuration team, or they may still need to be configured. However, having all of the relevant configuration steps in the list makes it less likely that any will be overlooked and may help with some of the integration points with other modules.

Before attempting to create a Project IMG, determine whether one has already been created for that purpose. There may be reasons at a project management level for not creating a Project IMG, so obtain agreement from the project manager(s) before attempting to create one.

If a Project IMG is created for Plant Maintenance, it will include configuration steps that are outside of the Plant Maintenance module. Some of those configuration steps are normally the responsibility of others and should remain so. They are included primarily to indicate that those configuration steps affect the Plant Maintenance module in some way. Depending on other modules that have been configured, are being configured, or are about to be

14 • Enterprise Asset Management

configured, there are few steps outside of the Plant Maintenance module itself that need to be configured by the Plant Maintenance team.

The Implementation Guide (IMG) can be found through transaction code SPRO or by following the menu path **Tools → Customizing → IMG → Edit Project** (see *Figure 1*).

```
▽ 📁 SAP menu
    ▷ 📁 Office
    ▷ 📁 Cross-Application Components
    ▷ 📁 Logistics
    ▷ 📁 Accounting
    ▷ 📁 Human Resources
    ▷ 📁 Information Systems
    ▽ 📁 Tools
        ▷ 📁 ABAP Workbench
        ▽ 📁 Customizing
            ▽ 📁 IMG
                📦 SPRO - Edit Project
                📦 SPRO_ADMIN - Project Management
                📦 SCU3 - IMG Logging
                📦 SST0 - Project Analysis
                📦 SE10 - Transport Organizer (Extended View)
            ▷ 📁 Business Configuration Sets
                📦 SCU0 - Customizing Cross-System Viewer
        ▷ 📁 Administration
```

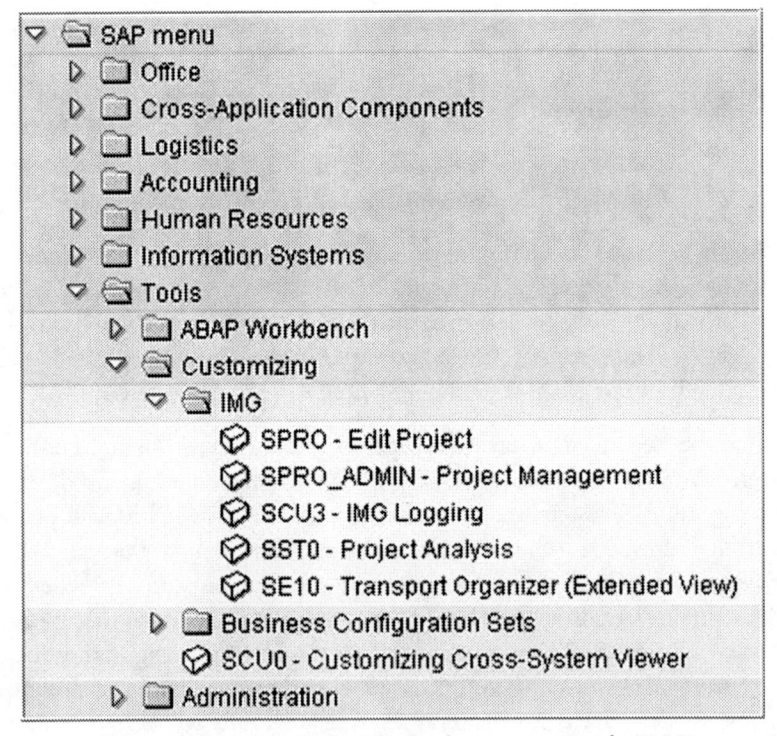

Figure 1. The Menu Path to the Implementation Guide (IMG)
© *SAP AG*

Note that the menu path displayed in *Figure 1* shows the transaction codes as well as the description of each transaction. For example, the transaction code "SPRO" is displayed next to the description "Edit Project." The display of the transaction codes can be turned on or off through the menus at the top of the screen (not shown in *Figure 1*). To do so, follow the menu **Extras → Settings** and check or uncheck the *Display technical names* checkbox. The first two other options in the Settings window are self-explanatory; while the option *Do not display screen* simply removes the "picture" that may be displayed alongside the menu. Checking this box is not recommended in cases where the "picture" may also contain information (the picture image can be changed and, in some cases, it may be used to provide information regarding the system).

Once in the transaction code (SPRO or Edit Project) mentioned above (or following the menu path shown in *Figure 1*), to create a Project IMG, follow the further menu path **Goto → Project Management**. When in the "Customizing: Project Administration" screen, click on the "Create Project" button (on the left) and, when prompted, provide an ID for the project. On the following screen, provide a name for the project. Depending on the level of actual project management to be performed with this functionality, there are additional options available in the tabs on this screen. For example, the ability to define status codes that can be used to indicate the status of each step of the project can be defined here. Save the project. On the "Scope" tab, although there is an option to specify the IMG steps to include if desired, click the "Generate Project IMG" button at the bottom of the screen.

A project IMG would be used primarily to ensure that each required step has been addressed, has been documented, and the status of each step is maintained and tracked. The project IMG provides a measure of tracking and control. The Reference IMG would be used when there is no need to plan, control and track which steps are to be configured or have been configured. For example, there is no need to record the steps' status, or to document the steps configured within the SAP R/3 system itself.

Although time-consuming, it is often a good idea to keep a log, outside of the SAP system, regarding which IMG steps have been configured and how, particularly during an implementation project. The initial configuration of a system is often performed first in a "sandbox" system (client), so that different types of configuration can be tested. Record in the log the "final" configuration performed. Once the intended final configuration is determined, the configuration is then repeated manually, with the assistance of previously-recorded log, in the "clean" client as previously discussed. This client becomes the source from which to transport the "good" configuration to the production/productive client. The benefits of having created such a log will become more apparent in time.

Transports and Change Requests

As discussed earlier, SAP "systems" are organized into "instances, " each of which contains one or more "clients." Examples of instances are DEV (for development and configuration), QAS (for quality assurance) and PRD (for the productive system). There may be more instances, but rarely less.

Each instance (DEV, QAS, PRD, etc.) may consist of more than one client. The clients are typically identified by a three-digit number, such as 100, 110, 120, 200, etc. Each client within an instance can share SAP R/3 programs, but will have its own transactional data. Some configuration will affect all of the clients in an instance, but some configuration will only affect the client in which it has been performed.

Each unique combination of instance and client is identified as "DEV100," "DEV 120" and "QAS100," for example. Since the productive/production instance normally contains only one (accessible) client, it is often referred to simply as "PRD." Instances and clients will be discussed again later.

In order to transport configuration changes to another SAP instance, the changes must be included in a "change request." One or more configuration changes can be included in the same change request, or each configuration change can have its own change request. Consult with the project team and/or the basis team to determine the best approach for transporting change requests. If each configuration change generates its own change request, many change requests can be time consuming for the basis team (or the person/group responsible for the correction and transport system (CTS)) to transport. However, many configuration changes included in the same change request can make it difficult or impossible to exclude a portion of the change request if later required.

Once a configuration step has been completed, when attempting to save the changes, a prompt, "Prompt for Customizing request," will appear. This prompt provides the opportunity to include the configuration change in an existing change request or to create a new change request for the change. To create a new change request, click on the "Create request" [Create request] button and provide a description of the change. Of course, if the change request will include more than one configuration change, the description should reflect that. It is a good idea to prefix the description with the two-character designation of the module being configured. For example, begin the change request description with "PM—" and continue with a description of the configuration change(s) (see *Figure 2*). It is not helpful to anyone if the description is "Change request," for example.

- NOTE: In some instances, the "Prompt for Customizing Request" window will not appear. This can happen if a change request has already been created for this step in the same session, if the object is not transportable, or if a change request must be manually created. If it is necessary, to manually create a change request, use the menu path Table View → Transport from the appropriate configuration screen.

Depending on the project, it may also be necessary to provide a "Target" system/client in the "Create Request" window. If not instructed to do so, leave the "Target" field blank.

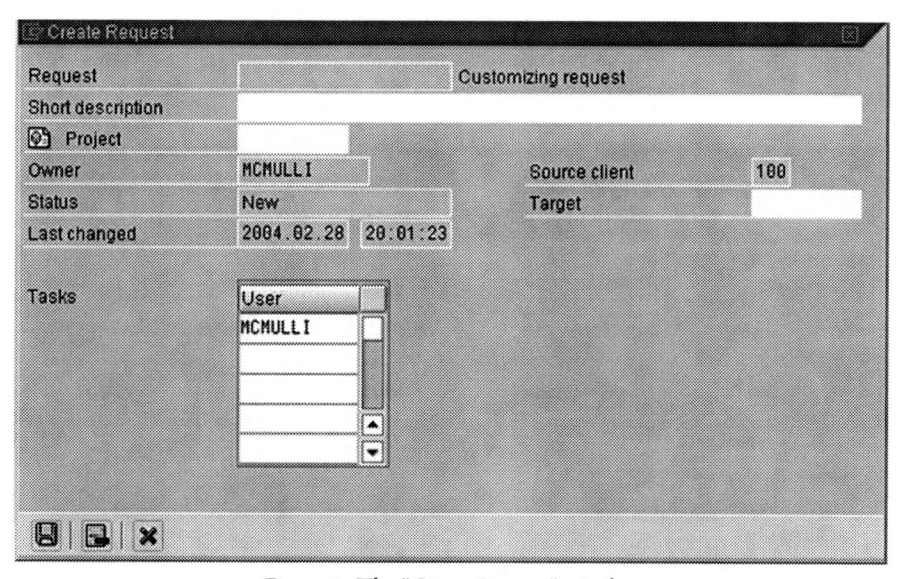

Figure 2. The "Create Request" window.
© *SAP AG*

When the change request is saved, record the change request number (assigned automatically after clicking the "Save" button) along with the description. Since the first transport of the change request will usually be to a test client, the change request will be required to be transported again to a different client. A list of change requests may be useful for this purpose.

Now that the configuration change is included in a change request, the change request must be released before it can be transported. Since this function is sometimes regarded as a security function, the responsibility of releasing change requests, and the tasks within them, may be assigned to the person who performed the configuration or someone else. Determine the proper procedure.

Releasing change requests and the tasks within them can be performed outside the IMG by using the transaction SE10 or by following the menu path (outside of the IMG) **Tools → Customizing → IMG → Transport Organizer (Extended View)**. For normal configuration steps not yet released that have been performed by the same person, the default settings on the screen are usually adequate. See *Figure 3*. Click the "Display" button at the bottom of the options. The list of change requests created by this user will be displayed as shown in *Figure 4*.

Although as noted previously, changes to the default setting are not usually required in order to view change requests that have not yet been transported. However, in order to view change requests that have already been transported to at least one other instance, the "Released" checkbox must be checked.

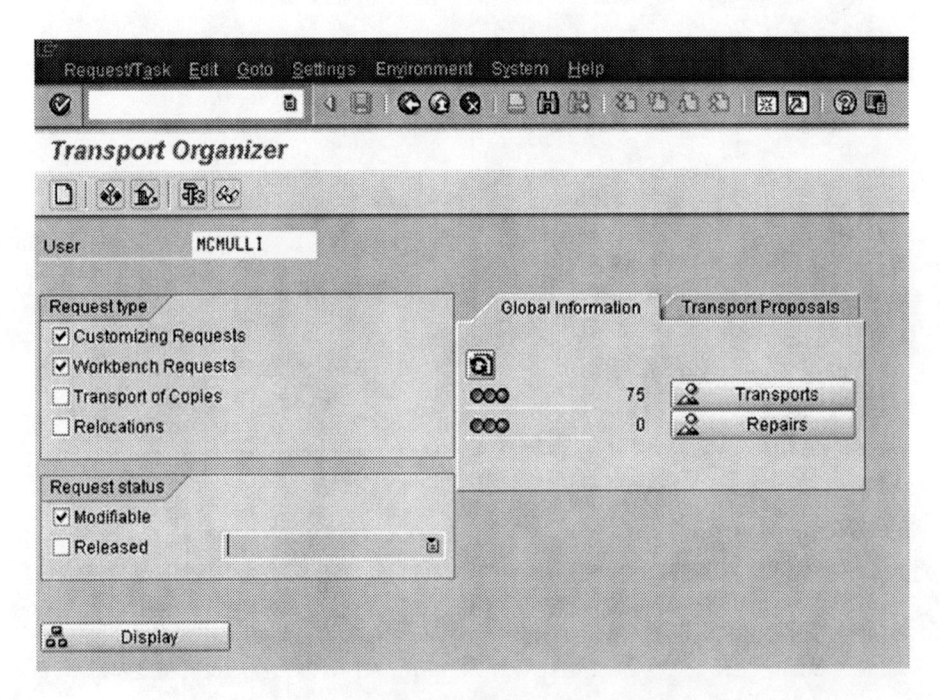

Figure 3. The "Transport Organizer" window.
© *SAP AG*

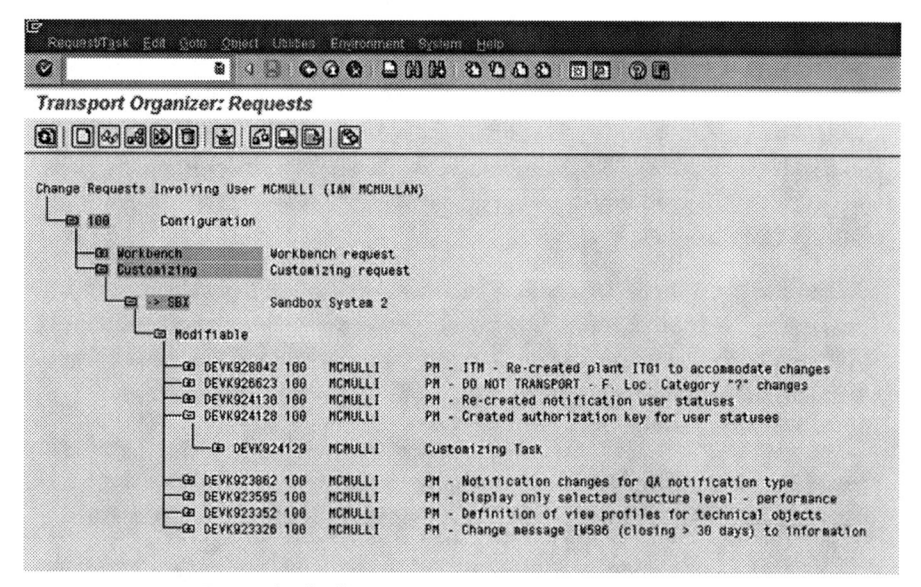

Figure 4. The "Transport Organizer: Requests" window.
© SAP AG

Before the change request can be released, each task within the change request must be released. Click the plus sign (+) to the left of the appropriate change request to expand the folder and display the tasks within the change request. *Figure 4* shows one change request where the plus sign (+) has been clicked and the task is now displayed. It is not necessary to click any further plus signs unless viewing the configuration data changed is desired.

Click once on the task (it will say "Customizing Task" to the right) to be released.

Click the "Release" button on the button bar near the top of the screen.

Depending on how the Correction and Transport System is defined, it may be necessary to save any required comments/reasons on a text screen, saving the text and exiting from the text screen before continuing. The task (not the change request itself) should now display a check mark beside it.

Back on the screen as displayed in *Figure 4*, click once on the change request itself (it will have the description previously entered beside it—in *Figure 4*, the change request with the task displayed is "PM—Created authorization key for user statuses.").

Click the "Release" button again.

Once again, the above steps may or may not be accessible, depending on whose role it is to release tasks and change requests. In some cases, the task may have to be released by someone with authorization to do so, while in other cases the task can be released by the owner, but the change request itself may have to be released by someone with the authorization to do so. In still other cases, the owner of the change request/task(s) may have the authorization to release both.

When the above steps have been completed, the change request(s) can then be transported to another system (instance). This is most often the responsibility of the basis team and there is often an approval process before the basis team can perform the transport, particularly into a productive/production client.

Note that transports are not reversible and cannot be "undone, " except by changing the configuration once again in the original system, creating a change request, and transporting the change request to the target system.

Usually, change requests are transported to a quality assurance type of environment (instance) initially. After the appropriate testing, including integration testing, has been satisfactorily performed in that instance, the same change request can then be transported to the production instance and any other instances and clients in which it is required.

For example, if the configuration/development instance is named DEV and the client for the source of "clean" configuration is 100, change requests will be transported from DEV100. The first transport of the change request might be to QAS100 (the quality assurance instance) for testing (as discussed before, if the change was client independent or cross-client, it will be transported to all of the clients in QAS). After successful testing, the change request can then be transported to the PRD instance (PRD100, for example). It is recommended at this point that the change request also be transported to any other instances and clients in order to maintain consistency. By doing so, it is more certain that if a test is performed acceptably in one instance/client, it will be performed acceptably in the other instances/clients.

In summary:

- Determine what configuration works in a "sandbox" instance/client (DEV200, for example)
- "Good" configuration is performed again in a "clean" instance/client (with little or no data. DEV100, for example).

- Configuration is transported from the "clean" instance/client (DEV100) to a "test/quality assurance" instance/client (containing data. QAS100, for example). Changes are made to the "sandbox" (DEV200) and "clean" (DEV100) clients if required, transported to the "test" client (QAS100) and re-tested.

- Configuration is transported from the "clean" instance/client (DEV100) to the "productive" client (PRD100, for example).

- Transports should not be performed from the "test" (quality assurance) instance/client to the "productive" instance/client.

- Direct changes to configuration should not be permitted in either the "test" (QAS100) or the "productive" (PRD100) instances/clients. All configuration changes to these instances/clients should be performed through transports from the "clean" (DEV100) instance/client. If configuration changes are permitted in QAS100 or PRD100, inconsistencies (which lead to more serious problems) are sure to occur.

Back to the Implementation Guide—Plant Maintenance Configuration

For the Plant Maintenance focus of this discussion, although the company structure, controlling area(s), chart of accounts, and so on must be configured and set up before the PM module can be used properly, those items will not be covered here. Before embarking on Plant Maintenance-specific configuration in the IMG, there are some other configuration items that must be configured and/or checked first:

Plants

One or more plants appropriate for a company's operations must be defined. In the Plant Maintenance module, these plants are often referred to as Maintenance Plants. It is best to work with those configuring other modules to determine what plants must be defined in R/3. For Plant Maintenance purposes, a plant can be any, usually static, location where maintenance can be performed. Groups of buildings at one facility are usually together referred to as one plant, but there may be exceptions.

Planning Plants

In the Plant Maintenance module, these plants may also be referred to as Maintenance Planning Plants. Planning Plants are "chosen" from the list of Plants defined previously as a plant where maintenance planning is carried out. If maintenance planning, including materials planning, is performed at every plant, then every plant will be also be defined as a Planning Plant. In some cases, more centralized planning for several plants will be performed at one plant. In this case, the plant where maintenance planning is performed will be defined as a Planning Plant, but those plants where maintenance planning is not performed will not be defined as Planning Plants.

Assignment of Planning Plants

Once the plants and planning plants have been defined, the assignment of maintenance plants to planning plants must be done. Beside each maintenance plant listed in the configuration step in the IMG, the appropriate planning plant is entered or chosen. In the case where each plant performs its own planning, the same planning plant number will be entered next to each maintenance plant number. In the case of centralized planning, the appropriate planning plant number must be entered for every maintenance plant.

Security: Authorizations and Roles

The responsibility for security, both setup and maintenance, in the SAP R/3 system is usually assigned to one or more individuals whose sole responsibility is security. If this is the case, those individuals will not likely be familiar with the Plant Maintenance module and will require some information in order to set up security for the Plant Maintenance module. It is not common for those responsible for configuring or using a particular module to also set up security for that module or other modules.

Some of the terminology used in SAP R/3 security includes:

Transaction Codes

There is a transaction code associated with each screen in the R/3 system. Some screens may share the same transaction code and there are some screens that are not accessible by menu paths, in which case the transaction codes must be used to access the screens. The transaction code for a particular screen may be found, in versions prior to 4.5, from the menu path **System → Status**, while later versions also make it available by right clicking with the mouse on the status bar near the bottom of the screen. Also in later versions, the transaction code may be displayed by default on the status bar.

Authorization

An authorization is comprised of one or more transaction codes. It may be useful to consider the job requirements of a particular position when defining authorizations. For Plant Maintenance purposes, an operator may require access to, and be restricted from, different transactions than a maintenance planner, for example. Grouping transaction codes into authorizations by job responsibility seems to make sense in most cases.

Roles

A role will consist of one or more authorizations, giving some measure of flexibility in building an authorization/group hierarchy, as desired. It is possible to include all of the operators' transaction codes in the authorization intended for maintenance planners, and then add the additional functions required, for example. It is also possible to make the transactions in the maintenance planners' authorization mutually exclusive from the transactions in the operators' authorization, and then assign both authorizations to an activity group intended for maintenance planners. In addition, composite roles can be defined, which consist of authorizations contained in other roles. In SAP versions prior to 4.5, profiles are used in a similar fashion to roles.

While there is plenty of room for flexibility in setting up security, it requires some planning. It may help to use a spreadsheet with Plant Maintenance-related transaction codes down the left side (because there will be many more transaction codes than roles) and job responsibilities (roles) across the top. The matrix can be used to determine which role requires access to which transactions. The ASAP methodology provides an excellent start to the creation of this matrix through the functionality of the BPML (Business Process Master List). Keep in mind, while creating the matrix, that some people will require access to change data in a transaction and other people will require "read only" access to the data. Specify in the matrix which type of access each role requires for each transaction.

Another matrix that will be helpful is one that represents which users will be assigned to which roles. Through the two matrices, a basis is formed for determining exactly which users have access to which SAP transactions.

In a multi-plant environment, discuss which, if any, roles require access to another plant's data. In addition, it is possible to impose security below the plant level. For example, data relevant to one maintenance planner may not be accessed by another maintenance planner. In addition, security can even be set at the status level. For example, if a piece of equipment has user status indicating that it has been scrapped, only specific people may then change that equipment master record. Determine whether the effort required to maintain security at the more granular levels is worth the benefit. If so, determine at what levels, including plants and planner groups, authorizations will be defined.

When the matrix is satisfactory, it can be used as a starting point to create authorizations and profiles for Plant Maintenance by those responsible for security.

The more complicated the authorization and role hierarchy, the more effort will be required to maintain security. Authorizations and roles should be kept as simple as possible while meeting the security requirements for a particular implementation.

When those responsible for security have completed the authorization setup for the Plant Maintenance module, testing must be performed to ensure that the authorizations have been defined properly. Ideally, test accounts can be provided, one for each defined role. Testers would log on to those accounts and determine whether they can access transactions that the role should be able to access as well as whether they can access transactions that the role should not be able to access. If authorizations are defined for plant-level security, planner group security, or any other authorization level, additional testing is required at the appropriate levels. For example, can a planner from one plant gain access to another plant's work orders? Properly testing security can be a time-consuming task. Plan ahead for the required time or accept the risk associated with incomplete testing.

While the security-related information above can assist with the planning of authorizations and roles, the actual definition of such authorizations and roles can be found in other publications such as *SAP Authorization System* by IBM Business Consulting GmbH, available on the SAP Press web site at www.sap-press.com or *R/3 Authorization Made Easy*, available in several versions from the SAP web site at www.sap.com/company/shop. Go to the SAP Knowledge Shop and find it in the Books section.

Engineering Change Management

Engineering change management provides a more formal method of reference to changes made, or changes that will be made, to materials, bills of materials, documents, or task lists. Although there are other object types to which engineering change management applies, such as classification objects, the same principles apply. This functionality is available to the various SAP R/3 Logistics modules, so co-ordination with the other logistics modules is recommended if this functionality is to be implemented.

While engineering change management is not required for a basic Plant Maintenance implementation, the importance of formal change tracking for a particular implementation should be considered.

When the engineering change management functionality is used, change master records are used in the system. Change master records include such data as the type of object, possibly the date of the change, and the reason for the change. The definition and assignment of *revision levels* and sequences may be made.

Engineering change management can be further formalized with the use of *engineering change requests* and/or *engineering change orders*. The SAP R/3 Online Documentation provides further information.

Number Ranges

Throughout the SAP R/3 system, there are many *number ranges*. Some of the defaults may be acceptable as SAP has provided, while other number ranges will need to be defined or adjusted.

A number range defines limits for the unique identifier for each item. In Plant Maintenance, for example, each piece of equipment (among other items) has a unique identifier, called Equipment Number. A number range for equipment numbers must be defined in order to identify valid equipment numbers.

A number range in SAP R/3 can be defined as an *internal number range* or an *external number range*.

Internal Number Range

An internal number range is numeric only, characters are not permitted, starting from a specific number and ending at a specific number. Internal numbers, when used, are assigned to an item automatically by the system. The next available number is always used and no selection of numbers is possible by the system users. Note that there are technical conditions under which the next number(s) in sequence may be skipped, based on buffer settings. Basis personnel may need to adjust buffer settings if this may be a problem for a particular implementation.

External Number Range

An external number range can be numeric, alphabetic, alphanumeric, and may contain certain special characters (consult the SAP documentation). This can be useful in cases where specific values need to be assigned to items. However, there is no provision for displaying the next available "number," and some planning may be required for each location to have its own range. In general, this method of "smart numbering" is discouraged, since there are many other methods of finding objects in the SAP R/3 system. In some cases, however, it may be required.

Mixed Number Range

A mixed number range is available in some rare cases such as document management. This type of number range, when available, permits the user to provide a prefix in the number field, after which the system assigns a sequential number.

If there is an inclination to use external (user specified) numbering, try to restrict it to more static data, such as equipment. For transaction-related data, such as work orders, it is often more beneficial to allow the system to assign the numbers.

Both internal and external number ranges can sometimes be active for the same items at the same time. In fact, it is possible, and in some cases preferable, to have more than one of each type of number range active at the same time, although it is not necessarily preferable to define internal and external number ranges for the same item. For example, different equipment categories can be assigned different number ranges. Alternatively, the equipment categories could share the same number range or a combination could be defined where some equipment categories share a number range and others are assigned their own number range. Multiple number ranges could be used if there is a reliance on "smart" numbering where the number of an object shows the type/category of the object. As discussed in more detail below, the more number ranges that are defined, the more consideration must be taken to avoid running out of numbers in any of the ranges.

When planning a number range, take into consideration all possible scenarios that could affect the future demands on the number range. When defining a number range for work orders, for example, consider how many work orders are used at each location, how much the number of work orders is expected to increase, whether work orders will be used for new types of work, whether other locations will be added through expansion or acquisition, and so on. Define the number range to be large enough to accommodate any foreseeable circumstances.

When naming a number range, make the description as meaningful as possible, given the space available for the description, especially in the case of number ranges that are shared between modules, such as the order number range. It can also be helpful, if space is available in the description, to include the "from" and "to" numbers of that range. This makes it a little easier to see at a glance what number ranges have been set up.

Some number ranges are "shared" by more than one module and should be configured in co-operation with other modules. The most notable shared number range table is the number ranges for orders. While used in Plant Maintenance for work orders, the same number range table is also used by other modules, for example, CO (Controlling) for internal orders, SD (Sales and Distribution) for sales orders, PP for production orders, and so on. Do not delete or make adjustments to shared number ranges without knowing the effect on other modules.

While it is possible to transport number ranges to other instances (systems), it is not easy to do so and it is strongly discouraged. When changes to a number range are made, a warning to that effect normally appears. The main reason is that internal number range configuration also includes a current number, which enables the system to determine the next available number. One potential problem is that the current number on the source system (transporting from) is lower than the corresponding current number on the target system (transporting to). When the lower current number is transported, the system will then attempt to assign a "next" number that has already been used, with the possibility of corrupting the data. Number ranges should be configured manually on each instance (system).

Refer to the SAP documentation regarding the definition of each type of number range, paying particular attention to the reasons for creating additional number ranges. For example, it is generally not a good idea to create different work order number ranges for different plants.

The steps usually involved in defining number ranges are:

1. Determine whether the number range is specific to Plant Maintenance or shared with other modules. Be considerate of other modules' requirements, current and future, when a number range, such as that for orders, is shared.

2. Determine the groups (separate number ranges) that will be required.

3. Determine whether internal (system-assigned) or external (user-assigned) number ranges will be required.

4. Determine the ranges that are available for numbering and plan for the ranges to be defined.

5. Determine the quantity of numbers required for each number range. Allow for that quantity and then add a substantial quantity more.

6. Determine whether the types of objects should each have their own number range or whether they should share a number range. For example, does each equipment category require its own number range or can equipment categories share number ranges?

7. Define the group(s) required to contain the number range(s).

8. Define the number ranges, if more than one, non-consecutively. That is, leave space between each number range to accommodate the

extension of a number range, if required in the future. If exceptionally good planning was used in determining the number ranges, of course leaving such space is optional.

9. Assign the object types (equipment category, for example, if defining number ranges for equipment) to the appropriate group(s). This can be performed by double-clicking on the object type(s) (their color will change), checking the box beside the appropriate group, and then clicking on the Element/Group button [Element/Group]. Note that the object type—equipment category code, for example—will appear at first at the bottom of the screen (scrolling down may be required) in a "group" that may have the title "Not Assigned."

10. When saving number range configuration, a window will appear, containing information that number range configuration will not be transported automatically. As previously discussed, it is generally not a good idea to transport number ranges, although a transport can be initiated manually. If number ranges are transported, be completely aware of the numbering, particularly "current numbers, " that will be affected by the transport.

As discussed previously, numbers may or may not be "buffered." Buffering numbers causes several numbers, the exact number depending on the buffer settings, to be retrieved from the database in advance. Doing so can save some time in the long run, since the system does not have to access the database each time a number is required. It can also, in some cases, help to avoid delays caused by "locks" when people or programs attempt to access the same numbers at the same time. On the other hand, if numbers are buffered, they may be lost if the system stops running unexpectedly. For example, if the equipment number range is buffered to retrieve 10 numbers at once and the system stops unexpectedly after the first two pieces of equipment, numbered 1 and 2, are saved, the next piece of equipment, when the system recovers, may be saved with the number 11.

If it is critical that numbers be sequential without gaps, ensure that buffering for that number range is turned off. If it is not critical that numbers be sequential without gaps, it may be beneficial to allow buffering.

Buffering number ranges or turning buffering off is usually performed by the Basis team.

Plant Maintenance-Specific Configuration

Although the information contained in this section will help in understanding the Plant Maintenance-specific configuration steps, it is in no way intended to replace proper training or experienced assistance. As with any software system, SAP R/3 changes from version to version, so the information provided may not necessarily apply to a specific implementation. There may be considerations for a specific implementation for which this book is unable to account, therefore additional training and/or experienced assistance is strongly urged. The cost associated with a proper initial implementation is small in comparison to the cost of re-doing an implementation properly or abandoning an implementation altogether.

Use caution. Some configuration can be changed later, while other configuration is very difficult, even impossible to change later.

If a specific implementation step does not appear in the following list, it is likely covered elsewhere in this book.

As previously mentioned, to access the Implementation Guide (IMG), use transaction code SPRO or from the SAP Easy Access menu, use menu path **Tools → Customizing → IMG → Edit Project**. If working from a project IMG, if the project does not appear on the next screen, *Customizing: Execute Project*, it can be added by clicking on the button with a + sign on it, below.

If working from a project IMG, some of the steps listed below may not appear on that IMG. If using a different version of SAP R/3 than version 4.7 (R/3 Enterprise), some of the contents may be different.

Master Data in Plant Maintenance and Customer Service

Basic Settings

Maintain Authorizations for Master Data

This configuration step is often entirely the responsibility of the security person or team. This step should only be performed with some knowledge of the SAP R/3 security structure, involving authorizations and roles.

The help button, which looks like a page with a pair of eyeglasses on it, leads to a description and basic steps to perform here. However, before attempting to define any security, see the Further Reading section of this book for recommendations or refer to the Education section of the SAP web site (www.sap.com) for security-related training.

This configuration step is not specific to the Plant Maintenance module and can be used to define authorizations throughout the R/3 system. It can also be found outside the Implementation Guide in the menu path **Tools → Administration → User Maintenance → Role Administration → Roles.**

Define User Status

Although the R/3 system has a *system status* field to indicate the current status(es) of equipment, functional locations, notifications, work orders, etc., in some cases more functionality centered on status is required. There is no need to configure user status profiles unless:

- The system statuses provided are inadequate
- Transactions are to be restricted based on status

Refer to the section "User Status for Notifications" on page 121 for further, more detailed information regarding user status definition.

Create Authorization Keys for User Status Authorizations

If user statuses have been defined in the previous step, this configuration step can be set to prevent a user from manually setting a user status without the proper authorization. If, for example, a user status is defined as an approval step, it may be desirable to allow only certain users access to set the user status. It is also possible to prevent certain business transactions based on user status settings. If this is desired, work with those responsible for security to define such restrictions. The authorization keys are defined in this configuration step, but are referred to in the previous step, "Define User Status."

Define Currency for Maintenance Statistics

Enter or choose a standard currency in which key figures will be reported. Maintenance costs in other currencies will be converted to this currency only for the purposes of reporting costs through key figures. Leaving this field empty may make it very difficult to report meaningful cost key figures after work orders have been created. Leaving this field blank or entering an incorrect value will not affect actual costs, but it may affect the reporting of those costs within the Plant Maintenance module.

Permits

Within the Implementation Guide, only permit categories and permit groups are defined. The actual permit definitions themselves are defined as master data, outside of the IMG, to more easily accommodate definitions and changes.

One or more permits can be associated with an object such as a functional location or a piece of equipment. When a work order is created based on that object, the restrictions associated with the permits will apply to the work order. For example, if an enclosed space permit that restricts the release of a work order is associated with a particular vessel, any time that a work order is created for that vessel, the release of the permit must be performed in the system before the work order can be released. Note that the restriction imposed by the permit can be an error message (which prevents the release of the work order) or a warning message (which can allow the release of the work order even though the release of the permit has not yet been recorded in the system). The restriction can also be placed on either the release of the work order, the completion of the work order, or even both.

Permits can be used to control whether a work order can be released and/or completed based on whether a permit has been issued. Outside of the IMG, in the definition of a permit, the permit can control whether a warning message or an error message is issued if a permit has not yet been issued. A warning message will allow the user to release or complete the work order after acknowledging the warning, while an error message will not allow the user to release or complete the work order until the permit has been issued.

Keep in mind that a computer system cannot ensure that a permit has actually been issued, only that a user has told the system that a permit has been issued. For this reason, permit functionality should not be the used as the sole method of ensuring that safety procedures are followed. Other processes outside of the system must be used, particularly where worker safety may be involved. Where safety is concerned, permit functionality may best serve as a reminder to issue something or to do something when a work order related to a specific piece of equipment or functional location is released and/or completed.

Define Permit Categories

A permit category is simply a logical grouping of permits. For example, permits related to safety could belong to the Permit Category "Safety."

Define Permit Groups

Defining Permit Groups allows the use of the classification system for permits. If permits are not to be classified further than grouping them into categories in the previous configuration step, this step need not be performed.

Set List Editing for Permits

In this configuration step, variants can be provided to save users time from filling in fields when making repeated requests for the same information. By default, the permit list display and change selection screens have little or no data provided. Any information required to limit the selection list must be provided by the user of the screen. A variant is simply a variation of the same screen with default information provided in one or more of the selection fields. The original default screen can be provided along with selectable variants or the original default screen can be replaced by one of the variants, if agreeable to all users of the screen.

Creation of the permits themselves can be found outside of the IMG by following the menu path **Logistics → Plant Maintenance → Management of Technical Objects → Environment → Permits**.

Once created, a permit can be assigned to an object. For example, to assign a permit to a piece of equipment, while creating or changing an equipment master record (outside of the IMG, of course, in transaction IE01 or IE02—menu path **Logistics → Plant Maintenance → Management of Technical Objects → Equipment Create or Change**), follow the menu path **Goto → Permits**...and specify the conditions for the permit.

Make System Settings for Measuring Points and Measurement Documents

This setting consists of a checkbox that should only be checked when large numbers of duplicate measurement readings are expected. For example, if there are 100 pieces of equipment installed at a superior equipment, and the same measurement is recorded at the same time for each piece of equipment at the same interval. The 101 records created each time a measurement is taken will eventually consume considerable database space. If this is a concern, and it is only recommended if it is a concern, this checkbox can be checked in order to use the same measurement document repeatedly for the sub-equipment. Refer to the Measuring Points section on page 43 for more information regarding measuring points.

Define Measuring Point Categories

This setting provides a means of grouping measuring points. A category controls several factors such as whether the measuring point should be unique for the object or for the system (client) as a whole, which catalog (if any) is used to provide possible valuation codes for readings, and whether the reading can be recorded as of a future time. Review any intention to create measuring point categories carefully, since the key field is only a one-character field, limiting the number of categories possible. Refer to the Measuring Points section on page 52 for more information.

Create Number Ranges for Measuring Points

Review the default setting, which is often acceptable. This number range controls the quantity of unique measuring points that can be defined in the system. A measuring point is a place at which a reading or measurement can be taken. More than one measuring point per piece of equipment or other object can be defined, if required. Refer to the Measuring Points section on page 52 for more information.

Create Number Ranges for Measurement Documents

A measurement document is created every time a measurement taken from a measuring point is recorded in the system. Since every measuring point will likely have more than one measurement recorded, the number range for measurement documents is significantly larger. Again, however, the default setting is usually sufficient. Consider how many measuring points might be defined, as well as how many measurements, on average, might be recorded in a month (or a year) and how many months (or years) the system could possible be used. If the resulting number is well within the default range, simply accept the default number range. If there is any doubt, however, change the range to accommodate a higher number of measurement documents. Refer to the Measuring Points section on page 52 for more information.

Define Field Selection for Measuring Points and Measurement Documents

This configuration step controls the field attributes (required, display only, hide, etc.) for the fields on the measuring point and measurement document screens. If it is critical for a field value to be entered when creating a measuring point, that field can be made "required, " for example. By using the "Influencing" option, the field attributes can apply to measuring points of a specific measuring point category instead of all measuring points, if desired.

Field Selection

Settings for Field Selection appear in several places in the Plant Maintenance sections of the Implementation Guide. Every instance of Field Selection is similar.

All of the Field Selection screens display a list of fields, along with their technical names to help avoid confusion. To find the technical name of a field (outside the IMG) in a screen, click once on the field and press the F1 key on the keyboard **or** right-click on the field and select Help. On the window that appears, one of the buttons looks like a wrench and a hammer and displays "Technical Information." Click on that button. In the "Technical Information" window that appears, look for the field labeled "Screen field." That is the technical name for the field and will provide a means to ensure that the appropriate field attributes will be changed in the IMG. It may be beneficial to keep two sessions open, one in the IMG and one outside the IMG, switching from one session to the other as a reference.

The options available to set field attributes are:

Input

This is the default setting for most fields and will allow the field and its contents to be viewed and, under normal circumstances, the contents to be entered or changed.

Req.

This setting will require an entry in the field. Note that on screens where there are multiple tabs, the user must often click on the appropriate tab before being required to enter a value in the field. However, once on the appropriate tab, a value will be required before the user can continue or save the record.

Disp.

This setting only allows the contents of the field to be displayed. No entry or change is permitted.

Hide

This setting actually hides the field from view entirely, not just the field contents. In order for the field and its label to be hidden, it may be necessary to set two fields to "hidden."

HiLi

This setting, which can co-exist with the settings above (where logical), changes the color of the field label. Depending on color settings, the change may be obvious or subtle.

Simply setting the field attributes on the main screen will set those attributes globally. For example, setting the Equipment Description field to "Required" will cause the Equipment Description to be required for all equipment categories. If setting the field attribute to "Required" for only one equipment category is desired, ensure that the setting on the main screen is "Input." Click on the "Influencing" button, double-click on Equipment Category, enter or select the desired Equipment Category and the press the "Enter" key on the keyboard. Now any attribute changes will apply only to equipment master records for the Equipment Category selected.

To see an overview of the influences already set, click on the "Influences" button.

The Field Selection functionality is similar throughout the Plant Maintenance section of the Implementation Guide. Only the individual screens and fields differ.

The Field Selection functionality can provide a guide for the user by hiding unnecessary fields, ensuring that required data is entered, and protecting sensitive field contents from being changed.

Note that "Field Selection for List Display" and "Field Selection for Multi-Level List Display, " also found in multiple locations in the Plant Maintenance part of the IMG, perform a somewhat different function. The instructions above do not apply to "Field Selection for List Display" or "Field Selection for Multi-Level List Display." Those configuration items control the fields that are displayed in lists.

Set List Editing for Measuring Point Lists

In this configuration step, variants can be provided to save users time from filling in fields when making repeated requests for the same information. By default, the measuring point list display and change selection screens have little or no data provided. Any information required to limit the selection list must be provided by the user of the screen. A variant is simply a variation of the same screen with default information provided in one or more of the selection fields. The original default screen can be provided along with selectable variants or the original default screen can be replaced by one of the variants, if agreeable to all users of the screen.

Set List Editing for Measurement Document Lists

This step is similar to the previous step, except that the default or variant data provided is used to select measurement documents instead of measuring points.

Check Warranty Categories

The default warranty categories are normally acceptable. Warranty category "I" allows the management of warranties that have been provided by a vendor or supplier. Warranty category "O" allows the management of warranties that are being provided to customers. One or the other may be deleted if that category of warranty will never be used.

Define Warranty Types

Different warranty types may be defined within warranty categories. While warranty categories differentiate between whether a warranty is provided by an external entity or to an external entity, warranty type can make further distinctions within either category. For example, a manufacturer and a vendor may both provide a warranty on the same piece of equipment. In this case, two warranty types can be defined, one for the manufacturer and one for the vendor, and both will be assigned to warranty category I. As of SAP R/3 version 4.6b, there are some unusable fields in warranty type configuration that are reserved for future use.

Define Number Ranges for Warranty Types

The default configuration is usually acceptable for this step. Review the settings if many warranty types are to be defined.

Maintain Transaction Start Default Values for Sample Warranties

A default field value for warranty type may be defined here for the transaction codes BGM1 (Create Master Warranty), BGM2 (Change Master Warranty), and BGM3 (Display Master Warranty). Defaults for the transaction codes are provided by default, but may be changed if a different warranty type is to be used more than the default.

Define Warranty Counters

A characteristic may be supplied here to provide a warranty-related counter. The characteristic must have already been defined in the Classification system. The counter may be used to represent, for example, operating hours. Another counter may be used to represent, for example, time. The counters can be checked each time that a piece of equipment breaks down in order to determine whether the equipment is still within its warranty period.

Partners

A partner, from a Plant Maintenance perspective, is a person or other entity that has anything to do with a work order (or other object), for example. Work order-related partners include, but are not limited to, person responsible, department responsible, vendor, and so on.

Define Partner Determination Procedure and partner function

In the vast majority of cases, the default settings for partner determination can be accepted as defaulted for Plant Maintenance purposes. The partner functions, as defined, need not all be used, but should be left intact in consideration of future requirements.

Copy Partner Functions to Master and Movement Data

This setting controls whether the partner function assigned to a technical object, such as a piece of equipment or a functional location, will be automatically copied to notifications and work orders. The default setting is for the partner function to be copied, which is normally preferred. If there is any reason why the partner function need not be copied to a notification or work order, uncheck the appropriate box(es) here.

Define Field Selection for List Display...

There are several configuration steps beginning with, "Define field Selection." These configuration steps control which fields are displayed, and in which order, when a list of the associated data is displayed on the screen. The lower the number entered beside a particular field, the more to the left it will be displayed relevant to other fields. For example, if only two fields have numbers entered beside them in this configuration step, those will be the only two fields displayed on the screen when a user displays a list of associated records. The lower numbered field will be displayed to the left of the higher numbered field. All the other fields are available to be displayed by the user, except for those fields whose "Invisible" boxes have been checked in configuration. There is no standard setting for the display position number, but leaving spaces between the numbers (5, 10, 15, etc.) will make inserting fields easier, should the need arise. Note that the number does not control the field's position on the screen, except as relevant to the other fields. For example, if only one field is numbered, it does not matter what the number is, the field will be displayed on the left side of the screen. Giving it a number of 50 instead of 5 will not cause it to be displayed any further to the right.

Search Helps in Plant Maintenance and Customer Service

The search help function was formerly known as *matchcodes*. While the default search helps are usually sufficient, at least until the system has been used long enough to identify deficiencies, this configuration step allows the alteration of pull-down, function key F4-related fields. If, for example, too many fields appear, causing confusion, when a pull down menu is accessed, some fields may be disabled using this configuration step.

Define Object Information Keys

This configuration step allows the display of recent relevant data regarding a technical object that is currently being referenced. For example, any work orders and notifications related to a particular technical object in the past 365 days can be shown in the object information window. Threshold values can be set in order for object information to be displayed only if, for example, the number of work orders in the past 365 days related to a particular technical object has exceeded 5. The default system allows two different object information keys to be defined, one for PM (Plant Maintenance) and one for SM (Customer Service, previously known as Service Management), although others may be added. Although object information can be displayed at any time from a technical object screen, checking the "automatically" box in this configuration step will cause the object information to display automatically when the technical object is referenced.

Technical Objects—General Data

Define Types of Technical Objects

Formerly known as "Equipment Type, "this configuration step has been expanded to include functional locations, so is now referred to as, "Object Type, " or, "Technical Object Type." For most implementations, however, it will still be used to list valid equipment types. When a technical object is created, it may be assigned an object type that has been defined in this list. No object types that do not appear on this list will be accepted. The object types defined may be used as a grouping function to analyze technical objects that have the same use. Typical object types may be, "Pump, " "Motor, " etc. Later, functional location categories and equipment categories will be discussed. Technical object types should be considered a lower level and more specific than functional location and equipment categories. There are normally considerably more technical object types than functional location categories and equipment categories.

Define Plant Sections

This configuration step may be used to define areas of production responsibility in a plant. From this list, a piece of equipment may be assigned to a plant section. When that equipment malfunctions, for example, the appropriate person responsible for the plant section may be notified. The configuration simply allows the definition of a plant section code, a person's position (preferably) or name and that person's phone number.

Define Planner Groups

In the same manner as the previous configuration step, maintenance planner groups may be defined here. A maintenance planner group may be composed of one or more people who have the responsibility for planning maintenance work. A maintenance planner group that has been defined for a piece of equipment, for example, will by default appear on work orders related to that piece of equipment. Note that later in the Implementation Guide, Task List Planner Groups are defined. Both this configuration step and the Task List Planner Groups configuration step must be performed, even if the same planner groups exist for both types of planning.

Define ABC Indicators

The ABC Indicator field can be used as a means of categorizing equipment. There is no definitive use for the field, but it is typically used to represent the importance or criticality of a technical object. Although the values A, B and C are provided by default, more may be added or any may be deleted as required.

Define Authorization Groups

This authorization group definition may be used to limit access to specific technical objects. In order to do so, the authorization groups defined must be assigned to the user master records of the appropriate users. The authorization groups defined must also be assigned to the appropriate technical objects. Once the authorization groups have been properly assigned, only those users whose user master records contain the same authorization group as the technical object may access that technical object. This configuration step is not performed unless security is required at the level of specific technical objects.

Set View Profiles for Technical Objects

Although for many implementations the default screen layouts for technical objects should suffice, this configuration step allows the manipulation of the tabs and the groups of fields on the screen. The "Icons and texts of views" section of this configuration step allows the texts and/or icons displayed on tabs to be changed. A tab is available for the display of warranty information through this configuration step.

Define Object Information Keys

Information regarding the recent history of an object can be controlled through this configuration step. When creating a notification (work request, for example) for a problem with a particular object (piece of equipment), information regarding any recent notifications and/or work orders can either be displayed automatically or be available on demand. The information can be displayed based on threshold values. For example, information can be made to display automatically if there have been five notifications or three work orders for that object within the past 365 days.

Check the box labeled "automatically" to force the system to display the information automatically.

In the "Info. System—time frame and threshold values" section, enter the number of days of history to search for notifications or orders. Also in this section, enter any threshold values. Object information will be displayed if the object meets or exceeds the threshold value(s) entered.

In the "Notifications—selection and automatic display" section, the two boxes on the left may be checked to display completed and/or outstanding notifications. The two fields (one numeric, the other a checkbox) on the right control whether completed notifications are displayed automatically and for how long (in days).

The "Classification" section of the screen is only relevant if the classification system is being used in conjunction with the Plant Maintenance module.

Ideally, the Object Information window should provide information to help prevent redundant work orders from being created, as well as to assist in identifying recently recurring problems. It should appear frequently enough to be of assistance, but not so frequently that it begins to be ignored.

Define Selection Procedure for Structural Displays and BOMs

Under some circumstances, when hierarchical structures and/or bills of material are large, system performance may be adversely affected when attempting to view such information in a hierarchical display. The reason is that the system may be "reading" more data than is actually displayed. If poor performance is experienced when attempting to display structural display or BOM information, check the appropriate checkbox(es) in this configuration step. Otherwise, the default setting (unchecked) will suffice.

The step-by-step discussion of the implementation guide will continue after the following section regarding the technical object hierarchy and associated information.

Defining Technical Objects

The Object Hierarchy

The object hierarchy in the Plant Maintenance module will usually start with individual plants, or even a group of plants, at the top level. The plants are usually subdivided into *functional locations* which may describe a physical area of a plant, an area of the plant with financial implications, or a logical process or function of the plant. Functional locations may be subdivided into lower level functional locations in a hierarchy until a functional location contains one or more pieces of *equipment*. The equipment may be subdivided into *sub-equipment, bills of material,* and/or *materials.*

The object hierarchy, particularly the functional location structure, can take a significant amount of time to determine, so the process to determine the structure should begin early in a project.

Functional Location, Equipment, Bill of Material

Determining the functional location hierarchy for any particular implementation can produce anguish for the participants. In some cases, many months have been spent on the task, in part because, once the hierarchy is in a production environment and in use, it is extremely difficult to change or delete. It is also difficult to prototype a functional location hierarchy, since properly testing it requires so much supporting data. Therefore, time must be spent to develop a functional location hierarchy that will properly meet the needs of a particular company. There is no "right" way to build a functional location hierarchy and it may be beneficial to seek experienced assistance to keep the process on track.

The following points can be used as guidelines only. Not all points discussed will be useful for all implementations:

- It may be beneficial to create a functional location hierarchy for each plant, with the plant code/number as the top-level functional location.

- Keep the number of levels to a minimum. It is rarely necessary to have a functional location hierarchy with more than six levels.

- The 30-character field for the functional location code may be expanded to 40 characters in version 4.5 and higher by invoking alternative labeling for functional locations. Turning this feature on also allows a secondary, perhaps more easily understood, label for functional locations. This feature does not allow a functional location hierarchy to be represented differently. Read the documentation provided by SAP and decide whether this feature will be beneficial.

- Do not use *reference functional locations* unless there is a requirement to make a change to several similar functional locations simultaneously. A reference functional location is not a "real" functional location and only serves to save time on data entry and modifications for similar functional locations. Making a change to a reference functional location will cause the change to be made to

- each functional location that refers to the reference functional location. To simply copy data from another functional location, refer to another functional location instead of a reference functional location. Changes made to one functional location will have no effect on those copied from it, however changes to a *reference* functional location affect all other functional locations that are based on the reference functional location.

- Define functional locations from the top down. When the functional locations are properly coded and entered into the R/3 system, they will automatically be assigned to the proper superior (parent) functional location as long as the superior functional locations are entered first. If the functional locations are entered with the subordinate (child) functional locations first, they must be assigned to the superior functional locations manually.

- Try to create as few functional location structure indicators as possible. It might even be possible to define one structure that is suitable for the entire organization. That doesn't mean that all of the organization's functional locations will be combined together, it simply means that they will share the same restrictions for numbering their functional locations.

- Try to avoid creating separate functional location structure indicators for each location/plant. Keep in mind that the functional locations themselves can define a location, even a plant or region, so creating a structure indicator for each location is often redundant. Create additional structure indicators for different structural requirements, not to define different locations.

Hierarchical Data Transfer (Inheritance)

When functional locations are assigned to other, superior functional locations, or pieces of equipment are assigned to functional locations, data may be "inherited" from the functional location to which it has been assigned. This is usually referred to as *data transfer* or *data inheritance*, and is defined and controlled in the Implementation Guide.

It is also possible to control which fields are inherited by equipment while the equipment is being assigned to a functional location.

Some consideration should be given to how much data inheritance is required. Making one simple change in a high level functional location to reflect that everything within that functional location is now assigned a different cost center will be much more complicated and time consuming if the inheritance of any objects within that functional location has been changed.

Functional Locations

A functional location can be used to organize equipment or other functional locations into logical groups usually based on function and/or geographic location. At its highest level, a functional location often depicts a plant or group of plants (or even a region), while at its lowest level it often represents a place in which one or more pieces of equipment may be installed.

Although there is a good example of a functional location hierarchy contained in the SAP R/3 Online Documentation, there is no standard format for defining a functional location hierarchy. It may be beneficial, in some cases, to determine the levels at which summarizing maintenance activity and history are desirable. It might make sense to compare a summary of maintenance between production line A and production line B, for example, in which case defining functional locations at that level seems to also make sense.

It is possible to operate the R/3 Plant Maintenance module without defining pieces of equipment by assigning all available functionality to functional locations. In some rare cases this may make sense. However, in the vast majority of situations, the wealth of information contained in an equipment record is invaluable.

One or more pieces of equipment may be assigned to a functional location, unless the functional location has been defined not to accept equipment assignment or not to accept more than one equipment assignment.

While more than one piece of equipment may be assigned to a functional location, sometimes it may be more desirable to define one more level of functional locations in order to assign one piece of equipment to one functional location (a one-to-one relationship). For example, if three pumps (equipment) are assigned to a pumping station (functional location), when the pumps are swapped out for repairs there is no record of the location in the pumping station at which each pump was installed. If one of those locations is a problem location, for whatever reason, it may be faster to pinpoint the problem if the pumps were assigned to specific locations within the pumping station. Defining a pump location A, B, and C in the pumping station will allow more specific tracking. Of course, the necessity for tracking installation locations will differ from implementation to implementation.

Work orders and task lists, which will be discussed later, can be assigned to functional locations as well as to pieces of equipment. When a piece of equipment has been assigned to a functional location, it may cause some confusion as to where to assign the work order or task list. Consider the functional location as a "place" at which the equipment is installed, and then consider whether the tasks are to be performed on the piece of equipment itself or to the place at which the equipment happens to be installed. If the work is to be performed on the piece of equipment, assigning the work to the functional location at which it is installed will cause the costs and history to avoid the piece of equipment.

Reference Functional Locations

A *reference functional location* is not a "real" functional location. It does not represent any particular object or location, but can be used as a reference for a functional location that does represent a particular object or location. It has the added benefit that any changes made to a reference functional location will be automatically made to all the functional locations created by using the reference functional location.

There is no need to use reference functional locations unless there is a requirement to make changes to multiple, similar functional locations all at once.

On the initial screen, when creating a functional location, the functional location being created can (optionally) refer to a functional location or a reference functional location. A functional location created with reference to another functional location will copy field values from the original functional location, but no further dependency exists. Any change made to either of the functional locations will have no effect on the other. A functional location created with reference to a reference functional location, however, will not only copy field values from the reference functional location, but will have a dependency on the reference functional location.

Changes made to the reference functional location will also be made to the functional location. Changes made manually to the functional location will have no effect on the reference functional location.

Equipment

Pieces of equipment are often the focal point for Plant Maintenance. A piece of equipment is most often the object for which work orders are performed and history is recorded. Pieces of equipment that are also assets can be linked to the SAP R/3 Asset Management module, if used, by providing the asset number on the equipment master screen.

Costs associated with the work performed on a piece of equipment can be accumulated, or "rolled up," to the functional location to which it is assigned and any superior functional location in the hierarchy.

Although it is possible to create an equipment hierarchy by assigning pieces of equipment to other pieces of equipment, in effect creating *sub-equipment*, it is difficult in the *Plant Maintenance Information System* (PMIS) to have costs roll up to superior equipment. Instead costs for a piece of equipment and any sub-equipment under it will roll up to the functional location to which it is assigned. If it is important to see a summary of costs at a certain level in the functional location/equipment hierarchy, it may be worth considering a different structure or an alternate method of reporting cost summaries.

If a piece of equipment is assigned to a functional location, the piece of equipment may inherit some field values (data) from the functional location, depending on configuration settings and options chosen while making the assignment to the functional location. If so, changes made to that data at the functional location level will also be made to the piece of equipment. Such changes may be considered advantageous or detrimental, so consideration should be made regarding the inheritance of data from functional locations.

Assets

Pieces of equipment may also be regarded as assets. There is no configuration to be performed in the implementation guide to link Plant Maintenance and Asset Management. To associate a piece of equipment with an asset in Asset Management, the asset number (and asset sub-number, if required) is entered in those fields in the equipment master record.

While the act of entering the asset number in the equipment master record seems simple, it may be worthwhile to consider the process by which a new piece of equipment is created in the R/3 system. Although SAP R/3 is an integrated system, there is data specific to Plant Maintenance that will not be known to Asset Management personnel or Materials Management personnel, requiring that some data be entered in each module. If a piece of equipment is required to be tracked as an asset and/or a material, at least for purchasing purposes, data must be entered in each of those modules, if used, as well as in the Plant Maintenance module. It may be preferable to enter data in the Asset Management and Materials Management modules before entering the associated data for the equipment in the Plant Maintenance module. The asset number, if available or required, can then be provided for entry into the equipment master record. Likewise, the material number, if required, can also be entered.

Note that the "Location" and "Room" fields available in Plant Maintenance are shared fields with other modules, including the Asset Management module. Reach an agreement on the use of these fields with other teams who may be using them.

Bills of Material

There are several different types of bills of material in the SAP R/3 system. The Plant Maintenance module is primarily concerned with equipment (and/or functional location) bills of material and material bills of material. The significant difference between the two is that materials are directly assigned to a piece of equipment in an equipment bill of materials, while materials are assigned to another, superior material in a material bill of materials. Combinations of the two are permitted and will be discussed in the following sections.

The advantage to taking the time to structure bills of material is that it is much easier on an ongoing basis to select the materials (parts) required from a list than it is to look them up and enter them each time they are required. Since the materials contained in the bill of materials are directly integrated with the Materials Management module, the cost of the materials is always current.

Although building bills of materials may seem like an overwhelming task, particularly if never done before, there are long-term benefits. If there are truly not enough resources or if there is simply not enough time to construct a complete representation of all bills of material required, provide bills of material for the most used, most repaired, and/or most complex pieces of equipment first. Work on the remainder as required or as time permits.

Functional Location Bills of Material/Equipment Bills of Material

While functional location bills of material are a relatively recent addition to the functionality of R/3, their usage is similar to equipment bills of material. Functional location bills of material will most likely be used where there is limited implementation of equipment records. Although the following information discusses equipment bills of material, the information also pertains to functional location bills of material.

The actual method of constructing a bill of materials will differ from implementation to implementation. The materials that make up a piece of equipment are specific to the piece of equipment, not the system used to track the bills of materials.

In its simplest form, an equipment bill of materials is a list of materials that make up the piece of equipment, along with the quantity of the materials required. When a work order is created for the piece of equipment, the bill of materials for the equipment can be displayed, allowing for the selection of the entire bill of materials or specific materials from the list.

Material Bills of Material

A material bill of materials is a list of materials that make up another material. In Materials Management, the "parent, " or superior, material is defined as well as the "child, " or subordinate, materials of which it is made up. It is quite possible to define assemblies through a hierarchy of material bills of material.

Once material bills of material are defined, one or more material bills of material and/or individual materials may be assigned to a piece of equipment. When materials (parts) must be assigned to the maintenance of the piece of equipment, the selection of materials individually or as bills of material will reduce the time spent creating the work order in addition to reducing possible errors in material selection.

Measuring Points

A measuring point, simply stated, defines a place on a piece of equipment at which some type of measurement is taken. The measurement may be pressure, cycles, miles, or one of many other types of measurements. Measuring points may also be defined for functional locations, if appropriate.

Usually, measuring points are defined in order to trigger maintenance when a certain measurement threshold is reached, although measurements may be taken as historical records.

Some considerations must be made before defining measuring points. Determine the unit of measure first. In the example of an automobile odometer, for example, will the measuring point be defined in miles or kilometers, five digits with one decimal place or six digits with no decimal places (or one for each)? To continue using the example of odometers, the measuring point can and should be defined to "roll over" when the odometer does. If the odometer can only count to 99, 999 miles before rolling back to 0 (zero), the measuring point must do the same.

Although the SAP R/3 Classification system will not be covered here, since it is not specific to the Plant Maintenance module, a slight detour into the Classification system will likely be required in order to define *characteristics* for measuring points. It is not necessary to define anything else in the Classification system for the purposes of using measuring points, but defining the necessary characteristic for a measuring point must be done before defining the measuring point itself. Because the Classification system is not specific to Plant Maintenance, identify PM characteristics by prefixing them with PM, for example. If a characteristic that has already been defined meets the requirements for a new measuring point, use the existing measuring point. It is usually not a good idea, for Plant Maintenance purposes, to use the SAP-provided default characteristics or any defined for use in another module.

Each measurement taken and recorded at a measuring point is referred to as a *measurement document* in R/3, and will be discussed later.

Back to the Implementation Guide (IMG)

The step-by-step discussion of the Plant Maintenance Master Data section of the implementation guide is continued below:

Functional Locations

Create Structure Indicator for Reference Functional Locations/Functional Locations

Determining the functional location structure can be one of the most time consuming tasks of an SAP R/3 Plant Maintenance implementation. Do not underestimate the importance of this step, especially since it is difficult, if not impossible, to correct later. Technically, it is possible to create a functional location hierarchy of 30 or more levels, but there is rarely a need to create a hierarchy of more than six or seven levels.

As discussed later, a functional location can be most conveniently thought of as a place. Smaller places are assigned to larger places, while equipment may be placed or "installed" at the smaller places, or lower level functional locations. Although this is a simple explanation of functional locations, it can help to distinguish them, in most cases, from equipment.

At the highest level of a functional location hierarchy, the functional location defined there will often represent a plant, but certainly not always. If the top level functional location represents a plant and there is more than one plant in the company, then multiple functional location hierarchies must be defined. Those multiple functional location hierarchies can all use the same structure indicator. A different structure indicator need not be defined for different functional location hierarchies unless there is a compelling reason to do so.

A different structure indicator need not be defined for different locations or plants, since functional locations defined with the structure indicator will likely represent those locations or plants.

In the IMG, the following step, *Activate Alternative Labeling*, if activated, will expand the Structure Indicator field from 30 to 40 characters, as well as providing other functionality. If the extra field length is required, alternative labeling may be activated whether alternative labels for functional locations will be used or not. Once activated, alternative labeling can be deactivated, but with potentially unexpected results, particularly with functional locations whose labels extend beyond 30 characters. Upon activating alternative labeling, an "Info" button will appear. Click on the "Info" button for important information regarding alternative labeling.

The first two fields in this configuration setting simply contain the code and description of the structure indicator.

The third field contains the edit mask. While the cursor is on this field, clicking on the F1 (help) key on the keyboard will display some useful information regarding valid characters that may be used.

The fourth field contains the indicators for the levels of the functional locations defined in the edit mask, above. If the top-level functional location represents a four-character plant code, for example, that may be defined in the previous field as XXXX (followed by a separator, such as "-" and other characters). In this field (hierarchy levels), the number 1 will be inserted immediately below the fourth "X". This pattern will be continued until all levels of the edit mask have been defined. An example follows:

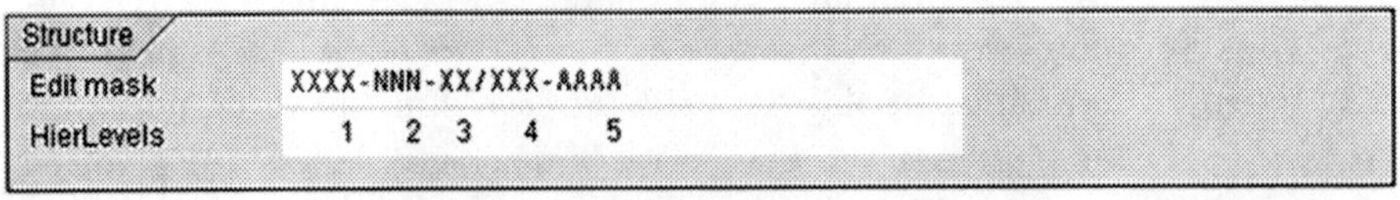

Structure	
Edit mask	XXXX-NNN-XX/XXX-AAAA
HierLevels	1 2 3 4 5

Figure 5. Defining a Structure Indicator
© *SAP AG*

In the example shown, the numbers indicate the end of each level of the hierarchy. There are two different types of separator shown, the "-" and the "/" although other separators may be used (press the F1 key or click the Help button to have a list of valid separators displayed). The character "N" indicates a space in the edit mask where the functional location label must contain a numeric value

(0—9). The character "A" indicates a space in the edit mask where the functional location label must contain an alphabetic value (A—Z). The character "X" indicates a space in the edit mask where the functional location label may contain either a numeric or alpha value (but not a separator).

More than one edit mask/structure indicator may be defined and used. It is a good idea, however, to use functional locations created with different edit masks in separate hierarchies.

Activate Alternative Labeling

Functional Location labels, as defined in the previous configuration step, can sometimes appear cryptic and difficult to understand. In this configuration step, alternative labeling can be activated to allow a different, perhaps more understandable, label to be used for the same Functional Location. Note that alternative labeling does not allow Functional Locations to be displayed in a different hierarchy. Functional Locations will be displayed in the hierarchy defined by the original Functional Location label.

As discussed in the previous configuration step, but well worth repeating, once it has been activated, alternative labeling can be deactivated, but with potentially unexpected results, particularly with functional locations whose labels extend beyond 30 characters. Upon activating alternative labeling, an "Info" button will appear. Click on the "Info" button for important information regarding alternative labeling.

Define Labeling Systems for Functional Locations

In this configuration step, any non-standard label systems may be defined for use with functional locations, on the condition that alternative labeling was activated in the previous configuration step. If alternative labeling was not activated, this configuration step can be skipped. If alternative labeling was activated in order to extend the length of the functional location label field from 30 to 40 characters with no intention of using alternative labeling, this configuration step can be skipped. Otherwise, define as many different labels as will be required.

Define Category of Reference Functional Location

Changes to the standard SAP settings in this configuration step depend on whether reference functional locations will be used, as well as whether any functional location categories are required in addition to the standard SAP category. Refer to the chapter on "Reference Functional Locations," for more information.

Define Structural Display for Reference Functional Locations

If reference functional locations are not being used, this step may be skipped, even if functional locations are being used. If reference functional locations are being used, enter a number corresponding to the order in which it will be displayed beside each field. For example, a 1 beside "RefLocation" will cause that field to be displayed first (on the left) when a list of reference functional locations is presented. If another field is assigned number 2, that field will be displayed immediately to the right of "RefLocation." Numbers may not be repeated. Keep in mind that this setting will simply be the default for a list of reference functional locations. The person using the list will be able to select other fields not included in the default unless the "Invisible" checkbox has been checked beside a particular field.

Define Category of Functional Location

Although there is a default functional location category, which should suffice in many cases, other functional location categories may be defined, particularly in cases where different partner determination procedures are required. An external customer's functional locations, for example, would likely have a different functional location category than a company's own functional locations.

Define Field Selection for Data Screen for Reference Functional Locations

Use this screen to make any necessary changes to the field attributes on the Reference Functional Location screens. For example, changing the attribute of the Maintenance Plant field to "Required" will require the user of the screens to enter a valid value in the Maintenance Plant field. Changing a field attribute to "Display" will prevent a value from being entered or changed in that field (display only). The "Hide" field attribute will cause a field to not appear on the screens at all. The "Highlight" attribute, which can be used in conjunction with some of the other attributes, causes the field (description) to appear in a different color. The color will depend on the GUI settings.

Define Structural Display for Functional Locations

These settings control which fields are displayed by default on screens where a list of functional locations is displayed. The field assigned "Display Position" 1 will be displayed on the left of the list display, the field assigned "Display Position" 2 will be displayed beside it, second from the left, and so on. The numbers do not indicate the number of characters to be displayed, and the numbers also do not indicate the number of characters from the left of the screen, they simply indicate a sequence. The eventual user of the resulting screen has the ability to select other fields not defaulted here. Checking the "Invisible" box to the right of a field here will prevent the user from seeing, and therefore selecting, a particular field.

Define Field Selection for Functional Locations

Use this screen to make any necessary changes to the field attributes on the Functional Location screens. As noted above, for Reference Functional Locations, changing the attribute of the Maintenance Plant field to "Required" will require the user of the screens to enter a valid value in the Maintenance Plant field. Changing a field attribute to "Display" will prevent a value from being entered or changed in that field (display only). The "Hide" field attribute will cause a field to not appear on the screens at all. The "Highlight" attribute, which can be used in conjunction with some of the other attributes, causes the field (description) to appear in a different color. The color will depend on the GUI settings.

Set List Editing for Reference Functional Locations

These settings can provide defaults for the selection of Reference Functional Locations. Fields on the selection screens may be made invisible, required, and so on. The system will allow one of these "variants" to be saved as an alternative to the system default, or it will even allow a "variant" to replace the system default.

Set List Editing for Functional Locations

This functionality is identical to the functionality in the previous step, except that these settings are for Functional Locations, not Reference Functional Locations.

Set List Editing for Functional Locations in Service

Again, this functionality is identical to the functionality in the previous two steps, except that these settings are for Functional Locations used in Service (customers' Functional Locations, for example).

Field Selection for Multi-Level List Displays of Functional Locations

The settings contained within this heading can be used to control the fields that are displayed in lists within the multi-level list displays of Functional Locations. For example, in the Functional Location multi-level list display, there is a checkbox for Equipment. If that checkbox is checked, a list of Equipment installed at the selected Functional Location(s) will be displayed. The settings for "Define Field Selection for Equipment Master Data Fields" will control which Equipment fields are displayed in the Multi-Level list. Each setting here corresponds to each checkbox on the Multi-Level List Display screen for Functional Locations.

Each of these settings determines which fields will be displayed and in which order. A field assigned "Display Position" 1 will appear leftmost on the List Display screens. A field assigned to "Display Position" 2 will appear immediately to the right of the field assigned "Display Position" 1. Once again, the numbers only indicate the order in which the fields will be displayed and do not control the fields' physical position on the screen. The eventual user of the resulting screen can change the order in which the fields are displayed, remove fields from the display, and add other fields to the display. Marking a field as "Invisible" here will prevent the user from seeing, and therefore prevent the user from choosing that field.

Equipment

Maintain Equipment Category

There are four default Equipment Categories. The most commonly used Equipment Category is M for Machines. The other three default Equipment Categories are P for Production Resources & Tools (PRT), Q for machines used with regards to Quality Management, and S (Service), which is used for equipment pertaining to customers. Other Equipment Categories may be defined as required. Different view profiles, usage history, functional location installation options, and separate number ranges are the main reasons for creating other Equipment Categories. A common Equipment Category to add, where appropriate, is one to accommodate vehicles (fleet). Do not mistake Equipment Category with Equipment Type, which is referred to as Technical Object Type in recent versions of SAP R/3. For more information on Technical Object Types, see the section "Define Types of Technical Objects." Equipment categories refer to a much higher level than technical object (equipment) types, so there should be relatively few equipment categories defined.

Define Additional Business Views for Equipment Categories

The settings here allow additional screens to be added (or removed, in some cases), if appropriate, for each Equipment Category. For example, if PRTs (Production Resources and Tools) are used, there is a tab on the equipment master screen that can be activated to show PRT-related fields. The "Other data" tab can also be activated, which can contain custom fields defined specifically for a specific implementation. Note that if "View Profiles" (page 43) are defined, some of the settings here may be overridden.

Define Number Ranges

Pieces of equipment can have their unique equipment number assigned manually by the user or automatically assigned sequentially by the system. Settings can be made to allow or disallow either manual equipment numbers or system assigned numbers. In the vast majority of cases, automatic assignment of equipment numbers by the system is preferred. Since equipment can be searched and sorted by a number of other means, there is rarely a need to manually assign "intelligent" numbers to equipment. As well, the extra effort required to track the next available number if numbers are assigned manually, is rarely worth the effort.

A number range may be defined for each equipment category (see above) or any combination of equipment categories may share the same number range. Initially, some equipment categories will be assigned to the group called "Group without text." This group may be changed to an appropriate name and its number range changed, if necessary, to accommodate any foreseeable equipment definitions. Alternatively, if not all equipment categories are to be used, but will be maintained for future use, a new group with an appropriate name may be created, the appropriate equipment categories assigned to it, and an adequate number range defined.

From the "Maintain groups" area:

- New groups can be created (Group → Insert)
- A group name can be changed (Group → Maintain text)

- A number range can be assigned (Interval → Maintain)
- The current number can be changed (Interval → Change current number)

Note that the current number should only be changed if specifically required, and should never be changed to a lower number. Changing the current number to one that is already in use may prevent the creation of new equipment for that group.

For the same reasons, that the current number could possibly be changed to one already in use, number ranges are not often transported (see the section titled, "Instances and Clients for more information regarding transporting.). As a common practice, number ranges are created or changed manually in each client.

- TIP: Keep a record of items to be performed manually in each client, possibly in a "cutover plan."

As of SAP R/3 version 4.6 and higher, number ranges can be manually created or modified in a system where the configuration is otherwise "locked down." Other security restrictions, however, still apply.

Usage History Update

This setting controls whether a history record of the equipment will be created if certain field values are changed on the equipment master record. The setting can be made independently for each equipment category.

Define History-Related Fields

Equipment history records can be created automatically by the system showing the status of an equipment master record at any point in time. The settings here control the changes by which an equipment history record is created. An "X" beside a field in this setting indicates that if that field value is changed in the equipment master record, a history record of the equipment is created showing the field value prior to the change.

Define Installation at Functional Location

A check mark beside an equipment category here indicates that equipment assigned to the equipment category can be assigned to (installed at) a functional location. Equipment assigned to one of the system default equipment categories, Machines, can typically be installed at a functional location, while equipment assigned to another system default equipment category, Production resources/tools, is typically not installed at a functional location.

Field Selection for Usage List

A selection variant (as well as a display variant) may be defined here. A selection variant is often a selection screen where one or more of the values are already filled, usually to save time avoiding entering those values. The selection variant can be defined as the new default (which affects all users) or as an optional selection screen, in which case the variant must be selected by the user. In some cases, the system will prevent the defaults from being overwritten. To save a selection variant, once the defaults have been entered, click on the "Save" button, make any desired changes to the field attributes, give the variant a name, and save it. The variant can then be used by the user through the "Goto → Variants → Get" menu path.

Likewise, clicking on the "Execute" button from the selection screen allows any equipment records available in the system to be displayed in a list. Fields can be removed from the display or added to the display, and otherwise changed. When the layout of the list is acceptable, the layout can be saved as a display variant in a similar manner by clicking the "Save" button and then naming the layout and specifying whether or not it is "User specific" and/or the "Default setting." Making the display variant user-specific makes it unavailable to other users. Making the display the default setting means that the variant will appear by default and will not have to be selected. Use caution when making a variant a non-user-specific default, meaning that all users will have the same default display layout.

Assign User Status Profile to Equipment Category

If a user status profile relevant to equipment has been created (see the section titled "Define User Status" for the definition of user statuses), the status must be assigned to one or more equipment categories in order to be used. This configuration setting allows the assignment of user status profiles to specific equipment categories.

Assign Partner Determination Procedure to Equipment Category

Although there are some default Partner Determination Procedures already defined, and default Partner Determination Procedures are already assigned, changes to the default assignments may be made here. See the section titled "Partners" for more information regarding the definition of partners and Partner Determination Procedures. The setting here allows any Partner Determination Procedures that have been defined to be assigned to specific Equipment Categories.

Define Field Selection for Equipment Master Record

The characteristics for fields on the equipment master record screens are controlled here. Specific fields may be made "required, " other fields may be made "display only" or "hidden." Fields may also be "highlighted." An "influencing" function may also be used here. For example, if an equipment master record is a specific technical object type, such as a pump, certain fields not pertinent to a pump may be hidden. Other fields may be made required for the same technical object type. Be advised of the trap of hiding some fields that may be desirable later and forgetting that they exist.

Allow Multilingual text Maintenance for Each Equipment Category

This setting simply allows or disallows the maintenance of the text in equipment master records of a specific equipment category to be maintained in other languages. The permission to maintain the text in multiple languages is indicated with a check mark.

Define List Structure for Structural Display

In this setting, a list of fields available for display in an equipment list is shown. A number beside a field indicates that the field will be displayed in a list of equipment. The field assigned to number 1 will be displayed leftmost in the list, the field assigned to number 2 will be displayed to the right of it, and so on. The numbers do not indicate the number of spaces from the left side of the screen, nor do they determine other formatting. The number simply indicates the order in which the fields will be displayed. The user of the equipment list screens can further determine the order in which the fields are displayed and can even control which fields are displayed and which fields are not displayed. The "Invisible" checkbox in this configuration setting controls whether a field is available to the user to be displayed at all.

Define List Structure for Structural Display of Installed Bases

Functionally, this setting is identical to the previous setting. Only the fields differ. One use of "Installed Base" is to structurally define a customer's equipment structures. A number beside each field indicates the order in which the field is displayed. Invisible fields cannot be displayed by the user.

Set List Editing for Equipment

When searching for one or more pieces of equipment, certain search criteria may be entered by the user. These settings control which fields are available for selection criteria, whether default criteria are already entered, and whether a field may be required. There is one setting for a list allowing display of equipment records only as well as a setting for a list allowing changes to the equipment. Selection variants can be defined for each of the settings, allowing the selection of the variant(s) from a list. Selecting a variant can often save time compared to entering all the search criteria values. Also, in this configuration step, a display variant may be defined that allows for a different display of the resulting equipment list. The display variant can be saved as the default for an individual or for all users, or as an alternative to the default display.

Set List Editing for Equipment in Customer Service

This configuration step is functionally identical to the previous step. It applies, however, to equipment used for the Customer Service (formerly Service Management) module.

Define Field Selection for Multi-Level List Displays of Equipment

The settings contained within this heading can be used to control the fields that are displayed in lists within the multi-level list displays of Equipment. For example, in the Equipment multi-level list display, there is a checkbox for Order. If that checkbox is checked, a list of orders related to the selected Equipment will be displayed. The settings for "Define Field Selection for Order Data Fields" will control which Order fields are displayed in the Multi-Level list. Each setting here corresponds to each checkbox on the Multi-Level List Display screen for Equipment. Refer to *Figure 6 The Multi-Level Equipment List.* The list and its legend display on the SAP R/3 screen in color, but are not portrayed in color here.

Each of these settings determines which fields will be displayed and in which order. A field assigned "Display Position" 1 will appear leftmost on the List Display screens. A field assigned to "Display Position" 2 will appear immediately to the right of the field assigned "Display Position" 1. Once again, the numbers only indicate the order in which the fields will be displayed and do not control the fields' physical position on the screen. The eventual user of the resulting screen can change the order in which the fields are displayed, remove fields from the display, and add other fields to the display. Marking a field as "Invisible" here will prevent the user from seeing, and therefore prevent the user from choosing that field.

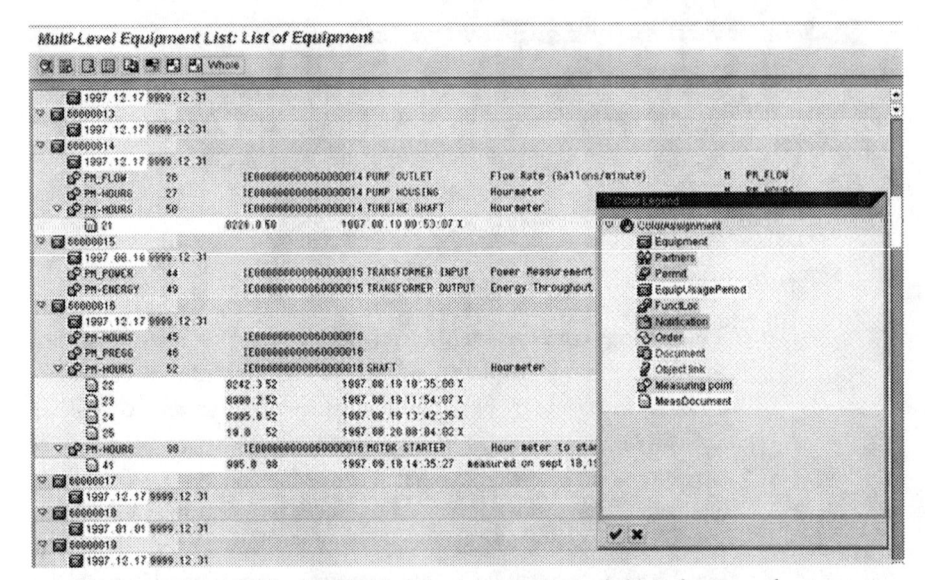

Figure 6. The Multi-Level Equipment List and the Color Legend
© SAP AG

Settings for Fleet Management

For fleet management to be implemented, certain settings must be configured in order to differentiate a Fleet Object from other equipment. Beginning with "Set View Profiles for Technical Objects, " a screen group must be defined for Fleet Objects. This will allow fleet-specific fields to be displayed. When a fleet-specific piece of equipment is created, it must be created with the "Create (Special)" option in the SAP menu (transaction code IE31) in order for the fleet-specific fields to be presented.

Assign View Profile and Equipment Categories to Fleet Object Types

Fleet Object types are defined in the configuration setting for "Define Technical Object Types, " along with other technical object types. This configuration step allows the defined Fleet Object types to be assigned to Equipment Categories and view profiles. View profiles are defined in the configuration setting for "Set View Profiles for Technical Objects." For example, the

Fleet Object types "Car" and "Fork Truck" may be assigned to the same Equipment Category and/or the same view profile.

Define Consumable Types

Fleet equipment may consume certain materials, such as gasoline (petrol), lubricating oil, and engine oil. Those consumables may be defined here.

Define Usage Types for Fleet Objects

The purpose of fleet objects may be defined here. An example of a usage for a fleet object might be "Company Business Only."

Define Engine Types for Fleet Objects

Engine types, such as gasoline, diesel, electric, etc. may be defined here.

Make Settings for Units of Measurement for Monitoring of Consumption

Here, settings can be defined to record consumption in terms of miles per gallon, liters per hundred kilometers, etc.

Define Special Measurement Positions for Fleet Objects

Positions can be defined that indicate the type of measurement that may be taken at that position. These settings may be used as a basis for the definition of measuring points and for evaluations. Further functionality may be available for this configuration setting in the future.

Define Calculation Method for Fleet Consumption Values

The most obvious consumption calculation methods are provided by default in the standard system (Miles/Gallon, for example). Others may be added, if necessary.

Set Field Selection for Specific Fields in Fleet Management

Functionally identical to the other Field Selection settings in the IMG, changes to the attributes of fields specific to Fleet Management may be made here.

Object Links

Although objects may be arranged in a hierarchy, such as a functional location/equipment hierarchy, objects in one branch of the hierarchy may affect objects in other parts of the hierarchy that may not be apparent in the structure of the hierarchy. Object linking allows those objects to be linked manually. Functional locations can be linked to other functional locations and equipment can be linked to other equipment.

The ability to link objects together may be useful for objects that share a "medium" such as water or natural gas, for example. Those pieces of equipment sharing the "medium" can be linked to show that a break in the flow of the "medium" affects downstream equipment as well as the equipment that may have broken down. If a piece of equipment breaks down, other equipment linked to it can be displayed.

Define Object Types

Additional categories relevant to object linking may be defined here.

Define Media for Object Links

The "medium," as discussed previously, may be defined here to provide a common linkage between objects. Two media that may be provided by default are "H2O" and "220v." Other media can be added as required.

Define Number Ranges for Object Links

In the default system, there may be an allowance for an internal (system assigned) number range and an external (user-assigned) number range for object links. Depending on needs, as with almost any number range, adjust, add, or delete number ranges as required.

Set List Editing for Object Links from Equipment

See "Set List Editing for Equipment" for more information. This setting allows defaults to be provided for searching for object links.

Set List Editing for Object Links from Functional Locations

See "List Editing for Equipment" for more information. This setting allows defaults to be provided for searching for object links.

Define Transaction Based Default Values for Object Types

This setting allows the default screens that appear for object type transactions to be changed to different screens. The default settings are usually acceptable, so changes should only be made here for very specific reasons. Note that although the descriptions of some screens are similar, some of those screens are specific to Plant Maintenance while the others are specific to Customer Service.

Define Structural Display for Material Data

Similar to other structural display settings, this configuration step allows the data displayed in lists of materials (in bills of material, for example) to be displayed in a specific order. See "Define List Structure for Structural Display" for more information.

Set List Editing for Material Data

See "List Editing for Equipment" for more information. Similar to that setting, this step allows the default selection for list displays but does not provide for list change.

Serial Number Management

Define Serial Number Profiles

Defines the method for applying serial numbers to materials. Often used in Customer Service in order to track specific pieces of equipment sold to customers as materials but to be maintained by maintenance staff, the functionality can also be used in the Plant Maintenance module for repairable spares, for example. There are also settings that determine whether serial numbers are/should be assigned at specific transactions.

Define Serialization Attributes for Movement Types

Changes to this configuration step are usually not required, but if changes to serialization attributes are required based on inventory management movement types, those changes may be made here.

Define Default Equipment Categories for Serial Numbers

The assignment of serial numbers within serial number ranges is defined for each equipment category here. There is a default setting for equipment category M, but others may be added, or the default setting removed, if required.

Deactivate Lock for Internal Assignment of Serial Numbers

Normally, only one user can assign serial numbers to a specific material at one time. Other users are prevented from creating serial numbers for the same material. In order to allow more than one user to "serialize" a material at the same time, this configuration step contains a checkbox for each equipment category. Check the box for each equipment category for which serialization is allowed by multiple users at the same time. Note that the number ranges are "buffered" and if such a user cancels a transaction without saving, a block of consecutive serial numbers may be skipped.

Transfer of Stock Check Indicator to Serial Numbers

If goods movements of serialized materials have already occurred and the Stock Check Indicator is changed for serial number settings, adjustments must be made to existing serial numbers. Although there are no configuration settings to be changed here, the documentation of this configuration step contains the name of the report that must be run in order to make the adjustments to existing serial numbers. Proper authorization is required to run reports/programs. One transaction code that can be used to run a report is transaction SA38.

Set List Editing for Serial Numbers

See "List Editing for Equipment" for more information. This setting allows default values to be provided for search criteria for serial numbers as well as allowing selection and display variants to be saved.

Field Selection for MultiLevel List Display of Serial Numbers

The settings contained within this heading can be used to control the fields that may be displayed in lists within the multi-level list displays of Serial Numbers. For example, in the Serial Number multi-level list display, there will be a checkbox for Maintenance Order. If that checkbox is checked, a list of maintenance orders related to the selected Serial Number will be displayed. The settings for "Define Field Selection for Maintenance Order Fields" will control which Maintenance Order fields are displayed in the Multi-Level list. Each setting here will correspond to each checkbox on the Multi-Level List Display screen for Equipment.

Each of these settings determines which fields will be displayed and in which order. A field assigned "Display Position" 1 will appear leftmost on the List Display screens. A field assigned to "Display Position" 2 will appear immediately to the right of the field assigned "Display Position" 1. Once again, the numbers only indicate the order in which the fields will be displayed and do not control the fields' physical position on the screen. The eventual user of the resulting screen can change the order in which the fields are displayed, remove fields from the display, and add other fields to the display. Marking a field as "Invisible" here will prevent the user from seeing, and therefore prevent the user from choosing that field.

Archive Serial Number History

With this setting, activity related to serial numbers can be kept in the system up to the specified number of days before it can be archived (deleted).

Bills of Material

Control Data for Bills of Material—Set Modification Parameters

Several default settings for Bills of Material may be made here. Although the SAP documentation recommends that the default settings be accepted, there may be some changes required, depending on project requirements. Some caution is required since some settings, such as "EC management active," will also affect the Production Planning module.

Control Data for Bills of Material—Define BOM Status

There are three default BOM statuses defined, which should suffice for most implementations. The SAP documentation recommends using the default configuration. The settings control which activities are permitted based on the status of a BOM.

Control Data for Bills of Material—Define Default Values

SAP recommends accepting the default values provided. These settings simply provide default values when Bills of Material are created.

General Data—BOM Usage—Define BOM Usages

The settings here allow Bills of Material to be "shared" between modules. A Bill of Material created for Production Planning purposes can also be used by Plant Maintenance, if appropriate. In most cases, the default setting where each department is responsible for defining and maintaining its own Bill of Materials is acceptable. Changes can be made, if desired and appropriate.

General Data—BOM Usage—Define Default Values for Item Status

The default settings are generally acceptable for Plant Maintenance use. For BOM Usage 4 (Plant Maintenance), the PM checkbox should be checked and the "Relevancy to costing" checkbox should be checked. The "Spare" indicator is applicable to Production Planning, not Plant Maintenance, and should be left blank for BOM Usage 4.

General Data BOM Usage Define Copy Default Values for Item Status

This configuration setting allows the creation of a Plant Maintenance BOM with reference to a Production BOM, as well as other types of creations with reference. If a Production BOM exists that could be copied with minor modifications, if any, to a Plant Maintenance BOM, a record showing a "1" in the "RefUsage" column, a "4" in the "UsageNew" column and a check mark in the "PM" checkbox should exist. If the BOM is relevant to costing, the appropriate setting (based on percentage) should be made in the "Relevant" field.

General Data—Define Valid Material Types for BOM Header

When a Material BOM (that is, a BOM with a material master record as its header) is to be created, certain materials can be marked as valid or invalid for the BOM header. By default, all material types are eligible as a BOM header for a Material BOM. If changes are required, for BOM usage 4 (Plant Maintenance), the second field should contain the material type and the third field should specify whether or not the material type can or can not be used as a BOM header. This configuration setting has no bearing on which types of materials can be included in the Bill of Materials itself.

General Data—Define Responsible Designers/Laboratories

This setting can be used to indicate the responsible party, or even the responsible individual for a Bill of Materials. Any entries made here will be available for entry into the appropriate field on the BOM. The maintenance of this field enables the searching and reporting of Bills of Material relevant to the responsible Designer/Lab/Individual.

General Data—Define History Requirements for Bills of Material

The settings here determine whether a change record is necessary when modifications to a BOM are made. A change record permits a historical "snapshot" of the BOM and also allows the creation of a "valid from" date for the BOM. Engineering Change Management must be active in order to use this functionality.

Item Data—Define Item Categories

The default settings provided by SAP are generally adequate for this configuration setting. Only if there is a specific requirement for which the SAP standard functionality is inadequate should additions or modifications be made here.

Item Data—Define Object Types

Once again, the SAP-provided default settings are adequate as provided and are provided for information only.

Item Data—Define Material Types Allowed for BOM Item

As with the earlier setting, "Define Material Types Allowed for BOM Header," the settings here indicate which material types are permitted to be used in the Bill of Materials itself. By default, all material types are valid for use in Plant Maintenance Bills of Material (as well as other types of BOM). If specific material types are to be included or excluded as valid material types for Bills of Material, make changes as required.

Item Data—Maintain Variable-Size Item Formulas

There are some default formulas provided that may meet the needs of those requiring such calculations for quantities of variable-sized materials. If additional formulas are required, they may be entered here. Note that variables in the formulas are indicated with the "ROMS" followed by a digit to identify one variable from another.

Item Data—Define Spare Part Indicators

This configuration setting can be ignored for Plant Maintenance purposes, since materials contained in a Plant Maintenance-related BOM are generally all spare parts.

Item Data—Define Material Provision Indicators

There are two default settings defined in this configuration step, which should be sufficient. The two defaults indicate that BOM materials can be provided by customers or vendors.

Determination of Alternative Bills of Material—Define Priorities for BOM Usage

For Plant Maintenance purposes, the default settings here can be accepted. If an additional BOM Usage was defined for Plant Maintenance, for some reason, the priority for each BOM Usage may be defined here.

Determination of Alternative Bills of Material—PM Specific Selection Criteria for Alternative Determination—Define Selection Criteria for Alternative Determination

Unless one or more additional BOM Usages have been defined for Plant Maintenance purposes, the default settings can be accepted here. If, for any reason, an additional BOM Usage has been defined for Plant Maintenance, the priority order of usages is defined here.

Determination of Alternative Bills of Material—PM Specific Selection Criteria for Alternative Determination—Check Selection Term for Alternative Determination

> Only a single setting can exist in this configuration step and one has been provided by SAP. Do not change the Selection Term provided unless there is a specific reason to do so, such as if the "INST" entry in the previous configuration setting has been changed.

Determination of Alternative Bills of Material—Define Alternative Selection by Material

> Alternative Bills of Material based on the material can be defined for Material Bills of Material, but not for Functional Location or Equipment Bills of Material. The setting here allows the selection of an Alternative BOM based on the material numbers provided.

Determination of Alternative Bills of Material—Make User Specific Settings

> Default settings specific to one or more users can be defined here, which may save time with repetitive entries. Note that if this setting is defined and must be changed in the future, it must be done in the Implementation Guide and possibly transported to the production SAP system.

Preventive Maintenance

Preventive Maintenance Overview

The Plant Maintenance module in SAP R/3 provides a very powerful, although somewhat complex, method of planning and organizing work to be performed on a regular schedule, when specific performance triggers have been reached, or a combination of the two.

Without launching into a detailed discussion regarding maintenance planning, a subject to which many books has already been dedicated, some description is necessary. In simple terms, reactive maintenance occurs when an event occurs that requires maintenance to be performed on a machine. Preventive maintenance attempts to minimize reactive maintenance by scheduling preventive maintenance work to be performed on a regular schedule. Preventive maintenance, however, may not be entirely cost effective, since some maintenance may be performed more often than is necessary. Predictive maintenance attempts to address that concern through analysis of the preventive maintenance and refining the preventive maintenance schedule in such a way that the preventive maintenance is performed at an optimal time. Of course, such maintenance concepts are more involved and more complex than described, but cannot be discussed more completely here.

SAP R/3 Plant Maintenance provides work order cycles for reactive (breakdown) maintenance and preventive maintenance, as well as providing analysis tools to assist with predictive maintenance. The primary advantage of preventive maintenance work orders is that they can be produced by the system automatically. The actual work order cycle is discussed later.

Discussion of the configuration for Preventive Maintenance in the Implementation Guide (IMG) will follow this section. Also, see page 210 for more detailed information regarding maintenance plans.

Maintenance Task Lists

Some of the terminology involved with SAP's maintenance planning may require some familiarization. A *task list* is required to provide a step-by-step instruction of the maintenance to be performed. In SAP's terminology, the tasks of a task list can be equated to the operations of a work order. When a work order is created from a maintenance plan, the tasks of the related task list become operations of the resulting work order. Each task on the task list may include labor requirements and material requirements.

Maintenance Strategies

A *maintenance strategy* consists of maintenance cycles usually grouped by a unit of measure common denominator. For example, a "Monthly" strategy may consist of cycles such as "Every month, " "Every 2 months, " "Every 4 months, " "Every 6 months, " and so on. The common denominator is one month. See *Figure 7 A strategy and some of its packages.*

A *maintenance package*, or simply *package*, is simply one of the cycles in a strategy. The example above of a maintenance strategy shows that the "Monthly" strategy includes the packages 1 month, 2 months, 4 months, and 6 months.

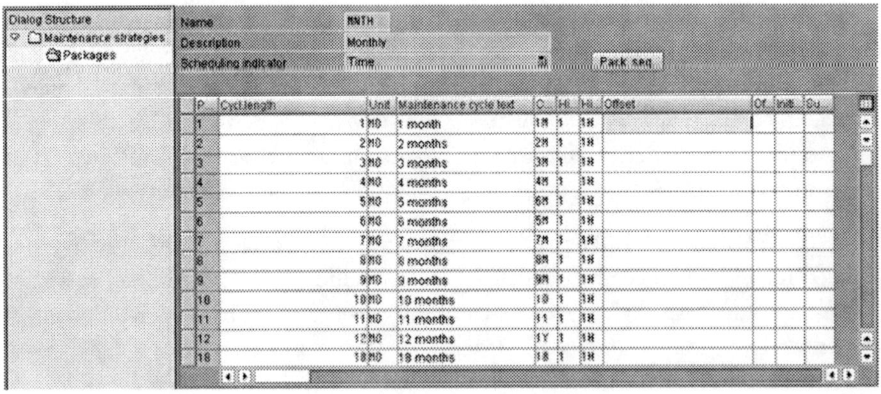

Figure 7. A strategy (MNTH) and some of its packages (cycles).
© SAP AG

Maintenance Items

In recent releases, SAP has attempted to make maintenance planning a little more simple where possible. A result of this is that the *maintenance item* is now less obtrusive than before. In instances where maintenance is to be performed on one piece of equipment and for only a single cycle, the user may be unaware that a maintenance item is involved, since its creation is automatic. A maintenance item serves to link the maintenance tasks and cycles to one or more pieces of equipment (or other technical object).

Maintenance Plans

The *maintenance plan* combines all of the previously mentioned terms into an overall plan. The maintenance plan itself simply provides a start date for the cycle(s) contained within, as well as some other default settings. Several *maintenance items* may be contained in the same maintenance plan if the start date of the required packages (cycles) can be the same.

Creating and Maintaining Maintenance Plans

The basic steps for creating a maintenance plan are as follows:

1. Ensure that the materials required for the tasks have been defined in Materials Management.
2. Ensure that the labor required has been defined (as work centers) in the system.
3. Ensure that the strategy and packages (cycles) required have been defined in the system (for a strategy-based plan).
4. Create the task list.
5. Assign materials as required to the tasks in the task list.
6. Assign labor as required to the tasks in the task list.
7. Assign the tasks in the task list to packages (for a strategy-based plan).
8. Create the maintenance plan.
9. Assign the equipment or other technical object to the maintenance plan. Add maintenance items for additional technical objects, if required.
10. Assign the task list to the maintenance plan.

Starting a Maintenance Plan (Scheduling)

Once the previous steps have been accomplished to create the maintenance plan, the plan must be assigned a start date (a proposed start date may have been entered during the creation or during the saving of the maintenance plan) and then must actually be started.

Initial Start

The term initial start is sometimes used to indicate the first time a maintenance plan is started. This is accomplished by simply clicking on a button marked "Start" on the "Schedule Maintenance Plan" screen, providing a date on which the plan will start, and then saving. See *Figure 8, The "Schedule Maintenance Plan" screen*, which shows the "Start" button. Although the "Scheduling Parameters" tab is available here for viewing, the scheduling parameters should have been set prior to scheduling the plan, since those parameters will affect the scheduling of the plan.

Note that the "Start" date does not indicate the date on which the first work order will be produced or released, but it does indicate the date from which all the packages (cycles) in the plan will be started. For example, if the strategy is weekly and one of the packages applied to a task is once per week, the first work order will be due one week after the start date of the plan. The work order may be created before the due date, depending on the scheduling parameters in the plan and/or the strategy.

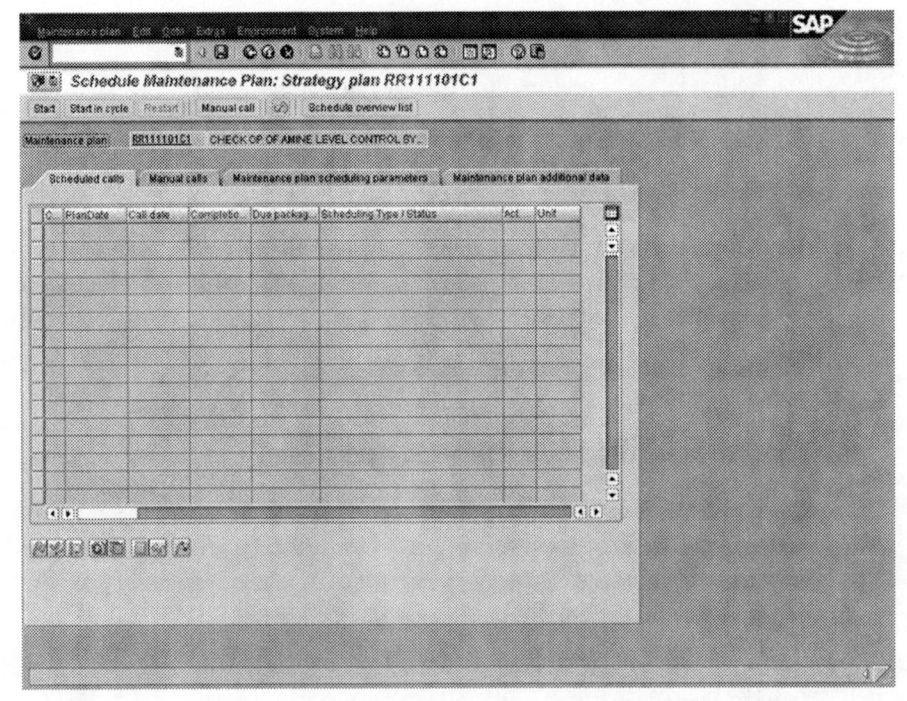

Figure 8. The "Schedule Maintenance Plan" screen before scheduling.
© *SAP AG*

Start In Cycle

If a convenient date to start the plan does not coincide with the logical start of a maintenance cycle for a piece of equipment, there is an option for the maintenance plan to *start in cycle*. In order to start a maintenance plan somewhere in its cycle, the procedure is much the same as the *initial start,* but with the addition of an *offset*. The offset indicates the amount of time into the cycle that the plan should be started.

Maintaining Maintenance Calls

Skipping Calls

In order to "skip" a call, which means that scheduled work will not be performed, the specific call to be skipped must be selected on the "scheduled calls" list and the "Skip call" button near the bottom of the screen must be clicked. Skipping a call may not cause the next call to be rescheduled. If the next call must be moved forward, it may be necessary to release the subsequent call manually.

Releasing Calls Manually

If it becomes necessary to release a call before its scheduled release date, a call can be manually release by selecting the call and clicking on the "Release call" button near the bottom of the screen.

Manual calls can be viewed from this screen via the "Manual calls" tab.

Deadline Monitoring

Deadline Monitoring, formerly known as "Date Monitoring," may be used to produce one or many preventive maintenance orders at once. The terms "Deadline Monitoring" and "Date Monitoring" are both misleading in that the functionality does not simply monitor calls and work orders. If not carefully used, Deadline Monitoring can produce and possibly release many work orders by mistake.

Taking scheduling and control parameters into consideration, if calls are due within the number of days specified in Deadline Monitoring, a work order will be created for each call due within that time period.

If security has not been implemented beyond the transaction code level, it is possible to produce work orders for another planner group or even another plant intentionally or by mistake. If implementing SAP R/3 Plant Maintenance for more than one planner group or for more than one plant, security at the appropriate levels is strongly recommended.

Deadline Monitoring is often used to group preventive maintenance calls and orders and is run on a regular basis, quite often as a regularly scheduled process, or "batch job." It prevents the necessity of updating the scheduling of maintenance plans manually.

Work orders created must be released before any actual goods issues or time (labor) confirmations can be charged to them. If work orders are not configured to release upon creation, it may be necessary to release work orders manually, including those created by Deadline Monitoring.

Back to the Implementation Guide (IMG)—Maintenance Plans

The step-by-step discussion of the Plant Maintenance Maintenance Plans section of the implementation guide is continued below:

Basic Settings

Maintain Authorizations for Planning

Maintaining authorizations, a security function of the SAP R/3 system, is best done in co-operation with the individual(s) whose responsibility it is to maintain security for the system. See the section "Security: Authorizations and Roles" for more information.

Define Plant Sections

This setting is typically used to represent individuals responsible for certain areas of a plant based on production responsibility. The intent is that, should a problem occur in a certain area of the plant, the person responsible can be determined and notified. This IMG entry is a duplicate of entries in the "Technical Objects" and "Maintenance and Service Processing" areas.

Define Maintenance Planner Groups

This setting is also a duplicate of settings in the "Technical Objects" and "Maintenance and Service Processing" areas. A maintenance planner group may be composed of one or more people who have the responsibility for planning maintenance work. A maintenance planner group that has been defined for a piece of equipment, for example, will by default appear on work orders related to that piece of equipment.

Define ABC Indicators

One more duplicate of settings in the "Technical Objects" and "Maintenance and Service Processing" areas, The ABC Indicator field can be used as a means of categorizing equipment. There is no definite use for the field, but it is typically used to represent the importance or criticality of a technical object. Although the values A, B and C are provided by default, more may be added or any may be deleted as required.

Maintenance Plans

Set Maintenance Plan Categories

There is an entry in this configuration step for Plant Maintenance work orders to be generated from maintenance plans, among other default settings. SAP R/3 versions from 4.5 onward also allow the creation of notifications from maintenance plans. By default, the PM *maintenance plan category* will specify that a PM maintenance plan will generate a maintenance work order. This can be changed here, if necessary.

Define Number Ranges for Maintenance Plans

This setting can be used to define a separate number range for each of the previously mentioned maintenance plan categories, if desired. The maintenance plans created in each maintenance plan category can be automatically or manually assigned a number from the same number range or from different number ranges based on the settings made here. See the section titled

"Number Ranges" for more information. Ensure that the number range is large enough to permit the assignment of numbers to maintenance plans into the foreseeable future.

Define Number Ranges for Maintenance Items

Maintenance items, simply stated, provide a means of assigning maintenance task lists to multiple objects based on the same scheduling start date. At least one maintenance item is created for each maintenance plan, so the number range available for maintenance items should never be smaller than the number range provided for maintenance plans. If there is even a small chance that multiple maintenance items will be assigned to a maintenance plan, the number range for maintenance items should be larger than that for maintenance plans to allow for the assignment of numbers to maintenance items into the foreseeable future.

Define Sort Fields for Maintenance Plan

Here, methods of sorting and grouping maintenance plans may be defined. The main advantage to providing sort fields for maintenance plans is to allow scheduling of multiple plans as a group in order to save time. The alternative may be to perform the scheduling individually. Some thought may be required to provide some convention or standard naming for the sort field values.

Define Field Selection for Maintenance Plan

When a list of maintenance plans is displayed, the settings here determine which maintenance plan fields are displayed, and in which order. As with other settings discussed previously, the field identified as #1 will be displayed first, on the left side of the screen displaying the list of maintenance plans. The field identified as #2 will be displayed immediately to the right of field #1 and so on. The numbers, as discussed previously, do not specify a position on the screen, just the order in which each field is displayed from the left.

Define Field Selection for Operation Data

As in the above setting, when a list of operations in the scheduling overview is displayed, this setting determines which fields are displayed by default, and in which order. Unless a specific field is checked as "invisible, " the user can still select which fields to display on the scheduling overview. These settings primarily control the default display.

Set List Editing

The next several configuration settings allow the control and defaults of selection criteria for the display of lists of maintenance plan and maintenance item data. Similar to "set list editing" steps discussed previously, these settings can be saved as an alternative to the default setting or in most cases can be saved as the default setting.

Work Centers

A work center, from an SAP Plant Maintenance perspective, is usually one or more people. If a work center is comprised of more than one person, those people should be equally qualified. That is, it doesn't matter which person is assigned to perform a task. In this way, several people with equal qualifications can be grouped together and their combined capacity can be used to more effectively schedule work.

Work centers are assigned to cost centers, from where valid activities and activity rates are derived. This is the source of planned and actual labor rates, multiplied by the number of hours, for example, that provides the cost of labor required to perform a task.

It is important to note that in the Production Planning module of SAP R/3, a work center is normally used to specify a place where work is performed, or to specify a machine that performs the work. In the Plant Maintenance module, a work center can also identify one or more similar machines that are used to perform maintenance work. This can serve as an alternative to defining the machine as a PRT (Production Resources and Tools). However, a Plant Maintenance work center most often defines a person or a group of people.

To determine whether the Plant Maintenance work center can define a group of people, first determine if it matters which of the people in the group is assigned to perform a particular task. If only a particular person in the group can perform the task, it is likely that the person does not belong to the work center.

For a group of people to belong to the same work center, it usually should not matter which of the people in the group is assigned to a particular task. They should all be capable of performing similar tasks and they should all be charged at the same labor rate to the work order, where applicable.

When configuring work centers, particularly the "Configure Screen Sequence for Work Center" step, remember that not all of the work center functionality and screens are relevant to Plant Maintenance. For example, if the "Technical Data" screen is active for Plant Maintenance and some of its fields are required, this may cause problems for the person creating a Plant Maintenance work center. The person may find themselves on the "Technical Data" tab, which is difficult to exit without losing data if the required information is not available, which it may not be for Plant Maintenance.

After the appropriate screen sequence has been defined, be sure to go back to the step described next, "Define Work Center Types and Link to Task List Application." This ensures that the proper field selection and screen sequences are assigned to the appropriate work center category.

When defining a work center (outside of the Implementation Guide), be sure to enter data on the Capacity Header screen and its subscreens, if applicable, to ensure that the proper capacity has been defined for the work center. Otherwise, assigning the work center to work orders will cause a warning message stating that not enough resources are available to perform the work. The Capacity Header screen can be accessed by clicking on the "Capacity" button near the bottom of the screen on the "Capacities" tab when creating or changing a work center. See *Figure 9*.

From the Capacity Header screen, the "Intervals and Shifts" button can be used to create a variety, or rotation, of shifts for the work center, if required.

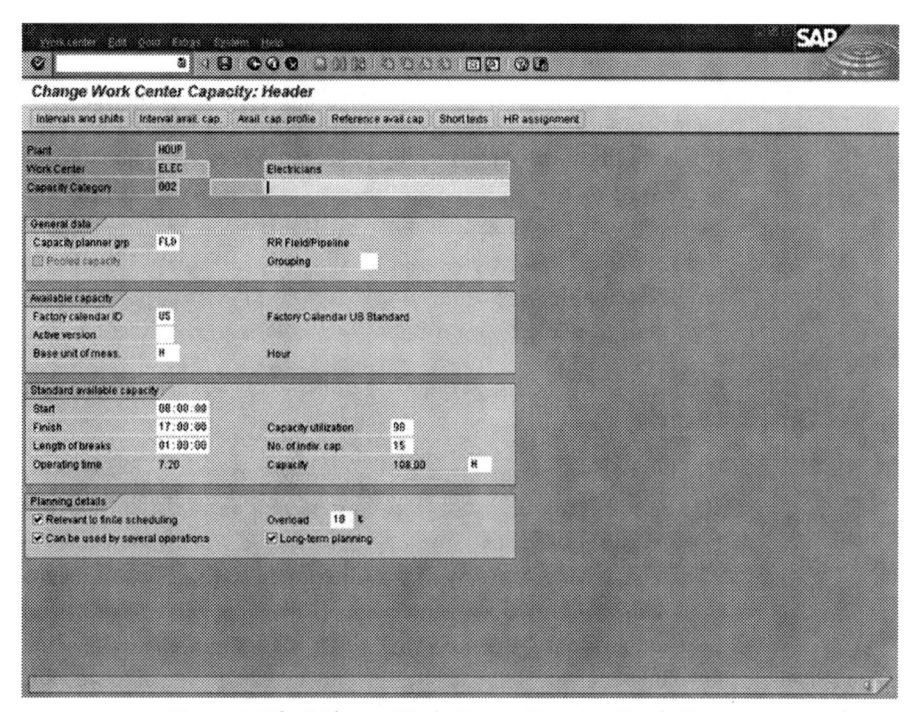

Figure 9. The "Change Work Center Capacity Header" screen.
© SAP AG

A description of the Implementation Guide configuration steps for work centers follows:

Define Work Center Types and Link to Task List Application

One primary function of this configuration step is to set the fields and screen sequences that are available when creating work centers. The Plant Maintenance work center category may default to the field selection and screen sequence for machines. Changing the field selection and screen sequence settings relevant to Plant Maintenance will help to present screens that better represent Plant Maintenance work center requirements. Whether the work center can be used in other applications may also be controlled here.

Define Field Selection

This setting can be used to control whether fields relevant to work centers are input fields, display only fields, mandatory input fields, and so on. The field attributes can also be set according to the value of specific influencing field values. For example, if the work order category is specific to Plant Maintenance, some fields may be hidden. This allows the fields to be available for other work center applications, such as Production, while being hidden for Plant Maintenance use.

Set Parameters

There is often no need to make changes to this configuration setting for Plant Maintenance. The parameters defined here are used in the subsequent configuration step, *Define Standard Value Keys*. This setting, along with the subsequent setting allow for standard setup and teardown times, which are often more appropriate for Production work centers than Plant Maintenance work centers.

Define Standard Value Keys

More often than not, the *standard value key* used for Plant Maintenance purposes is SAP0, which includes no parameters from the previous configuration step. If a standard setup, teardown, or other standard value is to be considered in scheduling, a different *standard value key*, along with one or more parameters from the previous configuration step, may be used.

Define Employees Responsible for Work Centers

Define a person or group responsible for the maintenance of work center master data for each plant. If an individual is identified, rather than a group, it may be beneficial to use a code, role, or position to represent the individual. Using an individual's real name will require maintenance of this setting when the individual's role changes.

Create Default Work Center

A default work center may be useful in order to reduce the amount of time required to create multiple work centers. Prior to creating one or more default work centers, it may be even more beneficial to create a default capacity, which can provide further default information to the default work center. Creating a default capacity, if desired, can be found (in version 4.6C) in the Implementation Guide (IMG) by following the menu path **Production → Basic Data → Work Center → Capacity Planning → Define Default Capacity.**

Define Task List Usage Keys

This configuration step can be used to control the types of task lists where a work center may be used. The default settings are most often acceptable. A common work-around when configuration of *task list usage* 004 (Only maintenance task lists) is not adequate is to refer to *task list usage* 009 (All task list types) when creating a work center. If *task list usage* 009 is used, however, the work center may be used in task lists in which it might be inappropriate.

Maintain Control Keys

There are several settings in this configuration step that control whether tasks related to the *control key* are relevant for scheduling, costing, capacity requirements, printing, confirmation, and so on. There are several default *control keys* relevant to Plant Maintenance. These begin with "PM" and in many cases may be adequate. Add others, if necessary, but take care not to alter or delete other control keys that may already be in use, or may be used in the future, by other SAP modules. When the system is in use, the *control key* in Plant Maintenance is assigned to each operation of a work order or task list.

Define Suitabilities

One or more qualifications may be defined here for later use to determine whether a person is suitable or qualified to perform a task. This setting is specific to each plant.

Configure Screen Sequence for Work Center

There are several screens involved in the definition of a work center. This setting controls the order in which the screens are presented as well as whether the screens are presented at all and whether data entry on any given screen is mandatory. If a change to this setting does not appear to work properly, it may be worth checking to see that the previous configuration step, *Define Work Center Types and Link to Task List Application,* is configured to the correct field selection and screen sequences.

Task Lists

Maintain Task List Status

For most basic uses of task lists in the Plant Maintenance module, the *task list statuses* provided as defaults are sufficient. For Plant Maintenance purposes, only two of the default statuses are required, 1 (Created) and 2 (released for order). Do not delete the other entries unless they will never be used by any other module, such as Production Planning. If there is a specific reason to create any additional statuses, they may be added here. In using the system, however, when searching for task lists, the system requires that a task list have the status of "2" to be found. Task lists with any other status cannot be found with the standard list display functionality.

Define Task List Usage

In most cases, particularly for Plant Maintenance purposes, the SAP-provided defaults are acceptable here.

Configure Planner Group

Individuals or groups responsible for task list planning are identified here. This is not necessarily the same as *planner groups* found in other sections of the IMG. A setting made in one planner group configuration step may not be carried over to another planner group configuration step. At least one planner group should be defined for each valid plant. Unless used by another module, such as Production Planning, the SAP default planner groups (Planergruppe 1, for example) can be deleted.

Define Number Ranges for General Maintenance Task Lists

There is a separate number range for each of the task list types. This number range setting is to provide a range of numbers for general maintenance task lists. This number range is not shared with any other SAP module or any other task list type. See the section on *number ranges* for more information on configuring number ranges.

Define Number Ranges for Equipment Task Lists

This number range setting is to provide a number range for equipment task lists. This number range is not shared with any other SAP module or any other task list type. See the section on *number ranges* for more information on configuring number ranges.

Define Number Ranges for Task Lists for Functional Locations

This number range setting is to provide a number range for functional location task lists. This number range is not shared with any other SAP module or any other task list type. See the section on *number ranges* for more information on configuring number ranges.

Define Profiles with Default Values

At least two profiles should be configured for use with Plant Maintenance task lists. Two appropriate default profiles may be provided with the system. One profile should be configured for use with primarily internally (employee) processed work and the other profile should be configured for use with primarily external (contract, for example). The profiles provide default values for the creation of task lists. If fields are not filled in a profile, some field values may need to be entered when creating a task list header or in each operation of the task list. Likewise, if a profile is not referenced when creating a task list, some field values may not be defaulted.

Define Presetting for Free Assignment of Material

This setting is normally acceptable as defaulted. There should be a "4" in the configuration table. This allows the free assignment of materials to a BOM, etc.

Define Field Selection

This setting, not available in some version 4.6 releases and older, allows task list field attributes to be set. For example, specific fields can be set to be "display only, " "required, " "hidden, " etc. There are numerous fields upon which the field attributes can be influenced. For example, a specific field could be hidden based on the planning plant.

Maintain Control Keys

This is a similar setting to the *maintain control keys* setting in the *work center* section previously discussed. There are several settings in this configuration step that control whether tasks related to the *control key* are relevant for scheduling, costing, capacity requirements, printing, confirmation, and so on. There are several default *control keys* relevant to Plant Maintenance. These begin with "PM" and in many cases may be adequate. Add others, if necessary, but take care not to alter or delete other control keys that may already be in use, or may be used in the future, by other SAP modules. When the system is in use, the *control key* in Plant Maintenance is assigned to each operation of a work order or task list.

Maintain Suitabilities

Changes made in this configuration step affect the same table in SAP as changes made in the *define suitabilities* section under *work centers*. One or more qualifications may be defined here for later use to determine whether a person is suitable or qualified to perform a task. This setting is specific to each plant.

Define User Fields

Additional fields that are not already defined by the system may be added in order to record additional data in the operations of a work order. There are several different types of fields in order to accommodate different types of data, such as character, numeric, date, etc.

The fields are given labels in the configuration step and the actual values associated with each label are assigned in the work order. The use of the user-defined fields is not suitable for recording readings during completion confirmation. Maintenance of the field values is performed during the creation or changing of a work order.

The *user field* functionality is shared among modules, particularly the PP (Production Planning) and SD (Sales & Distribution) modules, so coordinate definition of user fields between the modules according to the *field key*.

Set List Editing for Task Lists

This configuration setting allows the setup of variants to search for task lists. Although the standard system settings allow for task list searching, it may be preferable to have several search parameters predefined in order to save time repeatedly entering the same selection criteria when searching for task lists.

Presetting for List Display of Multi-Level Task Lists

Within this heading, there are settings for each of the lists that may appear when searching for task lists under the multi-level task list search. As with the other multi-level searches, when using the system, a group of check boxes representing objects that may be associated with task lists appears. To view the associated date, the check box for each object must be checked. The related data is then displayed with the task lists to which it is associated. These configuration settings define which fields are displayed in the list for each of the associated objects. The default settings are often a good starting point, but the default list displays may be expanded or restricted as necessary. If a field is not displayed by default, the system user can still display the field by selecting it in the display screen.

Production Resources/Tools

Define PRT Authorization Group

Production Resources and Tools master records may be protected from changes by unauthorized users by using this setting. Standard SAP security does not provide security down to the level of individual objects unless authorization groups such as provided in this setting are used. If protection at the object level is not required, changes are not required here. The creation and changing of PRT's in general can still be protected with standard SAP security by restricting access to the transactions that allow the creation and changing of PRT master records.

If security is required at the object level, determine which groups of PRT records will be restricted to which groups of users (roles), and then define the authorization groups in this setting. The authorization groups will then need to be assigned to the appropriate users/roles.

Define PRT Status

There are some default PRT statuses provided, which may be adequate. The PRT status controls whether a PRT can be used at all, and whether it can be used for planning and/or production. Other statuses, if required, may be defined.

Define Task List Usage Keys

There are several default *task list usage keys*. Although only one or two of the keys are normally useful in the Plant Maintenance module, the others are useful for other modules, particularly Production Planning. For this reason, it is recommended not to delete any of the default *task list usage keys*. *Task list types* are assigned to the *task list usage keys* as part of this configuration. The only two keys that have the Plant Maintenance *task list types* assigned to them are 004 (Only maintenance task lists) and 009 (All task list types).

When creating a piece of equipment that is a PRT (Production Resources and Tools), using transaction IE25 instead of transaction IE01, an extra tab containing PRT-specific fields will appear. One of the fields is the *task list usage* field. If the equipment is to be used for Plant Maintenance purposes, the task list usage must be 004 or 009, if the default *task list usage keys* are used.

Define PRT Group Keys

Production Resources and Tools (PRT's) can be grouped according to the groups defined in this configuration step. There may be some group keys already defined, which can be deleted if they are not useful. Note that PRT's defined as equipment cannot make use of this grouping. Searching for equipment PRT's based on the *PRT group key* cannot normally be performed. PRT's defined as materials, however, can use the grouping.

Define PRT Control Keys

This setting is used to control whether a PRT is included in the functions of a task list or an order to which it is assigned. An example of one of the functions is *scheduling*. A PRT may be excluded from such functions, if desired.

Formulas

The two settings contained in the *Formulas* heading are *Set Formula Parameters* and *Configure Formula Definition*. The first step is used to define formulas that are used or combined in the second step. The assignment of a PRT can be as exact and as complex as desired and with these settings, set up time, tear down time and numerous other factors affecting capacity planning and costs may be set. If such detailed tracking is not required, accept these settings as they are defaulted. Even if such formulae are required, examine the default formulas first. The formula required may already be defined.

Service Contracts

Set List Editing for Service Contracts

This setting is usually only relevant for Customer Service functionality, but it controls the list editing displays for information related to *service contracts*. This configuration step is similar to the other configuration steps involving the definition of list editing.

The Work Order Cycle

The complete work order cycle in the SAP R/3 system includes notifications, work orders, assignment of labor, assignment of materials, completion confirmation (possibly involving the Cross-Application Time Sheet, CATS), settlement, and business completion of the work order. The cycle may extend to the analysis of reactive maintenance work so that preventive maintenance can be scheduled to reduce the amount of reactive/breakdown maintenance.

Although, technically speaking, it is possible to use work orders without notifications, or notifications without work orders, in the R/3 Plant Maintenance system, to omit either will mean a loss of information. Notifications can maintain statistical information, such as mean-time-between-failures, that can be important in reducing breakdown maintenance work. Work orders maintain the essential integration with other modules, including cost information. In addition, the relationship between notifications and work orders provides a method for approval of requested work.

Determine, along with controlling and/or finance personnel, the method by which work orders will be settled. SAP allows work orders to be settled to a variety of receivers, including cost centers, projects, internal orders, other work orders, and so on. If equipment has been assigned to the appropriate cost centers, for example, work orders created for that equipment would, by default, settle to those cost centers.

Notifications

A notification in the SAP R/3 system is typically used to notify someone that some work is required, is requested, or was already done. Those three typical uses define the three default notification types for PM, although other notification types are available for QM (Quality Management) and CS (Customer Service), formerly SM (Service Management). Non-PM notification types should not be deleted without determining that other modules will never use them.

Notifications, in addition to the functionality listed above, track and compile statistical information and history regarding the objects against which they were created. A notification, however, retains no cost information and has no significant integration with other modules.

A *malfunction report* notification is, as the name suggests, a report that a malfunction has occurred. Usually, a malfunction report is used where it might be beneficial to record breakdown information such as mean-time-between-failures or mean-time-to-repair. The relevant piece of equipment may be completely stopped or its performance may be reduced.

A *maintenance request* notification is usually used to request maintenance work on a piece of equipment that may be functioning satisfactorily, but whose operator, for example, may see a potential problem.

An *activity report* notification is normally used to record work that has already been performed in order to maintain complete statistical history for the relevant equipment.

Although other notification types may be defined, the majority of implementations should find that the three default notification types described above would suffice. Since notifications can be identified as assigned to a particular plant, there is certainly no need to create different notification types for each plant, nor is there any need to specially number ("smart" number) the notifications for each plant.

The historical information recorded through the use of notifications is best done with the use of *catalogs*, which are described in the section on catalogs, below.

Catalogs

In the SAP R/3 system, catalogs represent a method of providing standard codes for damage, cause of damage, activities, and so on. The advantage of using standard codes and descriptions instead of allowing free-form descriptions is that when the information is summarized, it is possible to see how many times a particular problem has occurred with a particular piece of equipment within a specific time frame and how many times each maintenance activity was performed to resolve the problem. Further analysis allows the tracking of problems to a particular manufacturer, if manufacturer data is recorded for equipment. Without standard codes it would be difficult, at best, to summarize such information into a usable format.

A *catalog profile* provides a means of grouping catalog codes that are relevant to a particular function, for example. The codes within a catalog profile are made available to notifications based on the object (piece of equipment, for example) against which the notification is written. If a piece of equipment has a catalog profile assigned to it, only the codes within that catalog profile will be available to notifications written for that piece of equipment. A catalog profile, therefore, can be a method of reducing the number of codes to those relevant for an object.

Within a catalog profile are *code groups*, which can be used to further reduce the quantity of codes from which to choose. Codes can be grouped into equipment types, for example, so that the types of damage for pumps are contained in a separate code group than the types of damage for motors. The two main factors for separating the codes are:

- to avoid the use of codes that are not relevant to the object, and
- to restrict the choices to a manageable number. The more choices available in a list, the longer it will take to make a choice and the chance of a wrong choice being made will increase.

Finally, the *codes* within each code group are defined. Ensure that the codes are relevant to the group. Ideally, the number of code groups from which to choose should be minimized, as should the number of codes within each code group. In some situations, particularly where the use of codes is regulated, it may not be possible to minimize the number of codes.

For Plant Maintenance purposes, the *catalogs* typically used are *damage, cause of damage, object part, activities, tasks,* and sometimes *coding.* Other catalogs, if required, may be defined, but bear in mind that the catalog code can only be one character or digit. Since SAP reserves the right to use all the digits and the characters A to O inclusive, only the codes P to Z may be used to define other desired catalogs.

The information accumulated on notifications by means of using catalogs can be reported using the *Plant Maintenance Information System (PMIS)*, a subset of the *Logistics Information System (LIS)*, which is described in a later section.

Work Orders

A work order in the SAP R/3 system is typically used to plan work that is required, assign the work to resources who will perform the necessary work, accumulate labor and material costs, and track completion of the work.

A sequence of tasks (or operations) can be included on the work order. Labor and materials that will be required to complete the work are defined on the work order while it is in the planning stage. This provides planned labor and material costs.

If planned materials are purchased independently of work orders and are kept in stock, the work order will generate a reservation for such materials. If planned materials are not kept in stock and must be purchased specifically for the work order, the work order will generate a purchase requisition for such materials.

Planned labor can be performed by internal resources (employees) or by external resources (contractors). This will be discussed in more detail later.

During completion of the work, goods (materials) are issued to the work order, which causes actual material costs to accumulate on the work order. Confirmations of labor, either through the Human Resources module or directly in the Plant Maintenance module, cause actual labor costs to accumulate on the work order.

The three basic steps to complete and close a work order consist of technical completion, which usually indicates that all of the work has been completed, settlement, during which the accumulated costs on the work order are settled to a cost center or other cost receiver, and business completion (close).

A work order in SAP R/3 can be generated from a notification, it can be created independently, or it can be generated from a maintenance plan.

As with notifications, there are several work order types provided with the R/3 system by default. Many find that the default work order types are adequate for their needs, but additional order types can be defined if required. Since work orders can be identified by plant, there is no need to "smart" number the work orders to identify them by plant.

Unless there are circumstances requiring that work orders be manually numbered, it is usually recommended that the system assign work order numbers automatically. This is referred to as "internal" numbering. See the section on "Number Ranges" for further information.

Back to the Implementation Guide (IMG)—Maintenance and Service Processing

The step-by-step discussion of the Maintenance and Service Processing section of the implementation guide is continued below:

Basic Settings

Maintain Authorizations for Processing

Maintaining authorizations, a security function of the SAP R/3 system, is best done in co-operation with the individual(s) whose responsibility it is to maintain security for the system. See the section "Security: Authorizations and Roles" for more information.

Planning of Background Jobs for PDC

PDC, *Plant Data Collection*, can be used to automatically update information in the SAP system, possibly saving time and effort entering repetitive data into the SAP system. However, since there is more than one specific method by which to accomplish the automation, it is not possible to determine beforehand what these settings should be. The third-party data collection system and the method by which it will be interfaced with the SAP system will determine what the settings in this configuration step will be.

Since there may be some significant time involved in getting two systems to "talk" to each other and transfer data reliably, ensure that the scope of the implementation includes the integration of a plant data collection system and SAP R/3.

Define Download Parameters for PDC

As with the previous configuration step, this step also relates to the automatic collection and transfer of data from an external system to the SAP R/3 system. If this is required, work closely with the developers or programmers to determine how these settings should be set to meet the needs of the Plant Maintenance module in relation to the methods used to interface the two systems.

Define Plant Sections

This setting is typically used to represent individuals responsible for certain areas of a plant based on production responsibility. The intent is that, should a problem occur in a certain area of the plant, the person responsible can be determined and notified. This IMG entry is a duplicate of entries in the "Technical Objects" and "Maintenance Plans" areas.

Define Planner Groups

This setting is also a duplicate of settings in the "Technical Objects" and "Maintenance Plans" areas. A maintenance planner group may be composed of one or more people who have the responsibility for planning maintenance work. A maintenance planner group that has been defined for a piece of equipment, for example, will by default appear on work orders related to that piece of equipment.

Define ABC Indicators

One more duplicate of settings in the "Technical Objects" and "Maintenance Plans" areas, The ABC Indicator field can be used as a means of categorizing equipment. There is no definite use for the field, but it is typically used to represent the importance or criticality of a technical object. Although the values A, B and C are provided by default, more may be added or any may be deleted as required.

Define Shop Papers, Forms and Output Programs

This configuration step controls which shop papers, such as notifications and work orders, are available for printing. Within the configuration step, shop papers specific to notifications may be defined as well as shop papers specific to work orders. If a custom work order print form has been developed, that form must be defined in this configuration step (or another similar, later configuration step) in order to be available for printing.

Define Printer

This heading consists of three settings as follows:

- *Set User-Specific Print Defaults.* If a specific user (or a member of a specific planner group or planning plant) requires a different default printer, language, number of copies, etc., these settings may be made here.

- *Define Print Diversion.* If a specific shop paper must be printed on a different printer than the default printer, perhaps because it contains sensitive information, the setting for a different printer may be made here.

Print Diversion According to Field Contents

If a specific printer must be used, depending on the value of a particular field, then that setting may be made here.

Activate Printing in Online Processing

It may be necessary, during the programming of shop papers, to test the functionality during online processing rather than from the update program. The setting to do so may be made here. This setting should be made individually in the instance (system) in which the testing is required, and the setting should not be transported. The checkbox should not be checked in the production system.

Download

The two settings contained in this heading, *"Define Destination and Database for PC Download"* and *"Download Structures to PC,"* are used to define the method by which notifications and/or work orders (shop papers) may be downloaded to a Microsoft Access database. The online documentation in the Implementation Guide provides further information. Note that, since this setting is grouped under *Print Control,* The download of a notification or a work order is considered a printout and, as such, the status of the notification or work order will indicate that it has been printed.

General Order Settlement

This group of configuration steps should not be changed without the involvement of CO (Controlling) or FI/CO personnel. This section is a duplicate of that found in CO configuration, so any changes made here will be reflected in the CO module.

Maintain Settlement Profiles

This setting provides some integration with the CO (Controlling) module in the R/3 system. Although there are some reasonable defaults provided by SAP, review the defaults to determine whether any changes are required. The default settlement profile most often used by the PM module is "40—Maintenance measure." Do not make changes to, and do not delete, any of the other settlement profiles without consulting with a person responsible for the configuration or maintenance of the CO module or any other module that may be affected (such as those responsible for the QM (Quality Management) module in the case of "70—QM order").

In the default settlement profile 40, for example, it is presumed that work orders will be settled. If, for some reason, work orders are not to be settled, the provision for this is contained here. The default *object type is "CTR,"* which is a cost center. This presumes that the majority of Plant Maintenance work orders will be settled to a cost center. If this is not the case, the default settlement *object type* can be changed here.

Among the other settings contained here is a list of *valid receivers*. This determines whether the user may (or must) settle the work order to types of receivers. While in the majority of cases the receiver may be a cost center, orders can also be settled to a fixed asset, where work performed on the asset may increase the value of the asset, or the settlement may be made to a WBS element, where the work performed in the work order pertains to a Work Breakdown Structure element in a project in the PS (Project Systems) module. Other receivers may be allowed or disallowed as required.

Maintain Allocation Structures

This setting allows the assignment of costs to receiver types. Once again, this setting should only be changed by, or after consulting with, a person responsible for the CO module.

Maintain PA Transfer Structure

This setting allows the definition of cost allocation related to profitability analysis. This is mostly related to sales orders and projects and should only be changed by, or after consulting with, a person responsible for the CO module.

Assign Value Fields

These value fields are assigned to the PA Transfer Structure. If no changes were made to the PA Transfer Structure in the previous configuration step, then no changes are likely to be made in this configuration step. If changes are required, allow a person responsible for the CO module to make the changes, or do it after consultation with that person.

Define Number Ranges for Settlement Documents

Do not change this setting unless you are also responsible for the configuration of the CO module. It is unlikely that any Plant Maintenance requirements would require a change to the number ranges for settlement documents.

Settings for Display of Costs

This group of configuration steps is relevant to the Plant Maintenance Information System (PMIS) and, if applicable, the Customer Service Information System (CSIS).

Cost elements are used to group costs related to a specific purpose, internal labor for example. A value category can be defined (the R/3 system has a few defined by default) to reflect one or more cost elements. For example, if internal labor costs are actually reported through several cost elements, those cost elements can be grouped into a value category, perhaps called "Internal Labor."

Value categories can display the breakdown of costs in the cost display of a work order and are also used to report costs in the PMIS.

Maintain Value Categories

This setting simply allows the definition of value categories, and whether they are related to costs or revenues. Keep in mind, when defining value categories, that they may also be used by the Project Systems (PS) module.

Assign Cost Elements to Value Categories

Cost elements may be assigned to the appropriate value categories here. It may be necessary to work with personnel representing the CO module to determine the cost elements that make up a value category, although the CO representatives may be unfamiliar with the term "value category." Either one cost element or a range of cost elements can be assigned directly to a value category. If the appropriate cost elements have not been numbered sequentially, that is, there may be inappropriate cost elements in between the relevant cost elements, the appropriate cost elements must be grouped in a cost element group. The cost element group can then be assigned to the value category. The creation of cost element groups, if required, is usually performed in the CO module.

Check Consistency of Value Category Assignment

After configuring value categories and assigning cost elements to the value categories, this step can be used to evaluate the assignments. It is not restricted to Plant Maintenance-specific assignments, so it may take a few minutes to run, depending on several factors. Use this analysis to determine whether any appropriate cost elements have not been assigned, that the appropriate cost elements are assigned properly, and that cost elements have not been assigned more than once (unless intended, for some reason).

Define Version for Cost Estimates for Orders

This setting allows cost estimates to be entered for value categories on work orders. There is usually no need to change the default setting that was provided. In any case, only one cost estimate version can be maintained here.

Define Default Values for Value Categories

This setting controls the value categories that are displayed by default on the "Costs" tab within the "Costs" tab (yes, they both have the same name) on a work order. Other categories may be added when viewing the actual work order.

Quotation Creation and Billing for Service Orders

This group of configuration steps is related to Customer Service (formerly Service Management) and is not covered here. Nothing in this group is required for configuration of non-Customer Service Plant Maintenance.

Maintenance and Service Notifications

Overview of Notification Type

This item contains numerous options related to notifications. However, the following two sections, "Notification Creation" (beginning on page 109) and "Notification Processing" (beginning on page 119) are best completed before reviewing the options in this step. The options contained here are based on some of the settings available in the following sections.

The options available in this configuration item are as follows:

- *Screen Areas in Notification Header.* This allows the definition for the basic layout and information in the notification header. With this option, it is possible to provide a notification layout suitable for maintenance notifications, service notifications (CS module), or quality notifications (QM module). It is also possible to restrict the type of object (functional location, equipment, and/or assembly) for which the notification is created. In addition, certain custom-defined screen areas can be assigned to the notification type.

- *Screen Structure for Extended View.* This option allows control over which tabs appear on a notification, based on the notification type. Further, by selecting a tab and clicking the magnifying glass icon ("Details"), specific screen areas (groups of fields) can be assigned to a tab, deleted from a tab, or the order of screen areas on a tab can be changed. The name of the tab can be changed and an icon can be assigned to the tab. Any particular tab can be made active or inactive by using the checkbox.

- *Screen Structure for Simplified View.* This option can be used to defined a simple notification screen, usually with no tabs, and containing only the screen areas (groups of fields) that are entered here. In a later configuration step, "Defined Transaction Start Values," the simplified view can be assigned instead of the extended view to a specific transaction (Create, Change, or Display). This setting is also based on notification type.

- *Catalogs and Catalog Profiles.* Specific catalogs, which usually define damage, cause, activities, etc. available for notifications, can be assigned to the notification type here. Different sets of catalogs may be defined for different types of notifications. Catalog definition can be performed in the Implementation Guide under the "Notification Content" section, or outside of the Implementation Guide.

- *Format Long Text.* Long text control can be managed here. There is an option to log changes to long text in notifications as well as an option to prevent changes to long text in notifications. In addition, formatting of long text can be forced through the other options on this screen, which may be more of interest if long text is exported to other applications outside of SAP.

- *Priority Type.* There may be more than one priority type (which is not the same as priority level) defined in the system. For example, one priority type might apply to work orders, while another priority type might apply to notifications, or one type for maintenance notifications and another type for service notifications. Each priority type may contain a different set of priorities than other priority types. For example, the priority type for maintenance notifications might have only 1 to 3 (high, medium, and low) defined, while the priority type for service notifications might have 1 to 4 (emergency, high, medium, low) defined. This option allows a single notification type to be assigned to a notification type.

- *Partner Determination Procedure.* The SAP R/3 system is delivered with a default partner determination procedure for PM. Unless a different partner determination procedure has been defined for Plant Maintenance use, the setting here should be "PM" for Plant Maintenance-related notification types.

- *Partner Functions, Approval.* This option contains settings that can be used to control an approval process for a notification type. Partners can be defined for responsibility, and links to workflow processes can be defined (if Workflow is being used). There is a checkbox that should **not** be checked if an approval process is not required for notifications.

- *Standard Output.* Also referred to as "Standard text," this option can be used to define text that should appear on notifications by specifying the code of the standard text. This is particularly useful when printing notifications (or later, for work orders). Standard text itself is not defined within the Implementation Guide, but is defined in the SAP system in the menu Tools → Form Printout → SAPScript → Standard Text

- *Status Profile.* If user-defined statuses are to be used (and have already been defined) in addition to system statuses for notifications, the profile for the appropriate statuses can be specified here, for both the notification itself as well as for tasks in the notification, if required. User statuses, discussed later, can be defined when the SAP-provided system statuses are not sufficient.

- *Response Time Monitoring.* Used primarily for Customer Service, if response monitoring has been defined, this option can be used to assign a response profile to a notification type.

- *Allowed Change of Notification Type.* This option can be used to specify whether a notification can be changed from one notification type to a different notification type, and to specify the original notification types and target notification types for which this action will be permitted.

Notification Creation

This group of configuration steps consists of information relative to the creation of a notification.

Define Notification Types

Three Plant Maintenance-related notification types are delivered by default with the SAP R/3 system. These are:

- *Breakdown Report.* This notification type provides a means to report that an object, such as a piece of equipment, has broken down or failed in some manner. Usually, mean-time-between-failure and mean-time-to-repair statistics are associated with this type of notification.

- *Maintenance Request.* This notification type provides a means to request maintenance, often for a non-breakdown situation, although the "Breakdown" indicator is still available.

- *Activity Report.* This notification type is often used to report activity that has already been performed, in order to track statistical history. Because the activity may have already been performed, this notification type is sometimes created from a work order, while work orders are often created from the other two default notification types.

While additional notification types can be created in this configuration step, it is often found that the original three notification types delivered with the R/3 system by default are adequate for Plant Maintenance. Note that there are additional notification types for Customer Service (Service Management) and Quality Management.

Set Screen Templates for the Notification Type

This configuration step allows some flexibility in the way that a notification screen is organized and in which data it includes.

At least a notification type must be specified in the initial window that is displayed. The resulting screen will display an overview of the information that the notification type currently contains on its screen.

Those items whose "Register" begins with a 10 will appear as tabs on the main notification screen for that notification type.

Items whose "Register" begins with a 20 appear as tabs within the "Items" tab in the system as delivered.

A tab (register, in this case) can be selected, and its settings viewed, by using the "Details" (magnifying glass) icon. The title for that tab can be changed from this screen and, if desired, an icon can be added to the tab in addition to, or instead of, the tab description.

Some tabs consist of screen areas that can be changed. A screen area consists of fields that are usually grouped on the screen, often within their own "box." On some tabs, these screen areas are set and cannot be changed. On tabs where the screen areas can be changed, it is possible to remove groups of fields entirely from the tab, add other screen areas to a tab, or move screen areas from one tab to another. There are restrictions, however, on which tabs to which screen areas can be moved.

Each tab contains a checkbox which, when checked, activates that particular tab. When the checkbox is not checked, that tab will not appear for that notification type. So, it is possible for some tabs and screen areas to appear for one notification type, but not another.

Define Long Text Control for Notification Types

In addition to the short, 40 character field available to describe a notification, a "long text" field is available for longer descriptions. The primary purpose of this configuration step is to either prevent changes to the long text of a notification type or to log any changes to the long text of a notification type.

Set Field Selection for Notifications

As with the other configuration steps that address field selection, this step allows fields on the notification screen to be hidden, highlighted, display only, and so on. The fields can have different attributes, if desired, based on notification type, priority, or several other "influencing" values.

With the ability to change field attributes combined with the ability to change screen areas (groups of fields), a considerable amount of manipulation is possible with the notification screens.

Define Number Ranges

See the section on Number Ranges for more details regarding number ranges.

This configuration step allows the assignment of number ranges to notification types. It is possible to assign every notification type to the same number range, it is possible to assign each notification type its own number range, and it is also possible to combine notification types into number ranges.

As with other number ranges, internal (system assigned) and external (user specified) number ranges can be defined. Generally, external number ranges for notifications are discouraged, particularly where multiple people will be using the system, although there are always exceptions. A couple of reasons to let the system assign numbers to notifications are that it takes more time to enter a number than to let the system do it, and it can be difficult to determine the next valid number if more than one person is responsible for creating notifications.

The overall notification number range is shared with the QM (Quality Management) and CS (Customer Service) modules. Consider the requirements of those modules, whether they are used now or ever may be used in the future, when defining notification number ranges.

If several ranges are to be defined, ensure that the quantity of numbers is much more than adequate. Consider possibilities such as the acquisition of additional plants, etc. If there is even the slightest doubt, spread out the number ranges to allow expansion, if ever required.

The use of the configuration step is not necessarily intuitive. Define the number ranges first. To assign a notification type to a number range, double-click on the notification type(s), select the number range (check the box), and then click the "Element/Group" button.

Define Transaction Start Values

When a transaction is performed to create, change or display a notification, a specific screen appears first, along with a suggested notification type. This configuration allows the default screen and notification type to be changed, if required. The default values are often acceptable for this setting.

Assign Standard Texts for Short Messages to Notification Types

This configuration step is completely optional. It is possible to define a "standard text" for each notification type. This standard text can be used on notifications of that type simply by specifying the code for that standard text, instead of having to type the entire text each time it is required. The standard text obviously must be defined before it can be assigned to a notification type.

The standard text itself is defined elsewhere, not in the Implementation Guide, but in the standard SAP Easy Access menu under **Tools → Form Printout → SAPScript → Standard Text**. Note that in versions of R/3 earlier than Enterprise (4.7), the menu path will likely differ from that shown here.

After any standard texts have been defined, this configuration step can be used to assign the standard texts to notification types.

Allowed Change of Notification Type

This configuration step can be used to specify that a notification can be changed from one notification type to another. Only those changes will be permitted that are specified here.

Assign Notification Types to Order Types

This configuration step can only be performed after order types have been defined, which occurs a little later in the Implementation Guide.

Once order types have been defined, this configuration step can be used to associate notification types with a default work order type. This is not a restriction, but can save a small amount of time when creating a work order from a notification.

Define Order Types and Special Notification Parameters

This configuration step is only relevant to Customer Service (Service Management) module notifications. It allows a sales order to be created from a service notification and is not required for non-Customer Service-related notifications.

Notification Content

This group of configuration steps consists of information relative to catalogs, their contents, and how they are related to notification types. Catalogs contain information relative to damage, cause of damage, activities, etc.

Maintain Catalogs

Catalogs are used to encourage the recording of information that can be analyzed later. The information gathered through the use of catalogs is best analyzed over a period of time (months, for example) and the Plant Maintenance Information System, discussed later, provides a means of reporting the information. The information recorded can be used to identify patterns of damage, cause of damage, maintenance costs associated with types of damage, maintenance costs associated with a particular manufacturer's equipment, and so on.

The SAP R/3 system as delivered contains several catalogs by default. In most cases, these catalogs are sufficient, but their contents are not. A catalog has been predefined for each of the catalog-related fields that usually appear on the notification screen.

If the temptation to create additional catalogs arises, be advised that the catalog ID field is limited to one character, and SAP has reserved the characters A through O as well as the digits 0 through 9. That leaves only 11 possible additional catalogs that may be defined. Work with the default catalogs, if possible, before attempting to define other catalogs.

Creating and editing catalogs can also be performed outside of the Implementation Guide. SAP recommends that the creation and editing of catalogs be performed in the productive system rather than being transported to the productive system. Currently, however, it is still possible to perform this step either in the Implementation Guide or outside the Implementation Guide, and manually transport the catalogs individually. That means that, while editing a specific catalog, the menu **Table View → Transport** can be used to generate a change request for transport. More information regarding transporting configuration can be found in the "Implementation Guide" section on page 10.

Although the creation of catalogs, code groups and codes can be performed outside of the Implementation Guide, the following steps, "Define Catalog Profile" and "Change Catalogs and Catalog Profile for Notification Type, " must still be performed in the Implementation Guide.

With the delivered SAP R/3 system, the following catalog codes are most relevant to Plant Maintenance:

- A—Activities
- B—Object Parts
- C—Overview of Damage
- D—Coding
- 2—Tasks
- 5—Causes

Some of the other default catalogs are more relevant to QM (Quality Management) module use. However, other existing catalogs can be configured for use with Plant Maintenance notifications and, as previously discussed, a limited number of additional catalogs can also be defined if required.

With a little imagination, some other uses can be discovered and invented for using catalogs, code groups and codes. This discussion will be limited to those catalogs listed above and for basic purposes.

The *Activities* catalog should usually contain a list of activities that could have been performed to repair a piece of equipment, solve a problem, etc. For example, "Welded, " "Rewound, " and

"Replaced" are activities. The activities can be grouped as desired. An example of an activity grouping is to arrange the valid activities for a specific type of equipment into a group that reflects that equipment type.

The *Object Parts* catalog can be used to contain sections, parts, or areas of a piece of equipment for which to track damage and cause. If there is an interest in keeping track of damage to (or because of) a part of a piece of equipment, a list of Object Parts can be maintained. Often, the grouping of Object Parts is by the type of equipment, since the parts will vary depending on the equipment type. Note that Object Parts should not be confused with replacement parts, spares, parts used to repair the equipment, and so on, although there may be some overlap. This field is not used to keep track of the parts that were used during the maintenance of a piece of equipment.

The *Overview of Damage* catalog usually contains a list of possible damages. Examples of damage could be "Bent," "Cracked," "Melted," and so on. There are different methods of grouping damage codes. The best method of grouping damage codes will vary, depending on ease of use and the needs of the business. One example of grouping damage codes is, once again, by type of equipment.

The *Tasks* catalog is sometimes not used, since its most appropriate use is to provide a sequence of steps to perform the required or requested maintenance. Since, for many SAP R/3 Plant Maintenance implementations, the required sequence of steps is contained in the work order itself, entering a sequence of steps in the notification may be redundant. Of course, there are exceptions, and for some implementations, the Tasks catalog may be beneficial and even required, especially if the Plant Maintenance system is to be used without work orders. On the other hand, maintaining a catalog for tasks enables the creator of the notification to identify steps to be performed from a standard list. This can, where appropriate, save some time. If used, the Tasks catalog could, in some cases, almost match the Activities catalog, except for the "tense" (future tense, past tense) of the catalog entries. For example, the Tasks catalog could contain the entries "Weld," "Rewind," and "Replace," while the

Activities catalog could contain the entries "Welded, " "Rewound, " and "Replaced." Again, the catalog can be grouped as best suits the requirements of the implementation.

The *Causes* catalog can be used to contain a list of the possible causes of damage. Some examples of causes of damage could be "Impact, " "High Temperature, " "Vandalism, " and so on. Causes can be grouped in a number of ways, including by type of equipment.

Three of the basic catalogs are used on the standard notification screen in the "Item" screen area (this being on the notification transaction screen while creating, changing, or displaying a notification, not in the Implementation Guide). These are the "Object part, " "Damage" and "Cause" catalogs.

The two fields beside each of those catalogs are for a code group and a code, respectively. Ideally, the three fields, "Object part, " "Damage, " and "Cause" will flow together to make a sentence. For example, the *casing* (Object part) was *cracked* (Damage) because of an *impact* (Cause).

It is important to note that the catalog/code structure is not exactly hierarchical. The codes for each catalog are arranged by code groups, but additional levels or groupings (groups of groups, for example) are not possible.

Ideally, it might be desirable to plan and organize the groups and codes in such a way that the list of groups would be short enough to all appear on the screen without scrolling and, likewise, the list of codes in each group would be short enough to all appear on the screen without scrolling. However, real-life requirements often overshadow convenience. Try to provide enough codes for meaningful reporting and analysis, but not so many that it is difficult for the user to select the most appropriate code.

Display Catalog Directory with All Sub-Items

There is nothing to configure here. This step simply provides an overall view of the catalogs, groups and codes selected.

Define Catalog Profile

Catalog profiles can be assigned to functional locations, equipment and other objects. This configuration step provides a means of assigning a different selection of codes to different types of equipment, for example.

If two different sets of code groups had been created, one group with the code group ID beginning with "PM" (PM0001, PM0002, etc.) and the other with the code group ID beginning with "QA" (QA0001, QA0002, etc.), the PM code groups can be assigned to a PM catalog profile and the QA code groups can be assigned to a QA catalog profile. The appropriate catalog profile can then be assigned to the appropriate pieces of equipment or other object. A notification created for a piece of equipment will inherit the catalog profile assigned to that piece of equipment (or from the notification type), so when the damage, cause and other codes are accessed, only the codes relevant to that catalog profile will be displayed.

This configuration can also be used by the QM (Quality Management) module and the CS (Customer Service) module, so assign the appropriate code groups to at least one relevant Plant Maintenance-related catalog profile.

Change Catalogs and Catalog Profile for Notification Type

In this configuration step, the appropriate catalog profile previously created can be assigned to one or more notification types. In addition, the appropriate catalogs can be assigned to notification types. If a different catalog was previously defined for a specific use, the catalog can be associated with one or more specific notification types here. Any catalogs that are definitely not desired on the notification screen can be removed here.

In Summary:

- Determine which catalogs to maintain (Object part, damage, cause, tasks, activities).
- Create a selection of groups and codes for each catalog (can take some time).

- Assign the catalogs and groups to one or more catalog profiles.
- Assign the catalogs and profiles to notification types

Define Partner Determination Procedure and Partner Function

In SAP terminology, a partner is an entity that can be associated with an object in any way. In this instance, the object is a notification. For most implementations, the default settings for this configuration step will provide the required functionality.

Regardless of whether changes are made to partner determination procedures, review this configuration step to ensure that the PM (Plant Maintenance) partner determination procedure (or a different partner determination procedure, if more appropriate) is assigned to the relevant PM-related notification types, particularly if additional notification types have been defined.

Review the partner functions that have been assigned to the notification types if changes are required. If desired, an approval process can be assigned to notifications. To use the approval process function, check the "Approval required" checkbox and press the "Enter" key on the keyboard. The additional fields will appear. Do not check the "Approval required" checkbox if this type of approval process is not required.

Field Selection for List Display of Partner Data

This configuration section can be used to control which data appears in lists of various partners. For example, when a list of vendor data is displayed, the vendor-relevant fields that appear are those specified in this configuration setting. Some defaults are provided.

Notification Processing

This group of configuration steps consists of information relative to the processing of a notification.

Response Time Monitoring

This configuration section is more suited to use with the CS (Customer Service) module rather than with standard Plant Maintenance functionality.

The first setting, also found elsewhere in the IMG, allows the creation and assignment of priority types and priorities. The second setting allows the definition of a sequence of tasks to be performed within a specific time period that can be proposed on a notification. The sequence of tasks is based on a response profile.

Additional Functions

This configuration section is primarily suited for workflow functionality. These settings provide a gateway to additional functions that can be performed with notifications, some provided by SAP, others that can be added as required. If workflow functionality is not required, no changes to these settings are required. Since workflow functionality is not discussed in this publication, changes to these configuration settings will depend on workflow requirements.

If, by default, the "Action box" appears on notification screens, it can be adjusted or removed by changing the settings in this section of configuration.

Notification Print Control

This configuration section can be used to define and control which "shop papers" can be printed and where.

Define Shop Papers, Forms and Output Programs

If the standard default SAP R/3 notifications are being used, this setting will contain some default shop papers that can be printed from notifications. Whether or not the default notifications are used, additional and/or alternate shop papers can be defined.

If interested in printing notifications, review the shop papers that are available by default. If the default shop papers are not adequate, determine the layout that will be required. The development of the shop papers is usually performed by programmers.

If non-default shop papers are created, the shop papers can be made available (linked) from the notification with these settings.

Within this setting, it is also possible to link specific shop papers to specific notification types, if there is a reason to do so.

In addition, shop papers can be set to print by default when the print functionality is accessed from a notification.

Define Printer

This configuration setting contains three sub-settings:

- *User-Specific Print Control.* This setting can be used to control which shop papers are printed on which printer(s) based on the user ID and the shop paper. Additional print options can be set.

- *Define Print Diversion.* This determines whether print diversion (directing a shop paper to a different printer) is active for specific shop papers.

- *Print Diversion According to Field Contents.* This setting can be used primarily to control whether a shop paper is diverted to a different printer based on the value contained in a specified notification field. For example, if the notification contains a specific equipment number in the equipment field, a specific shop paper can be diverted to a different printer than usual. Print diversion, when it applies, overrides user-specific settings.

User Status for Notifications

The configuration settings contained in this section need not be changed unless the system statuses for notification are not adequate.

Define Status Profile

This configuration setting can be found in several places throughout Plant Maintenance configuration as well as configuration for other modules.

A default profile may already exist for notifications. If an additional profile is created, prefix the status profile with the letter Z. Although conflicts with SAP named objects are rare, beginning configuration objects with the letter Z guarantees that there will be no current or future conflicts with SAP named objects.

Determine what statuses are required before proceeding further. Then determine whether only one status at a time will be permitted and which status will be the initial user status when a notification is created.

From this point, there are two methods of defining status profiles. One allows a single status at a time, while the other allows multiple statuses to be active at the same time.

To limit the user status field on a notification to one status at a time, use the "Lowest" and "Highest" fields. These fields refer to the status numbers, the first field on the list of user statuses. From any given user status, the only other user status that can be set is determined by the "Lowest" and "Highest" fields. Refer to "Figure 10: User Status Profile Configuration."

For example, if the user status "Completed" (status number 5) has the "Lowest" and "Highest" fields both set to 5, no other user status can be set. However, if the "Lowest" field is set to 4 and the "Highest" field is set to 5, then the user status can be changed to 4 ("Active, " for example) or remain at 5 ("Completed").

If multiple user statuses are required at the same time, the "Position" and "Priority" fields must be used instead of the "Highest" and "Lowest" fields.

There is enough space in the user status field on a notification to contain several user statuses. Each status that appears at the same time occupies a "position." The leftmost position in the status field is Position 1, the next status occupies Position 2, and so on. In this configuration step, one or more user statuses can be assigned to position 1, one or more to position 2, etc.

If more than one status is assigned to position 1, which one is displayed on the notification screen is determined by its Priority and whether or not it has been set by the user.

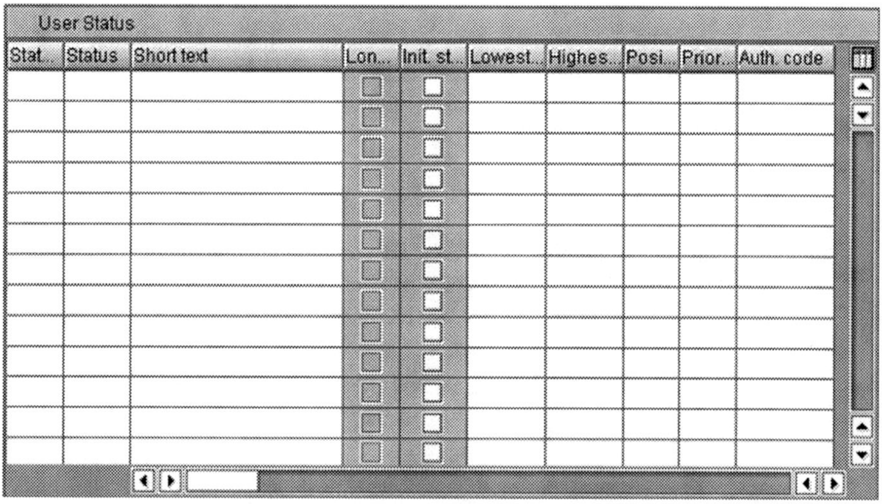

Figure 10. User status profile configuration.
© *SAP AG*

Regardless of which method is used, some time should be taken to organize the statuses and determine the combinations and the order in which statuses will be set. Test the settings to ensure that the user statuses will function as required.

In addition, an authorization code can be set for each status. This can be used to control who can change a user status, but must be defined in co-operation with SAP security. The security person/team must ensure that the specified authorization codes are included in the authorizations for the appropriate users.

There is one additional step to be performed in this configuration setting. This is to assign the user status profile to the appropriate notification types. Note that, if required, status profiles can be assigned in this step to notification tasks as well as to the notifications themselves.

Create Authorization Keys for User Status Authorizations

This configuration step can be used to create the authorization code/key as previously mentioned. This is only required when only specific users should be permitted to change user statuses on notifications.

It is possible that only those responsible for security will be permitted to set this configuration. If this configuration is not restricted, work with those responsible for security to at least ensure compatibility with security standards and procedures.

Maintain Selection Profiles

This configuration setting can be used to define a combination of statuses for use in searching for, in this case, notifications. On the "List display" or "List change" screens, there is a field to specify a selection profile. If a selection profile has been defined here, that selection profile can be specified instead of the user being required to determine and specify each desired status.

Object Information

The Object Information window can be configured with the settings in this section. The Object Information window is available from the notification and work order screens and contains information relative to the object (equipment or functional location, for example) for which the notification or work order were created. The Object Information window can also be configured to appear automatically when notifications or work orders are created. See *Figure 11. The "Object Information" window.*

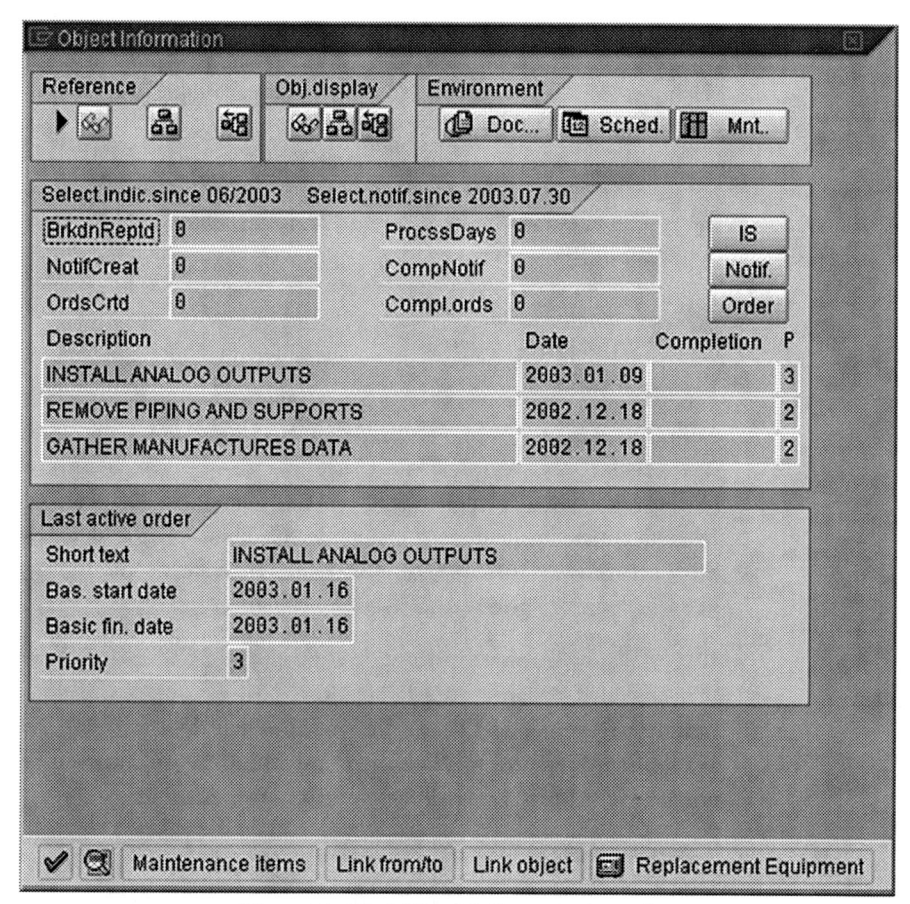

Figure 11. The "Object Information" window.
© SAP AG

The Object Information window can show recent notifications and/or work orders for the same object within a specified time period. It can also draw attention to thresholds that have been met or exceeded, such as number of breakdowns, number of orders created, etc. within the specified time period. For example, if more than three breakdowns have been reported for the same piece of equipment over the past 90 days, attention will be drawn to that statistic, if the Object Information window has been configured as such.

The Object Information window, as shown in *Figure 11*, does not appear in the Implementation Guide. The configuration settings in the Implementation Guide control whether or not the Object Information window appears automatically, under what conditions, and what information is displayed in the window. The window itself, as shown, appears during the creation of a notification or a work order, for example.

Two benefits of the Object Information window is that duplicate reporting of a problem for which a notification has already been created can be reduced, as well as attention being drawn to an object that seems to have a recurring problem.

Define Object Information Keys

A default Object Information Key, PM, is provided for Plant Maintenance purposes. If the Object Information window seems useful, the default Object Information Key can be modified as required. An alternate Object Information Key can be created to use instead of the default provided and, if desired, multiple Object Information Keys can be created for various purposes and assigned to different notification types.

If the Object Information window does not seem useful, confirm that the "automatically" checkbox is unchecked in this configuration step. The Object Information window will still be available on demand by clicking a button on the notification or work order screen, but will not appear automatically.

The other areas in this configuration step are as follows:

- *Reference for notification and class selection.* Specify whether the information contained in the Object Information window pertains to the object itself, the object and its superior object, or to the object's structure (presuming one exists).

- *Info. System—time frame and threshold values.* Specify the number of days for which the other six fields in this area are relevant. For example, number of breakdowns in the past X days. For the other six fields, specify the thresholds at which attention will be drawn to that number on the Object Information window. For example, if the "No. days" field contains 60 and the "Orders created" field contains 5, attention will be drawn to the "Orders created" field in the Object Information window when five or more work orders have been created for that object in within the past 60 days.

- *Notifications—selection and automatic display.* As with the previous area, the number of days must be specified for the system to consider previously created and/or completed notifications for the object. A 30 entered in the "Sel. days" field will cause the system to consider notifications for the object from the previous 30 days. The "SelComplNotifs" checkbox will cause completed notifications to be displayed as well as outstanding and/or in process notifications. The other two checkboxes will cause the Object Information to be presented automatically if outstanding notifications and/or completed notifications, respectively, exist for the object for the time period specified.

- *Contract—automatic display.* This area is more relevant to the Customer Service (CS) module and controls whether information is displayed if a contract has been created for an object.

- *Classification—views and display.* If views have been configured for classes, views may be specified here for relevant classification data to be displayed for the object. The "Characteristics" checkbox will allow the display of characteristic information pertaining to the class.

Assign Object Information Keys to Notification Types

This configuration step simply allows the assignment of a specific Object Information Key to one or more notification types.

Condition Indicator

This configuration section contains two settings as described below.

Define System Conditions

This configuration setting is usually used to set up a standard selection for the condition of a "system" (piece of equipment, for example). The system condition can be used to indicate the condition of a piece of equipment before and after maintenance, for example. "Operational, " "Limited Operation" and "Out of Order" are often used, but alternates or additional conditions can be defined.

Define Operation Effects

This setting can be used to provide standard descriptions of the effect that maintenance of an object might have on production. "No effect, " "Production Restricted" (or reduced) and "Production Stopped" are usually adequate, but alternatives or additional effects can be defined.

List Editing

This configuration section controls the selection and display of lists of notifications.

Define List Variants

This configuration setting can be used to provide default values on selection screens for notifications. A variant (predefined selection criteria) is usually only defined here if it applies to many, if not all, users. Even if a variant is not provided with this configuration step, variants can still usually be defined by each user, if required.

Variants can be created for a variety of notification-related items. In addition, separate variants can be created for display or change mode.

Define Field Selection for Multi-Level List Displays of Notifications

This configuration setting can be used to define which fields appear by default in lists of objects associated with notifications. When the user selects "List Editing → Display (Multi-Level) from the menu, objects associated with notifications can be displayed with the notifications. The fields that appear for each associated object by default depend on this configuration setting. The users can select additional fields themselves unless the "Invisible" checkbox has been checked for a field. In that case, the field will not be available for the user to select for display.

Set Workflow for Maintenance Notifications

Workflow functionality is not covered here, but a workflow template for determining workflow functionality from a notification can be specified here.

Set Workflow for Service Notifications

This setting is relevant to workflow functionality from Customer Service (CS) notifications. Neither workflow nor the Customer Service module will be covered here.

Maintenance and Service Orders

Functions and Settings for Order Types

This section contains many options related to the configuration of work orders. The individual configuration steps are discussed below.

Configure Order Types

The configuration of order types is central to Plant Maintenance and provides most of the integration between the Plant Maintenance module and other SAP R/3 modules. Although advice regarding the configuration and definition of order types cannot apply to every implementation, some basic recommendations are in order.

Since there are a number of configuration steps to be performed when additional order types are created, and to reduce confusion, try to keep the number of order types to a minimum. It is sometimes possible to substitute an "activity type, " a field on work orders, instead of creating an additional order type. The "maintenance activity type" field can be used instead of an additional order type, especially if grouping, selecting or reporting is the primary reason for considering an additional order type.

Try to avoid creating different order types for different plants. Since the work orders themselves are plant-specific, there is little reason for a plant to have its own order type(s).

In the configuration itself for order types:

- Work with the CO (controlling) team or personnel to determine the most appropriate settings for the "Cost accounting parameters" and "Cost accounting profiles" screen areas.

- In the "Reorganization" screen area, "Residence Time1" refers to the time, in months, that must pass before a work order marked for deletion can be permanently marked for deletion (prepared for archiving/deletion) by the archiving and physical deletion functionality of the system. Until the time a work order is permanently marked for deletion, the delete flag on the work order can be reset so that the work order is no longer marked for deletion. Once permanently marked for deletion, however, the delete flag can no longer be reset on the work order.

  "Residence Time2" refers to the time, again in months, that must pass before a work order that has been permanently marked for deletion can physically be archived and deleted.

  Regardless of the residence time settings and the running of the archiving and deletion process, no work orders can be deleted unless the delete flag for the work orders has been set first.

- The "Release immediately" checkbox controls whether a work order is released automatically when it is created. Releasing work orders immediately upon their creation may be beneficial to some, but detrimental to others (implementations as well as work order types).

- The "Screen RefObject" field controls the type of object information that is displayed on the work order screen. The functional location, equipment and assembly fields are selected by default, but other settings can be selected, if appropriate.

Credit Limit Checks, Sales Document Types for Service Orders

This configuration step is only relevant for Customer Service. In any case, as long as the default order types for Customer Service have not been altered, SAP recommends starting with the default settings.

Indicate Order Types for Refurbishment Processing

A special type of work order, a refurbishment order is treated somewhat differently than other work order types, so it is important to identify to the system which work order type(s) are intended to be used for refurbishment. Refurbishment work orders should not be used as other maintenance work orders and regular work orders cannot be used as refurbishment work orders.

On a typical, non-refurbishment work order, materials are often issued to the work order and "consumed" in the maintenance of an object such as a piece of equipment. On a refurbishment order, materials are issued to the work order from stores, but with the understanding that they will be returned to stores as part of the refurbishment order process.

This configuration step simply consists of a checkbox to indicate which work order types will be used exclusively for refurbishment orders. A refurbishment work order type may be provided by default with the standard SAP R/3 system.

Order Types and Investment Management

This section of configuration is only relevant to capital investment orders. Consult with personnel representing the areas of CO (Controlling), AM (Asset Management) and PS (Project Systems) prior to changing any configuration in these steps.

Each of those areas may have an interest in capital investment orders that may affect this configuration, if required.

Configure Number Ranges

Refer to the "Number Ranges" section for more information about number ranges in general.

Additional care must be taken when configuring order number ranges than other number ranges, since the numbers available for work orders are shared with other modules.

It is not recommended that an external number range be configured for use with work orders. There are always exceptions, of course, but exceptions should be rare here.

The same number range can be used for multiple order types, order types can be combined into different number ranges, and each order type can have its own number range, if required. There is usually little consequence in having order types grouped into the same number range. "Smart numbering" of work orders is not likely necessary, since there are numerous methods of finding work orders, including by plant. Defining a separate number range for each order type also leads to uncertainty whether numerous number ranges are adequate.

Keeping in mind that the available number ranges for orders is shared with other modules, including the CO module, for internal orders, some preferred lower number ranges may already be reserved. Avoid the temptation to "squeeze" an order number range between two other number ranges. If the range is underestimated, it may be impossible to expand the range if additional numbers are required in the future.

When reserving one or more number ranges for Plant Maintenance use, consult with, in particular, representatives from the modules CO (Controlling), PP (Production Planning), QM (Quality Management), CS (Customer Service) and PS (Project Systems) to ensure that no conflicts will occur over number ranges.

Use the "Overview" function in this configuration step to view the existing number ranges. Then determine the most appropriate number range(s) to allow more than enough numbers.

For configuring number ranges, the number range is actually assigned to a "group." In the "Maintain Number Range Groups" screen, for example, the menu option Group → Insert allows the creation of a group. The assignment of a number range is also performed here, as well as indicating whether the number range is internal (no check mark) or external (check mark). The system will not permit the assignment of a number range that overlaps an existing number range. The "Current number" can be left at 0 (the default). The first time the number range is used, the appropriate current number will be set properly.

Once a group has been created with a number range, the appropriate order types must be assigned to the group. Select each of the appropriate order types by double-clicking on them (the color of the order type will change, but it may be subtle). Next, select the group to which the order types will be assigned, by checking the checkbox for that group. Then click the "Element/Group" button. The selected order types will be assigned to the selected group.

When work orders of those order types are created, they will be assigned the next sequential number of the specified number range, if the number range is internal. If the number range has been defined as an external number range, it will be the responsibility of the user to determine a valid number within the assigned number range.

More than one number range cannot be assigned to a group at the same time, whether internal or external.

Assign Order Types to Maintenance Plants

The order types that have been defined must be assigned to the maintenance plants at which they will be used. Unless there is a reason to restrict a plant from using one or more specific work order types, this setting will consist of assigning every order type to every plant.

Assign Inspection Types to Maintenance/Service Order Types

This configuration step applies primarily to QM (Quality Management) functionality and allows quality inspection types to be assigned to work order types.

Define Default Value for Planning Indicator for Each Order Type

This configuration step simply sets a default for each order type to "Unplanned" (non-emergency and non-preventive), "Immediate" (emergency or rush), or "Planned" (preventive).

Create Default Value Profiles for External Procurement

At least one profile type should be defined/maintained here. External procurement involves materials (parts) that are not stocked or external services such as contractors. When externally procured materials or services are included on a work order, this configuration will provide at least some defaults, which can reduce the need to enter some purchasing information each time the information is required. A person responsible for the MM (Materials Management) module may need to provide the appropriate purchasing information, and possibly a person responsible for the CO (Controlling) module may need to provide the appropriate cost element(s). The profiles are assigned later.

Define Access Sequence for Determining Address Data

No configuration is necessary here unless a purchase requisition should be able to derive an alternate address for delivery of materials. If the address to which the materials should be delivered is the standard address of the equipment/functional location/plant, or if the address will be provided manually, no changes are required to this configuration step.

If alternate addresses may be required, define as required for each plant/order type combination one or more address sources.

Create Default Value Profiles for General Order Data

This configuration step allows the creation of one or more profiles that are used to provide default values for work orders. A "Field key," when one has been defined, provides field names for user-defined fields. The "Calculation key" instructs the system to calculate a value, such as duration, from two other values, such as effort ("man-hours") and number of resources (people). The "Relationship view" determines whether a task relationship is seen from a successor or predecessor point of view. "Level of detail" can usually be left untouched. "Overall profile ID" is relevant to capacity leveling which, if used, the appropriate profile ID can be provided as a default. "Checking WBS activity" is only relevant if using work order integration with the PS (Project Systems) module, in which case a default can be entered instructing the system what to do if the work order dates fall outside the WBS (Work Breakdown Structure) element's dates in the PS module. The "Graphics profile" is usually defaulted adequately. If not, set it appropriately.

Default Value for Task List Data and Profile Assignments

This configuration setting consists of two levels. The initial setting simply defines for which plant and order type(s) the subsequent settings apply. On the initial screen, the plant(s) must be specified, but the order types field can contain wildcards. For example, if the subsequent setting will apply to all of the order types at a specific plant, the order type can be defined as ****. This reduces the number of entries that need to be made in this setting.

The subsequent level is accessed by selected a line (plant/order type combination) and using the "Details" (magnifying glass) button.

The "Short text" field simply contains the description of the order type selected. This field will be blank if a wildcard was used in the previous setting.

Enter the appropriate profiles that should already have been configured in the "Profile" fields for each plant/order type combination.

When task lists have been created in the system, it is possible to copy the task list into a work order so that the same tasks/operations need not be entered again. The "Operation selection" checkbox, when checked, allows the selection of individual tasks, if desired. If this checkbox is not checked, the entire task list is copied into the work order.

Operations on task lists can be assigned to different work centers (people or groups of people). If the "Work center selection" checkbox is checked, it is possible to select tasks/operations from the task list that are assigned to specific work centers. Only tasks/operations assigned to the selected work centers will be copied into the work order. If this checkbox is not checked, no selection of tasks/operations is permitted.

The "Renumber" checkbox allows operations to be renumbered (0010, 0020, 0030, etc.) according to the configured numbering sequence for the work order.

The "Include once completely" checkbox limits a task list in its entirety to being copied only once into a work order. If this checkbox is unchecked, a task list may be copied more than once into a work order.

The "Operation sorting" checkbox cannot be used at the same time as the "Renumber" checkbox. It allows operations copied from a task list to have the same sequence that the operations had on the task list.

Settlement Rule: Define Time and Creation of Distribution Rule

Each work order created requires a settlement rule in order for it to automatically settle the costs of the order to a cost center or other cost receiver. This configuration setting determines at what point in the work order cycle the settlement rule is required before further processing of the work order is permitted. A settlement rule or distribution rule is required either at the point of order release or order completion. There is an additional setting for use with distribution rules.

Define Proposed Reference Time for Order Completion

This configuration setting simply defines a default date/time that the system will provide for the completion of a work order. The selections are:

- *Today's date*—The current date and time when completing the order
- *Created on*—The date on which the order was created
- *Basic start*—The date contained in the order basic start field.
- *Basic finish*—The date contained in the order basic finish field.

For the majority of implementations, "Today's date" seems to be the most likely date/time for the default setting for completion of the order. Regardless of the selection made here, the actual completion date can be changed by the user.

Define Transfer of Project or Investment Program

No configuration is necessary here unless also using the PS (Project Systems) module and/or IM (Investment Management). If using either PS or IM, this configuration setting allows the automatic copying of the project or capital investment program into the work order type specified.

Define Relevant Fields for Assignment of IM Program

Once again, this configuration setting is only relevant if work orders are relevant to IM (Investment Management). The configuration allows the system to attempt to automatically determine an investment program from the settings entered.

Assign IM Assignment Key to Order Types

If the previous step was configured for IM Investment Management) use, this configuration step can be used to assign the assignment key(s) to the appropriate order type(s).

Define Default Order Types for Maintenance Items

Maintenance Items, which are assigned to Maintenance Plans, are the source of preventive maintenance work orders (orders produced by the system from a schedule). The order type(s) to be created from maintenance plans/items must be defined. This configuration step contains a list of Planning Plant/Planner Group combinations. The appropriate order type should be provided for each of the combinations, where preventive maintenance orders are expected to be created.

Define Notification and Order Integration

This configuration step allows the assignment of a specific notification type to an order type. A default order type was assigned to a notification type in the notification configuration section, which defaulted the work order type to be created from the notification.

This integration between a notification and a work order is for a somewhat different reason. The "Notification type" field and the "Notification" checkbox allow the system to create a notification of the specified type when a work order of the specified type is created (if a notification does not already exist for the work order) and to include several notification fields on the work order screen.

The "Long Text" checkbox provides long sought-after functionality that was missing from releases of SAP R/3 Plant Maintenance prior to R/3 Enterprise (4.7). When the "Long Text" checkbox is checked, long text from a notification is copied to the long text of a work order, when a work order is initially created from the notification. Subsequent changes to the notification long text will not be transferred, nor will long text from additional notifications.

If the "Long Text" checkbox is not checked and the work orders are created from maintenance plans/maintenance items, the long text will be copied from the long text of the maintenance item (in the plan).

Maintain Control Keys

This configuration step contains several default control keys, which should be sufficient as they are for most implementations. The configuration is shared among several modules, but the two primary settings for Plant Maintenance are PM01 and PM02. These two control keys contain standard settings for operations that are performed internally (by employees, for example) or externally (by contractors, for example), respectively.

Review the settings for the standard PM-related control keys. If any of the settings are not adequate, create an additional control key, leaving the standard control keys as they are.

Maintain Default Values for Control Keys for Order Types

One control key can be specified as the default for work order operations for each Planning Plant/Order Type combination. Ensuring that a default control key exists for each Planning Plant/Order Type combination will eliminate the need to enter or look up a control key for each operation on a work order. Of course, the default setting can be changed on the work order itself.

Maintenance Activity Type

This configuration section contains the steps necessary to create Maintenance Activity Types and associate them with work order types.

Be careful not to confuse Maintenance Activity Types with CO Activity Types, which appear on work order operations. Maintenance Activity Types are used to identify the type of work that will be/has been performed on a work order. It is sometimes used as a substitute for a type of order where there is no need to create a separate order type. The Maintenance Activity Type exists at the header level of a work order (once per order). The CO Activity Type, defined in the CO module, but used in work order operations, is used to determine the rate at which a work center will be charged to the work order. A work center can be charged to a work order at different rates, depending on the type of work performed, when the work is performed, and so on. The cost center, to which the work center is assigned, is linked to the activity types and rates.

Define Maintenance Activity Types

This configuration step simply allows the definition of Maintenance Activity Types.

Assign Valid Maintenance Activity Types to Maintenance Order Types

This configuration step must contain one entry for each Maintenance Activity Type that will be assigned to each order type. For example, if there are five order types and there are six Maintenance Activity Types to be assigned to each order type, this configuration setting will contain 30 entries. Wildcard entries are not allowed.

Default Value for Maintenance Activity Type for Each Order Type

Although all of the possible Maintenance Activity Types for each order type were defined in the previous step, this configuration step can be used to define which Maintenance Activity Type will appear as the default Maintenance Activity Type for each order type.

If a default is provided, there is a possibility that the user may overlook changing the Maintenance Activity Type to the most appropriate type. If it is critical that the proper Maintenance Activity Type be selected, consider not setting a default, but change the field attributes to "required" (in the IMG setting "Define Field Selection for Order Header Data (PM)").

Costing Data for Maintenance and Service Orders

The entries in this configuration section also appear in the CO (Controlling) section of the IMG and are usually configured by a representative of the CO implementation team. Do not configure this section of the IMG without knowledge of the CO functionality contained within. Since this functionality is more CO-related than PM-related, this configuration will not be discussed here. If an attempt is made to alter this configuration, it should only be performed after consulting with a person responsible for implementing or maintaining the CO module.

> - Note: If overhead surcharges are to be applied to work orders (instead of being applied as part of "standard" rates), some changes to this configuration may be required with the co-operation of the CO personnel.

Define Change Docs, Collective Purc. Req. Indicator, Operation No. Interval

This configuration step contains some miscellaneous settings related to work orders. For each plant/order type combination, the settings are as follows:

- *Increment*—This determines the default numbering for work order operations. For example, the first operation will be numbered 0010, the second, 0020, and so on. This is set to "0010" which should be fine. Setting it to 0001 would sequentially number the operations, but leave no space to insert operations between existing operations.

- *OrdStChgDoc*—This checkbox controls whether changes to the status of a work order are recorded. If the checkbox is checked, each time the work order header status is changed, the change of status is recorded, along with when the change was made and who made the change.

- *CollReqstn*—This checkbox, when checked, allows all of the non-stock materials of a work order to be included in the same purchase requisition. If the checkbox is not checked, multiple purchase requisitions will be generated for non-stock materials. Confirm whether those responsible for purchasing (a function of the MM (Materials Management) module) have a preference between one purchase requisition or multiple purchase requisitions from the same work order before committing to checking or unchecking the checkbox.

- *Res/PurRq*—This setting determines whether, and when, purchase requisitions and/or material reservations are generated from a work order:
    - **Never**—Self-explanatory
    - **From release**—Reservations (for stock material) and/or requisitions (for non-stock material) will be generated when the work order is released/put in process.
    - **Immediately**—Reservations and/or requisitions will be generated upon creation (saving) of the work order.
- *PDC active*—This checkbox should only be checked if a Plant Data Collection (PDC) system is to be interfaced with the Plant Maintenance module. Plant Data Collection is not a function of the standard SAP system, but an external PDC system can be used to automatically gather information, such as measurement readings, and transfer that information to the SAP Plant Maintenance module.
- *Workflow*—This checkbox should only be checked if workflow is to be triggered by changes to a work order. Workflow, which is not covered in this text, allows information and announcements, for example, to be sent to people upon an event being triggered.
- *Change document*—This checkbox forces the system to record changes to certain fields on work orders. This allows the system to record the value of the field before the change, the value of the field after the change, and who made the change.
- *Net order price*—This checkbox restricts the ability to change the net price for this work order type between the purchase requisition and the purchase order. Consult with a person representing the MM (Materials Management) module before committing to this setting.

Set workflow for orders

This configuration need not be set unless workflow will be used in relationship to work order changes. Workflow, being a cross-application function not restricted to Plant Maintenance is not discussed in this text. If using workflow, this configuration may be used in relation to work order changes according to the workflow requirements. The IMG documentation for this configuration step contains useful information should this configuration step be required.

Goods Movements for Order

This configuration section is related to goods movements related to work orders:

- *Define Documentation for Goods Movements for the Order*—This configuration step can allow the system to document specific types of goods movements related to specific order types. For example, the system can record whether goods have been received for a relevant purchase order, or whether goods have been issued to the work order, depending on the settings made here.

- *Set List Editing for Goods Movements for Orders*—This setting is similar to the many other settings that control list change and list display options. General, or global, selection options, for example, can be made here.

- *Reorganization of List for Goods Movements for Orders*—This is not a configuration step, but instructions for reorganizing/resetting list editing for goods movements after goods movement configuration changes have been made. This is not required when initially configuring the system, and if no changes are made to goods movement configuration, should not have to be performed in the future.

Availability Check for Material, PRTs and Capacities

This configuration section contains three steps that set up the definition and control of availability checking for materials, production resources and tools, and capacities (people, in Plant Maintenance). It may be beneficial to consult with people responsible for the MM (Materials Management) module and, possibly, the PP (Production Planning) module when performing this configuration.

- *Define Checking Rules*—There is a default checking rule for PM provided with the system. Unless additional checking rules will be required, no changes are required here.

- *Define Scope of Check*—Some default settings are provided for the PM module here, but those default settings should be reviewed to determine whether they are appropriate. If MRP (Material Requirements Planning) is being used, usually by those responsible for the MM (Materials Management) module, determine which settings should be maintained in order to coordinate with MRP.

  If MRP is being used, review the PM-related settings. If additional requirement checks have been defined for MRP, additional checking controls may need to be defined for PM.

  For each of the PM-related settings, the magnifying glass icon provides details for each of the settings. The groups of fields contained in availability checking control are:

  o **Stocks**—It is presumed that availability checking will consider general stock that is available for use (unrestricted use). However, if the stock is not available for unrestricted use, these settings control whether other stocks are considered available. For example, if the "Incl. blocked stock" checkbox is checked, any quantities of the requested material that are marked as "blocked stock" will be shown as available.

  o **In/outward movements**—Not all of the options in this screen area are directly relevant to the PM module. Some of the settings are more appropriate for PP (Production Planning) use. However, in determining the quantity of materials available, materials on purchase requisitions, purchase orders, and even reserved materials can be taken into account.

- o **Replenishment lead time**—This checkbox, when checked, allows the system to consider the time it should take for a material to actually be available for use after its receipt. In order to use this function properly, some information must be maintained on the appropriate material master records. Consult the SAP help for this checkbox for more information, if required.

- o **Storage location inspection**—This setting allows availability checking at the storage location level to be turned off, in which case availability checking is performed at the plant level.

- o **Missing parts processing**—This field can be used to contain the number of days in advance to check for a goods receipt for a missing part. This is most useful if workflow is being used, in which case the MRP controller can be notified by email when a missing part is received. Review the SAP help for this field for more information.

- o **Receipts in the past**—The default setting, blank (Include receipts from past and future) is normally adequate for Plant Maintenance use.

Define Inspection Control

This configuration setting specifies, for each plant/order type combination, whether availability checking is carried out for materials, PRTs, and/or capacity. These settings must be maintained for each plant/order type combination, especially if changes are made. The screen areas are:

Material availability:

- *No avail. check*—If this checkbox is checked, automatic availability checking for materials is turned off for this plant/order type. Manual availability checking is still permitted.

- *Status check*—This is normally checked and specifies that, prior to release of the work order, the system will only check for missing parts. If this checkbox is unchecked, it may have an impact on system performance.

- *Check material availability when saving order*—This checkbox, when checked, allows the system to perform an automatic availability check for materials when an order is saved, but only if specific fields have been changed. See the SAP help for this checkbox for a list of the specific fields.

- *Checking rule*—Usually, this field will contain PM, indicating that the PM checking rule will be used. If additional checking rules have been defined for Plant Maintenance use, enter the appropriate checking rule here.

- *Type comp. check*—Consult with a person responsible for the MM (Materials Management) module to determine whether ATP (Available To Promise) checking is appropriate here.

- *Mat. release*—This field controls whether an order can be released if parts (materials) are missing. The order can be released regardless of missing parts, the order can be released if the user decides it can be released, or the order can be blocked from release if materials are missing.

PRT availability:

- *No check*—If this checkbox is checked, automatic checking for PRTs will not be performed. The checkbox should be checked if PRTs will not be used. Likewise, if PRTs will be used, but availability checking for PRTs should not be performed, the checkbox should be checked. If PRTs will be used and should be checked for availability, ensure the checkbox is not checked. Note that there may be a slight impact on system performance related to work orders if PRT checking is enabled (the box is not checked).

- *Checking rule*—For Plant Maintenance purposes, the standard status check is usually sufficient.

- *PRT release*—As with the material release field discussed previously, this field can be used to allow or block the release of a work order based on a missing PRT.

Capacity availability:

- *No check*—If this checkbox is checked, automatic checking for capacities will be disabled. For Plant Maintenance purposes, capacity checking usually involves determining whether the people required to perform the work will be available, however additional types of capacity can be defined.

- *Overall profile*—If capacity availability checking is to be performed, enter an appropriate profile here. Appropriate profiles available with the default system are those in the pull-down list with the prefix "SAPPM_". If no profile is entered, the system will use a default profile as specified in the help for this field. The default may not be appropriate.

- *Rel. capacities*—As with the previous similar settings, this field can be used to allow or restrict the release of a work order for which insufficient capacity is available.

Batch assignment:

This setting is not normally relevant for Plant Maintenance use, but allows some control over materials that are handled in "batches."

Assign Standard Texts for Short Messages to Order Types

This option can be used to specify text that should appear on work orders by specifying the code of the standard text. This is particularly useful when printing work orders (shop papers). Standard text itself is not defined within the Implementation Guide, but is defined in the SAP system in the menu Tools → Form Printout → SAPScript → Standard Text.

General Data

This section contains work order-related options that are not restricted to order types. The individual configuration steps are discussed below.

Define Default Values for Component Item Categories

Determine the material type(s) that will be used for Plant Maintenance purposes. This determination is usually done in cooperation with those responsible for the MM (Materials Management) module. Once the material type(s) designation has been determined, it is possible to define a default item category for the material type/plant combinations here. The item categories most often used are L (for Stock items) and N (for non-stock items). Those item categories, along with some others that can also be used, are provided with the standard system. So, if this configuration step is performed, the item category will default for the material type/plant combination, which may or may not be desirable.

Define Movement Types for Material Reservations

This setting is often acceptable as defaulted. Again, consult with those responsible for other modules, particularly the MM (Materials Management) module and perhaps the PP (Production Planning) module, to determine whether changes have been made or if additions will be required here. These settings control which movement types will be used for goods issues for stock material reservations. The relevant "Package" for Plant Maintenance is IW01. Confirm that an appropriate goods issue movement type and that an appropriate goods issue cancellation (reversal) movement type have been specified.

Other settings in this configuration step may be required by other modules and should not be modified or removed.

Define Account Assignment Cat. and Document Type for Purchase Requisitions

In this configuration setting, ensure that an appropriate entry for Plant Maintenance purposes has been maintained. An entry should exist, or should be created, for order category 30 (maintenance order), document type NB (purchase requisition). The standard settings should be as follows:

© SAP AG

Acct.Assgmt.Cat.Gen   F

Acct.Assgmt.Cat.Proj   Q

AccAssgmtCat S.Order   E

Sales Doc.—Project   D

- For further information regarding the settings shown above, refer to SAP OSS (Online Service and Support) note number 575491.

Define Accounting Indicators

This configuration setting is only required if orders are to be settled to profitability segments, usually only applicable for

Customer Service. In addition, the CO (Controlling) component PA (Profitability Analysis), or CO-PA, must be used.

Define Priorities

This configuration step occurs in multiple places in the IMG. For example, a different set of priorities can be used for notifications and work orders, or different sets of priorities can be used for Plant Maintenance and Customer Service. While the same set of priorities can be used for notifications and work orders, using or defining the same set of priorities for Plant Maintenance and Customer service is not recommended. If the requirements for one module changes at a later time, it will be easier to accommodate if each module has its own priorities.

There are three steps contained within this configuration step:

- *Define Priority Types*—Priority types should not be confused with priorities themselves. A priority type can be "PM, " for example. In that case, all of the priorities within the "PM" priority type will be used for the Plant Maintenance module. Some default priority types are provided with the standard SAP R/3 system, including a "PM" priority type. If no additional priority types are required, the "PM" priority type can be used. The actual priorities will be defined in the next step.

- *Define Priorities for Each Priority Type*—In this step, the actual priorities are defined for the previously created priority type. Note that the default priority types already contain priorities. These may be used as provided, but some changes are likely required.

    The "Relative start" and "Relative end" days are used by the system, when possible, to initially schedule work orders that are assigned a priority. For example, when a work order is assigned a priority with a relative start value of 0 (zero), the system will attempt to schedule the work order for the current day. Note that some other parameters may be involved in work order scheduling. Priorities can also assist in grouping and sorting work orders, but consider the role that the priority may have in initially scheduling work orders.

- *Define Priority Type for Orders*—The standard system will contain defaults that assign the default PM priority type to the default Plant Maintenance order types. If other work order types will be used or if other priority types will be used, this configuration step must be used to assign the appropriate priority type to the appropriate work order type.

Create System Conditions or Operating Conditions

This configuration step allows the definition of operating conditions. The standard system may provide two operating conditions, essentially on and off, or operating and not operating, but different conditions or additional conditions can be defined to indicate whether a piece of equipment, for example is running.

In addition, this configuration step provides some integration with the PP (Production Planning) module. If the PP module is being used, or will be used, the "Reservation by PM" checkbox can be used to indicate that, when a piece of equipment is not in operation, a capacity requirement will be issued for the piece of equipment (as a PP work center) in the PP module.

For this integration to take place, the PP work center identifier must be defined in the master data record for the piece of equipment, on the "Location" tab. Do not confuse this with the field for the Plant Maintenance work center, which is located on the "Organization" tab of the equipment master record.

Activate Default Value for Current Date as Basic Date

This configuration step simply allows the current date to be defaulted into the basic date field on a work order, based on the planning plant. The basic date may be the start or finish date, depending on the scheduling type used.

Define Default Values for Units for Operation

This configuration step provides default unit of measure values for work and duration in work order operations. This configuration is not necessary, but can save some time in entering or looking up the appropriate units of measure for work and duration for each operation.

Since "hour" is likely the most common unit of measure for work and duration, it is possible that the system contains both "H" and "HR" to represent hours. Settle on one or the other and use that unit of measure consistently throughout the Plant Maintenance module, unless there is a compelling reason not to. Keep this in mind when defining work centers (outside of the IMG). If a work center is defined to use the unit of measure "HR, " for example, setting the default to "H" in this configuration setting will cause a conflict that must be changed for each operation.

User Status for Orders

This configuration step is mostly similar to the configuration for user statuses for notifications. The only difference is in the second step, "Assign User Status to Order Types, " where the user statuses defined can be assigned to work order types.

For more information on defining user statuses, refer to the section on user statuses for notifications.

Define Partner Determination Procedure and Partner Function

This configuration step is very similar to that in the IMG section for notifications. In SAP terminology, a partner is an entity that can be associated with an object in any way. In this instance, the object is a notification. For most implementations, the default settings for this configuration step will provide the required functionality.

Regardless of whether changes are made to partner determination procedures, review this configuration step to ensure that the PM (Plant Maintenance) partner determination procedure (or a different partner determination procedure, if more appropriate) is assigned to the relevant PM-related order types, particularly if additional order types have been defined.

Review the partner functions that have been assigned to the order types if changes are required. If desired, an approval process can be assigned to orders. To use the approval process function, check the "Approval required" checkbox and press the "Enter" key on the keyboard. The additional fields will appear. Do not check the "Approval required" checkbox if this type of approval process is not required.

Scheduling

This configuration section contains some parameters that allow the system to assist with the scheduling of work orders. This functionality is based on, and shared with the PP (Production Planning) module. Some settings and functions within this section are specific to PP, so it may be beneficial to discuss any changes to this configuration with a person responsible for the PP module.

Maintain Scheduling Types

Usually, the default configuration provided with the system is adequate. Deleting unwanted scheduling types is not recommended, since one may be required in the future or by another module, particularly PP (Production Planning). Most often, forwards scheduling is used in Plant Maintenance. Simply stated, forwards scheduling means that the work progresses from a start date. See the SAP help for each of the buttons in this configuration for more information regarding the different types of scheduling.

Set Scheduling Parameters

Scheduling parameters can be configured for each plant/order type combination. Although there is a field for "Production Controller, " that field is more relevant to Production Planning and is not necessary for Plant Maintenance. There should be an asterisk (*) in the "Production Controller" field for each plant/order type combination relevant to Plant Maintenance.

The magnifying glass icon leads to the detailed settings for each plant/order type. The fields in the detailed scheduling parameters settings are described below:

- *Adjust dates*—Select from the available options, which allow the system to adjust basic start dates of orders or restrict the system from adjusting the basic start dates.

- *Scheduling type*—As discussed before, forwards scheduling is often the most appropriate scheduling type for Plant Maintenance purposes, however other scheduling types can be used where appropriate. For example, when work needs to be finished by a specific date, the system can perform backwards scheduling to determine when the work should start.

- *Start in past*—This field contains the number of days that the system is permitted to schedule a work order in the past. Consider a reasonable setting for this field. If an attempt is made to schedule a work order in the past beyond this setting, the system will override the scheduling type with "Today" scheduling, meaning that the start date for the work order will be the current date. To the user attempting to back-date the start date of a work order, for whatever reason, it may cause some frustration when the system changes the user's specified date to the current date.

- *Automatic scheduling*—This checkbox, when checked, allows the system to perform automatic scheduling of a work order when the work order is saved.

- *Automatic log*—This checkbox, when checked, will cause the scheduling log to be displayed automatically after each time scheduling is performed.

- *Scheduling with breaks*—The checkbox, when checked, indicates that specified breaks should be taken into consideration when scheduling is performed.

- *Shift order*—This checkbox controls whether the actual dates of partially confirmed operations is taken into account when subsequent scheduling is performed. If this checkbox is checked, the system will ignore any actual dates on partially confirmed operations.

- *Latest dates f. material*—This checkbox controls the requirement date for materials required for the work order. The SAP help for this checkbox provides sufficient information regarding whether or not the checkbox should be checked.

External Scheduling

The settings in this configuration section are only relevant if scheduling will be performed by an external program and the dates passed to the SAP R/3 system. The settings may depend on the functionality of the external program and are not discussed here. Refer to the SAP help for these configuration steps for a better understanding of this functionality, if required.

- It is worth noting that SAP has an approved interface to project management/scheduling software. At the time of this writing, the SAP web page with more information, along with a downloadable document that includes the necessary configuration settings for this functionality can be found at *www.sap.com/partners/icc/scenarios/plm/cs-sdl.asp* at the time of this writing (Include the hyphen between cs and sdl).

Create Revisions

This configuration setting allows the definition of shutdowns, for example. The intention is that work orders can be grouped into a "Revision" for the purposes of scheduling the work orders within the dates specified by the Revision. An added benefit is that, since the appropriate revision must be entered on the relevant work orders, the work orders can be grouped and reported according to Revision. In this configuration step, the Revision is simply given a unique identifier, a description, a start date and time, and an end date and time.

The unique identifier can be somewhat challenging, considering the field is only eight characters in length. There is no need to include the relevant plant in the identifier, since a separate field contains the plant ID (this is not necessarily true in some older versions of SAP R/3). Once a Revision has been defined, the revision can be assigned to work orders. When a Revision has been assigned to a work order, the work order dates will be changed, if necessary, so that the work order dates are within the revision dates.

Production Resource/Tool Assignments

This configuration section contains some settings that control how PRTs (Production Resources and Tools) are handled on work orders. PRTs are typically special equipment or materials, for example, that are assigned to a work order to assist with performing the required work. A good example of a PRT is a crane. There may be multiple demands for the crane, but the crane cannot be in more than one place at a time, so there may be a need to schedule the crane's time for a work order.

Define PRT Control Keys

There are two control keys provided with the standard SAP R/3 system, one that permits scheduling, costing, confirmations, printing, and printing additional information, and the other that only permits printing. These may be sufficient or additional control keys may be defined to allow a combination of those options, if required. Refer to the SAP help for the checkboxes if more information is required.

Formulas

Generally, the SAP-provided formula parameters and formula definitions are sufficient for most PM-related requirements. Some of the formulas are more relevant to the PP (Production Planning) module. Even if it seems as though some of the formulas may never be used, deleting any formula information is not recommended.

Print Control

This configuration section can be used to define and control which "shop papers" can be printed and where. This is similar to the previous "Notification Print Control" step discussed earlier, but in this section, shop papers can be assigned to orders.

Define Shop Papers, Forms and Output Programs

If the standard default SAP R/3 work orders are being used, this setting will contain some default shop papers that can be printed from the work orders. Whether or not the default work orders are used, additional and/or alternate shop papers can be defined.

If interested in printing work order shop papers, review the shop papers that are available by default. If the default shop papers are not adequate, determine the layout that will be required for a custom work order shop paper(s). The development of the shop papers is usually performed by programmers. Shop papers can include job tickets for each work center, pick lists for materials, time tickets for confirming time, etc.

If non-default shop papers are created, the shop papers can be made available (linked) from the work order with these settings.

Within this setting, it is also possible to link specific shop papers to specific work order types, if there is a reason to do so.

In addition, shop papers can be set to print by default when the print functionality is accessed from a work order.

Define Printer

This configuration setting contains three sub-settings:

- *User-Specific Print Control.* This setting can be used to control which shop papers are printed on which printer(s) based on the user ID and the shop paper. Additional print options can be set.

- *Define Print Diversion.* This determines whether print diversion (directing a shop paper to a different printer) is active for specific shop papers.

- *Print Diversion According to Field Contents.* This setting can be used primarily to control whether a shop paper is diverted to a different printer based on the value contained in a specified notification field. For example, if the work order contains a specific equipment number in the equipment field, a specific shop paper can be diverted to a different printer than usual.
- Print diversion, when it applies, overrides user-specific settings.

Message Control

This configuration setting can allow changes to the severity of some error and warning messages. For example, some error messages can be downgraded to warning messages and some warning messages can be upgraded to error messages. Not all messages can be changed in this way, and some thought should be given before changing others.

To change the severity of a message, determine the message number (it's usually displayed right on the message when it appears) and its application area. Determine whether the message already appears on the list in this configuration step and, if so, change its message category appropriately. If the message does not appear on the list, its severity cannot currently be changed in this configuration step. However, it may be possible for the severity of custom (not standard SAP) messages that may have been added to the system to be changed here.

Changing the severity of messages is not normally required.

Assign Default Values for Settlement Areas to Order Types

Unless "Accounting Areas" have been set up by someone responsible for the CO (Controlling) module, no configuration is required here. This configuration, if accounting areas have been defined, allows the grouping of work orders for collective settlement. Refer to the SAP help for this configuration step for further information regarding collective settlement of orders.

Object Information

The Object Information window, which has been discussed previously, can be configured with the settings in this section. The Object Information window is available from the notification and work order screens and contains information relative to the object (equipment or functional location, for example) for which the notification or work order were created. The Object Information window can also be configured to appear automatically when notifications or work orders are created.

The Object Information window can show recent notifications and/or work orders for the same object within a specified time period. It can also draw attention to thresholds that have been met or exceeded, such as number or breakdowns, number of orders created, etc. within the specified time period. For example, if more than three breakdowns have been reported for the same piece of equipment over the past 90 days, attention will be drawn to that statistic, if the Object Information window has been configured as such.

Two benefits of the Object Information window is that duplicate reporting of a problem for which a notification has already been created can be reduced, as well as attention being drawn to an object that seems to have a recurring problem.

Define Object Information Keys

A default Object Information Key, PM, is provided for Plant Maintenance purposes. If the Object Information window seems useful, the default Object Information Key can be modified as required. An alternate Object Information Key can be created to use instead of the default provided and, if desired, multiple Object Information Keys can be created for various purposes and assigned to different notification types.

If the Object Information window does not seem as if it would be useful, confirm that the "automatically" checkbox is unchecked in this configuration step. The Object Information window will still be available on demand by clicking a button on the notification or work order screen, but will not appear automatically.

The other areas in this configuration step are as follows:

- *Reference for notification and class selection*—Specify whether the information contained in the Object Information window pertains to the object itself, the object and its superior object, or to the object's structure (presuming one exists).

- *Info. System—time frame and threshold values.* Specify the number of days for which the other six fields in this area are relevant. For example, number of breakdowns in the past X days. For the other six fields, specify the thresholds at which attention will be drawn to that number on the Object Information window. For example, if the "No. days" field contains 60 and the "Orders created" field contains 5, attention will be drawn to the "Orders created" field in the Object Information window when five or more work orders have been created for that object in within the past 60 days.

- *Notifications—selection and automatic display.* As with the previous area, the number of days must be specified for the system to consider previously created and/or completed notifications for the object. A 30 entered in the "Sel. days" field will cause the system to consider notifications for the object from the previous 30 days. The "SelComplNotifs" checkbox will cause completed notifications to be displayed as well as outstanding and/or in process notifications. The other two checkboxes will cause the Object Information to be presented automatically if outstanding notifications and/or completed notifications, respectively, exist for the object for the time period specified.

- *Contract—automatic display.* This area is more relevant to the Customer Service (CS) module and controls whether information is displayed if a contract has been created for an object.

- *Classification—views and display.* If views have been configured for classes, views may be specified here for relevant classification data to be displayed for the object. The

"Characteristics" checkbox will allow the display of characteristic information pertaining to the class.

Assign Object Information Keys to Order Types

This configuration step simply allows the assignment of a specific Object Information Key to one or more order types.

Define Field Selection for Order Header Data (PM)

This configuration step allows changes to the attributes of fields contained on the work order screen. For example, a specific field can be made mandatory (an entry is required before the system will allow the user to continue) while another field can be hidden. The attribute options, also found elsewhere in Plant Maintenance configuration are:

- *Input*—The normal status of a field. This allows, but does not force, the user to enter a value in the specified field.

- *Required*—This setting forces the user to enter a value in the specified field before being permitted to continue. Each field appears on a specific tab on the work order screen. If the tab containing the specified field is not accessed by the user, the user is not forced to enter a value in the field. The user must click on the appropriate tab before the field is actually required.

- *Display*—The value already contained in the field is only displayed and cannot be changed in any way. If no value exists for the field, a value cannot be entered.

- *Hide*—The field will not appear on the work order screen.

- *HiLite*—The label for the field will appear in a different color than the other field labels. Depending on the color scheme used, the different color may or may not be obvious.

It is also possible to base the attributes of one or more fields on the value of a specific field. For example, by using the "Influencing" function of this configuration, a specific field can be hidden for a specific plant or for a specific order type. To do so:

1. Click on the "Influencing" button.
2. Select the field whose value will determine the attributes of the other field(s).
3. Enter the value that will trigger the attributes of the other field(s).
4. Press the "Enter" key (or click the "Enter" button/icon).
5. Make the necessary attribute changes.

When making changes to influencing attributes or to review influences, always press the Enter key after entering the influencing field value.

Define Field Selection for Order Header Data (CS)

This configuration step, as with the previous step, allows changes to the attributes of fields contained on the work order screen. In this case, the attributes are relevant to the CS (Customer Service) module and are not required specifically for Plant Maintenance purposes.

Define Field Selection for Order Operation (PM and CS)

This configuration step, as with the previous steps, allows changes to the attributes of fields related to work order operations. See the previous steps for more information on the functionality of this configuration step.

Define Field Selection for Components (PM and CS)

This configuration step, as with the previous steps, allows changes to the attributes of fields related to work order components (materials). See the previous steps for more information on the functionality of this configuration step.

List Editing

This configuration section controls the selection and display of lists of work orders and is quite similar to the previous "List Editing" configuration section for notifications.

Define List Variants

This configuration setting can be used to provide default values on selection screens for work orders. A variant (predefined selection criteria) is usually only defined here if it applies to many, if not all, users. Even if a variant is not provided with this configuration step, variants can still usually be defined by each user, if required.

Variants can be created for a variety of order-related items. In addition, separate variants can be created for display or change mode.

Define Field Selection for Multi-Level List Displays of Orders

This configuration setting can be used to define which fields appear by default in lists of objects associated with work orders. When the user selects **List Editing → Display (Multi-Level)** from the menu, objects associated with work orders can be displayed with the orders. The fields that appear for each associated object by default depend on this configuration setting. The users can select additional fields themselves unless the "Invisible" checkbox has been checked for a field. In that case, the field will not be available for the user to select for display.

Completion Confirmations

A completion confirmation can be thought of as entering the actual time spent performing an operation, or confirming the time spent performing the required work. Depending on whether the HR (Human Resources) module of SAP R/3 is also being used, completion confirmations may be entered in the Plant Maintenance module, or the confirmations may be performed through CATS (Cross Application Time Sheet) functionality if required by the HR module. It is also possible that a third party, external time collection system is being used. In this case, it is usually important that the actual times are communicated back to the Plant Maintenance module in order to determine the actual costs of maintenance.

The time spent performing the work is related to an activity type as defined in the CO (Controlling) module. The CO activity type determines the rate at which the labor will be charged to the work order and subsequently settled to a cost center (or other settlement object). For example, the planned labor costs on the work order may be based on regular time, but the actual labor may have been performed as overtime. The planned hours will be based on one CO activity type, but the actual hours reported in the completion confirmation may be based on a different CO activity type, allowing for planned vs. actual cost analysis later.

The following configuration descriptions may be based on the assumption that completion confirmations will be performed in the SAP R/3 Plant Maintenance module. Consult with someone responsible for the HR (Human Resources) module, if appropriate, to determine whether CATS will be used for time entry/confirmation. If so, work with those responsible for the HR module to ensure that the process of entering actual hours/confirmations is appropriately defined.

Define Control Parameters for Completion Confirmations

This configuration step primarily sets defaults that will appear on the completion confirmation screen for the user. Control parameters can be defined for each plant/order type combination and can be the same or different from each other, as required. The magnifying glass icon leads to detailed configuration for each plant/order type combination. The screen areas of the detail screen are described below.

Default Values:

- *Final Confirmation*—When this checkbox is checked, the Final Confirmation checkbox on the completion confirmation screen will default to being checked. Unless the user removes the check mark, the first completion confirmation will also serve as the last completion confirmation for that operation. If this checkbox is not checked, the Final Confirmation checkbox on the completion confirmation screen will not be checked and the user should check it during the last confirmation for that operation.

- *Post open reservs.*—This checkbox does not cause materials to be issued (goods issued) to a work order. It causes the Final Issue checkbox to be checked for the appropriate materials on a work order indicating that no further goods issues are expected for each material associated with this operation on the work order. The Backflushing checkbox for the material, however, will cause goods issues for outstanding reservations to a work order.

- *Propose dates*—When checked, allows the system to provide a date default on the Completion Confirmation screen.

- *Propose activities*—This checkbox, when checked, allows the system to provide a default for the "Actual Work" field on the completion confirmation screen. The default used will be the remaining planned time for that operation. The default can be overridden by the user. Regardless of whether this checkbox is checked, the system can calculate the "Remaining Work" field value by subtracting the actual time entered from the remaining planned time.

- *Milestone automatic.*—This checkbox, when checked, will enable the system to automatically transfer a percentage complete for an operation for project management purposes. If it is not important to track operations to the level of percentage complete, it is not necessary to check this checkbox. This functionality is only relevant for work order operations related to projects in the SAP PS (Project Systems) module.

Checks:

- *Date in future*—When this checkbox is checked, the system will allow a completion confirmation to be entered for a future date. If a confirmation is attempted to be entered for a future date, an error message will be presented. If the box is not checked, confirmations for future dates may not be entered.

- *WrkDev. active*—This checkbox allows the system to validate the actual time entered against the actual time expected. The next field, "Work deviation, " controls the percentage within which a deviation is acceptable. If the "Work deviation" field is blank (the same as zero), then no deviation should be acceptable. That is, the actual time entered must be the same as the planned time. However, setting a zero deviation appears to be a problem on at least some systems, so it may be beneficial that it is rarely, if ever, required.

  When the "WrkDev. active" checkbox is checked and a percentage value is entered in the "Work deviation" field, a warning message stating that the actual work plus the remaining work deviates by more than the percentage from the planned work. The message will appear if the user attempts to enter a final confirmation outside the deviation percentage, or any confirmation greater than the planned time plus the acceptable deviation.

  A final note: Setting the deviation to zero would effectively eliminate the possibility of planned vs. actual analysis.

- *Work deviation*—This field operates in conjunction with the previous field. See the previous field, "WrkDev. active, " for a description of this field.

- *DurtnDev.active*—This checkbox operates in much the same way as the "WrkDev. active" checkbox, except it pertains to duration instead of work time. If this checkbox is checked, the system issues a warning during completion confirmation if the duration of an operation will exceed the planned duration by more than a specified deviation. The deviation is specified in the following field, "Duration deviation."

- *Duration deviation*—This field works in conjunction with the previous checkbox, "DurtnDev.active, " and provides an acceptable deviation between the actual duration (elapsed time, not work time) and the planned duration of an operation.

Logs/Error handling:

- *Actual costs*—When this checkbox is checked, the system can generate a log of actual costs during every confirmation.

- *Termination for Incorrect Act.Costs*—This checkbox, which is only active if the previous checkbox is checked, allows the system to stop (terminate) the confirmation if actual costs are presumed to be incorrect. This is based on certain conditions, which can be found in the SAP help for this checkbox.

- *Goods movement*—When this checkbox is checked, the system can generate a log of goods movements during every confirmation.

- *Termination for Incorrect Goods Movt*—This checkbox, which is only active if the previous checkbox is checked, allows the system to stop (terminate) the confirmation if goods movements are presumed to be incorrect. This is based on certain conditions, which can be found in the SAP help for this checkbox.

Mass Confirmation:

- *Rough Reversal*—When this checkbox is checked, the system can perform a reversal for many operations with as little impact on system performance as possible. The trade-off is that information specific to individual operations may no longer be accurate. This type of reversal should only be performed when performance is more critical than the detailed information at the operation level.

- *Simplified Forecast Work Canceltn*—This checkbox is only required when cancellations of confirmations cause problems with the "Forecasted Work" field on the completion confirmation screen. Checking this checkbox causes the "Forecasted Work" value to equal the planned work value. See the SAP help for this checkbox for further information.

- *Execute Milestone Functions*—This checkbox is only relevant for PS (Project Systems) module-related work order operations. For confirmations performed in the background (batch), the system will only permit milestone-related functionality if this checkbox is checked. If this plant/order type combination is not relative to the PS module or if milestone activity is not required during the confirmation, then this box should not be checked.

Material Movements:

- *All components*—This checkbox applies to individual time confirmation, not to overall time confirmation. When this checkbox is checked, the system is permitted to display all of the materials relevant to the operation, not only those materials for which the backflush indicator is set.

Selection:

When performing completion confirmations in the Plant Maintenance module, it is possible to obtain a list of operations to be confirmed for a specific work order. The following checkboxes control the defaults as to whether confirmable operations appear in the list and/or whether operations that have already been confirmed appear in the list.

- *Confirmed ops*—Operations that have already been confirmed will also appear in the list of operations.

- *Confirmable*—Confirmable operations will also appear in the list of operations. This option is more useful for other modules that use the confirmation process. Plant Maintenance operations that have not yet been confirmed will normally appear in the confirmation list regardless of the setting of this checkbox.

HR update:

- *No HR update*—This checkbox controls whether confirmation data is transferred from the PM (Plant

Maintenance) module to the HR (Human Resources) module. The checkbox should only be unchecked if both the PM and HR modules are in use and the HR module depends on the PM module for time data. If CATS (Cross Application Time Sheet) functionality is being used in conjunction with the HR module, it is likely that the process is reversed and the PM module will inherit time confirmations from the HR module, in which case this checkbox can be checked. Regardless of whether this checkbox is checked, additional functions must be performed to actually transfer data from the PM module to the HR module. See the SAP help on this checkbox for additional information.

In short, the "No HR update" checkbox should be checked unless confirmations entered in the PM module should be transferred to the HR module. If confirmations will not be transferred to the HR module, leaving this checkbox unchecked may cause an "Unprocessed future change recs" error message when attempting to close a work order, usually a work order with confirmations associated with an employee number.

- *No date update*—Unless the previous box is unchecked, this checkbox has no effect. If HR updating from the PM module is performed, this checkbox prevents actual dates from being updated in the HR module.

Control Data:

- *Process control*—There is no need to enter any value in this field unless there is a need to affect automatic goods receipt, backflushing, and posting of actual costs in the background. A process control key must have been defined in order for one to be entered here. See the item "Define Execution Time for Confirmation Processes, " below. If no control key is entered, the aforementioned items are performed in "real time." See the SAP help for this field for more information regarding the definition and use of the process control keys.

Define Causes for Variances

If it is important that the reasons for variances between planned and actual time be tracked, this configuration step can be used to define standard reasons for variances. If the same variance reasons are to be used at multiple plants, the reasons must be defined for each plant.

Define Execution Time for Confirmation Processes

This configuration setting can be used to define controls for the timing of automatic goods receipts, backflushing of components, and the posting of actual costs. Even if keys are defined here, they must still be assigned to plants and order types (see the item "Control Data, " above). If no keys are assigned, the confirmation processes listed above will occur during interactive processing, not later in the background.

Parallelized Confirmation Processes

This is a technique that can be used to spread CPU-intensive confirmation processes (many confirmations at once) among processors/servers. This is not usually required for Plant Maintenance-related confirmations. However, the SAP help for this IMG step can provide further information, if required.

Schedule Background Jobs Confirmation Processes

This configuration setting simply allows a background job/process to be started and/or scheduled. This transaction is also available outside of the IMG. If scheduling a background job is required, it may be necessary to have a person with the appropriate authorization actually perform the scheduling. If background job scheduling is not restricted, provide a name for the background job that appropriately identifies the module and/or the person responsible and/or the process. Proper identification of the background job enables those responsible for Basis to react more quickly to problems, if they occur.

Set Screen Templates for Completion Confirmation

This configuration setting affects the "Overall Completion Confirmation" screen, or transaction code IW42. It is possible to configure a confirmation screen that combines time entry, goods issues, and catalog code (damage, cause, etc.) entries, as well as providing one-button access to measurement readings.

Define as many profiles as required. Don't define an item as a screen area and also check the same item as an "Active pushbutton." For example, if a screen area is defined for "Cause of damage, " there is no need to provide a pushbutton for "Cause of damage." Experiment with the settings, viewing each setting in the "Overall Completion Confirmation" screen to determine the best setting.

Set Field Selection for Completion Confirmation

This configuration setting, as with other similar settings, allows the attributes of the fields on the completion confirmation screen to be altered. For example, specific fields can be hidden, required, display only, normal, or highlighted, if required.

The following two settings are similar in that each relates to a list of confirmations, but one controls search parameters for a list of operations while the other controls search parameters for a list of confirmations.

Set List Editing for Confirmations Using Operation List

This configuration setting can be used to provide default list editing values for confirmations accessed through a list of operations. Multiple variants can be saved and used as necessary. For example, specific fields can be made required, so that the user must enter a value each time, while other fields can have a default value already provided.

Set List Editing for Completion Confirmations

This configuration setting can be used to provide default list editing values for confirmations accessed through a list of confirmations. Multiple variants can be saved and used as necessary. For example, specific fields can be made required, so that the user must enter a value each time, while other fields can have a default value already provided.

Information Systems for Plant Maintenance and Customer Service

The Plant Maintenance Information System (PMIS)

The Plant Maintenance Information System (PMIS) is a subset of the Logistics Information System (LIS) in the SAP R/3 system. It allows some flexibility in the updating of information as well as the ability to report on data trends gathered over time.

Rather than providing list editing-type reports that allow a view of specific work orders or pieces of equipment, for example, the PMIS is more suited to reporting accumulated figures such as "How many times did this manufacturer's equipment break down in the past year and how much did it cost to maintain?"

Define Currency for Maintenance Statistics

In order for the system to provide figures that can be used for comparison purposes, a standard currency must be defined. Regardless of how many currencies are in use within the system, this setting allows the system to convert the currency for each transaction to the standard currency. If all of the transactions in the system are performed in the same currency, then that currency should, of course, be defined as the currency for maintenance statistics. If the transactions take place in a variety of currencies, select the currency in which the statistics should be compared.

Assign Value Categories to Maintenance Cost Key Figures

A value category may be comprised of one or more cost elements, depending on which cost element groupings make sense. See the section "Settings for Display of Costs" on page 105 for further information on defining value categories.

There are several Cost Key Figures provided by default by SAP and these may be adequate. However, in the case that a more granular breakdown of costs in the PMIS is required, additional Cost Key Figures may be defined. If required, additional Cost Key Figures should be defined in the next section, "Define Customer-Specific Key Figures." Once they have been defined, continue to the following setting to properly assign the Value Categories.

> - TIP: Spend some time to become familiar with at least how the Standard Analysis section of the PMIS works before the system is actually used in a "production" environment, if possible. Determine how to obtain the most benefit from the analysis and then define the appropriate value categories and, if necessary, additional key figures. If the value category/key figure structure is changed later, it is not a simple process to reset the cost reporting.

Customer-Specific Key Figures

This configuration section allows the definition of Cost Key Figures and the assignment of Value Categories. If the default key figures are adequate, this section need not be configured.

Define Customer-Specific Key Figures

Although there are a few key figures provided as a default by SAP, which provide some basic analysis through the Plant Maintenance Information System (PMIS), this configuration step allows the creation of additional key figures. The default key figures provide data for costs such as internal employees, external "employees, " internal material, etc. "Customer-Specific" in this case refers to a customer of SAP.

Value Categories and/or Accounting Indicators for Internal Key Figures

If additional key figures were defined in the previous step, use this configuration step to assign the appropriate value categories to the key figures.

Configure Measurement Document Update

It is not necessary to perform this configuration step if the Plant Maintenance module is not being used for fleet management. This configuration step allows some control over the updating of key figures related to measurement documents (readings taken from measuring points, such as an odometer). Refer to the SAP help for this configuration step for more information.

System Enhancements and Data Transfer

Develop Enhancements

This configuration step provides access to perform customizing of the Plant Maintenance module beyond SAP standard functionality. The SAP documentation for this configuration step provides a comprehensive list of the standard enhancements available. These standard enhancements have also been referred to as customer exits or user exits.

This customizing is usually performed by programmers. In addition to the SAP documentation in the Implementation Guide, further information on how to take advantage of this additional functionality can be found within the "Develop Enhancements" configuration step by clicking on the (i) button.

Business Add-Ins

This configuration step provides an additional method of customizing and adding functionality beyond that provided by SAP. Each of the Business Add-Ins listed in the IMG has its own documentation provided by SAP. Refer to this documentation if additional functionality is required.

Execute Data Transfer

This configuration step provides access to the transaction IBIP, which can be used for the mass loading or changing of data. It is most commonly used for Plant Maintenance purposes to perform an initial load of functional location and/or equipment data. Although it can be used to load or change other objects, it is sometimes so difficult to organize the data in the correct format(s) that other data manipulation and loading techniques, possibly including manual entry, are preferable.

Although there is extensive documentation provided by SAP, it can be difficult to follow. An example, for a "simple" data load for equipment is as follows:

> Perform transaction SE12 to obtain a data layout for the view "IBIPEQUI." (IBIPEQUI is the equipment layout for the IBIP (data load) transaction as found in the SAP documentation). This shows a complete listing of the fields and the field lengths.
>
> The input data must be arranged into the format provided in the previous step. The first two fields, TCODE and RECORDNAME should contain IE01 and IBIPEQUI respectively. IE01 is the transaction code for creating a piece of equipment, while IBIPEQUI is the data layout provided.
>
> However the data is accumulated (Microsoft Access is one option), the data must be provided to the IBIP transaction as a text, non-delimited file. That means that no commas, tabs, or other characters can be used between fields and that a 10-character field must be 10 characters in length, even if some of the characters are spaces.
>
> Every field is treated as a text field, just as if the data was being entered manually. Additionally, each field will be subjected to the R/3 system's normal data validation. That means that any invalid data cannot be loaded into the system.
>
> Once the file is in the correct format, a test load can be performed. Provide a file with only one record on the first

attempt. This attempt will serve to ensure that the field lengths are aligned correctly. On subsequent attempts, load perhaps three records once or twice before attempting to load the entire file. If it is important not to load the same piece of equipment more than once, be sure to remove those records already loaded from the input file on subsequent attempts. Keep a full version of the data file for subsequent full data loads, but create partial data files for partial data loads as required.

To perform a data load, there are very few changes required to the settings in the IBIP transaction. Experiment with the other changes, if required, but listed here are the critical fields:

Process mode—There are three modes:

o A—This processing mode requires user input on every screen. If four screens/tabs are involved for every equipment to be loaded, the "Enter" key must be pressed for each screen, regardless of whether an error exists. Not recommended for loading many records.

o E—This processing mode only requires user input when an error is encountered. Error correction can be made "on the fly" as the data is being loaded. However, as data corrections are made as the data is loaded, be sure to make the same changes to the original data file to allow error-free entry on subsequent data loads. This is recommended for when the data file is reasonably error-free but may still contain some problems. This setting is a good compromise, but still requires some watching over the load process.

o N—This processing mode is performed in the background and requires no user intervention until its completion. If this processing mode is used, be sure to check the "Save errors" checkbox below and review the log for errors upon completion of the data load. Selecting this option eliminates the need to watch over the process, but requires that the error log be reviewed after completion of the process. Any data records for which there were errors will not be loaded, but will have been ignored by the system. All error-free data will have been loaded. Those records for which there were errors must be extracted from the original data load file, corrected, and then loaded by themselves.

The other important field is the "Physical file name" field in the "File access: Source" data group on the "File Management" tab. Use the "pull-down" to the right of this field (click on the field first) to find the data file. If the data file is on a desktop computer, the "Presentation server" button should also be active.

In addition, a file in which to save errors can be specified in the "Physical file name" field in the bottom data group, "File access: Objective/saving incorrect transactions."

For functional location loading, once a functional location has been loaded, it cannot be loaded again, since the functional location must be unique in the system. If testing a functional location load and a subsequent load must be performed, perhaps change the first character or two for every record in the input file. This will create another functional location hierarchy in the system. Perform the load in a test system as many times using this technique as necessary in order to eliminate all errors from the load. Once the load is certified error-free, it can be loaded into the "production" system cleanly once only.

For equipment loading, depending on whether internal or external numbering is used, the data may or may not be loaded more than once without changing the data. If internal (system-assigned) equipment numbering is enabled, it is possible to load equipment records more than once. While this simplifies testing the data load, caution is advised when performing a data load into the "production" system to ensure that the data is not loaded more than once. If external equipment numbering is used, a portion of the equipment number must be changed in order to test load the data more than once.

Regardless of whether the IBIP transaction is used to load data or whether a different method is used, the test loads can follow the same technique described above in order to perform more than one test load. With any method of data loading, ensure that the data loads cleanly in its entirety before performing a data load into the "production" system. Once an entire data load has been cleanly performed, any subsequent changes to the data must trigger a new round of testing before a "production" data load can be performed, no matter how simple the change may seem.

It is not a simple process to delete functional locations and/or equipment records from the system, so ensure that the process need only be performed once into the "production" system.

Note: There are several alternatives to transaction IBIP for data loading. One of the best alternatives is the Legacy System Migration Workbench (LSMW), which can be accessed through transaction code LSMW. SAP recommends searching for updated documentation for LSMW on the SAP Service Marketplace (service.sap.com) web site. A user ID, normally available through SAP system administrators, is required to access the web site.

LSMW provides an easier method of transferring data from other sources into the SAP R/3 system than developing programs for each data conversion. Although LSMW can make the data conversion process easier, an understanding of data tables and field mapping is recommended.

Updating the PMIS

Activate Update

This configuration step can be found in the IMG by following the path:

Logistics—General → Logistics Information System (LIS) → Logistics Data Warehouse → Updating → Updating Control → Activate Update

Select the Plant Maintenance option and review the settings. The settings can be changed by selected a particular info. structure and clicking on the magnifying glass button. Usually, for statistical reporting and analysis, monthly updating is adequate, but that can be changed here.

Consult with those responsible for the CO module to determine whether a fiscal year variant should be used. Typically, this is used to align PMIS reporting periods with financial reporting periods.

Although there are other settings that can be made in the configuration for the Logistics Information System, of which the Plant Maintenance Information System is a part, the setting of primary concern is mentioned above.

End of Configuration

It is important to note once again that the settings as previously described are typical, but do not apply to every implementation of the SAP R/3 system. It is impossible to predict what the best settings for a particular implementation will be, so the descriptions serve as familiarization for the Plant Maintenance section of the Implementation Guide and should not be considered a substitute for qualified assistance.

Just because a setting can be configured does not mean that it should be configured. The vast array of configuration settings for just the Plant Maintenance module of SAP R/3 are meant to accommodate a variety of implementations. While it is important to know which configuration settings should be changed for a particular implementation, not all configuration settings should be changed.

CHAPTER 3
ADMINISTERING SAP R/3 PLANT MAINTENANCE

In this chapter

- Master Data in the Plant Maintenance Module
- The Work Order Process
- The Preventive Maintenance Process
- Reporting

Master Data

In the SAP R/3 system, master data is primarily contained within the menu "Management of Technical Objects." Master data, as mentioned previously, is data that is fairly static in the system. That is, it can change but is not usually considered transactional data.

Examples of *configuration data* are equipment types and work order types. Configuration data is created and changed least frequently. Changes to configuration data usually require that the changes be made in one system (instance) and transported to the production system (instance) once tested and approved. Very few people should have authorization to create and change configuration data, and changes to configuration data should be prevented in the production system.

Examples of *master data* are functional location and equipment master records. These types of records are created and changed occasionally and, while more people will have authorization to create and change master data, that authorization will usually still be somewhat restricted.

Examples of *transactional data* are notifications and work orders. Transactional data is created quite frequently, more often than master data. While it is sometimes common for many people to have the authorization to create and change notifications, there are often more restrictions on the work order, since the work order can be used to authorize work and accumulate costs.

Master data and transactional data will be discussed further in the next several sections.

Good representative examples of master data, including those previously discussed, are:

- Functional locations
- Equipment
- Materials
- Bills of materials
- Work centers

although other data elements may be considered master data.

Functional Locations

Functional locations are most often used to define a physical "place" or "location." However, they can also be used to define where a process occurs.

Functional locations are usually related to each other within a hierarchy and it is not uncommon for more than one hierarchy to be defined. Most often, the hierarchy reflects where functional locations occur within other functional locations. For example, if the functional location at the top of a hierarchy reflects a plant, the functional locations directly below the top level (plant) might reflect areas of the plant or even buildings. As functional locations are defined downwards in the hierarchy, they might, in turn, reflect production lines, logical groupings of equipment, on down to the places where individual pieces of equipment can be "installed."

If the top level of a functional location hierarchy represents a plant and there is more than one plant in a company, it stands to reason that there would be more than one functional location hierarchy defined. It is possible to create an even higher level to represent a region, country, division, etc. but only do so if it makes sense from a maintenance perspective. The cost center hierarchy in the Controlling (CO) module will take those into account from a cost perspective. Whatever the highest level functional locations, create those first and then create others downwards in the hierarchy. This will ensure proper "inheritance" of values from the "parent" functional locations.

The functional location to which another functional location is assigned is known as a *superior functional location*. Although not as commonly heard, functional locations assigned to another functional location are *subordinate functional locations*. The relationship between the levels of functional locations are also sometimes referred to as parent/child relationships.

Functional locations are created according to the structure indicators and edit masks defined in the Implementation Guide. If functional locations are created from the top level down in the functional location hierarchy, the lower level functional locations will automatically adopt the appropriate higher level functional location as their superior (parent) functional location. This allows the functional locations to "inherit" values (also as defined in the Implementation Guide) from their superior functional location.

If lower level functional locations are created before the higher level functional locations, the link between a functional location and its superior functional location must be created manually.

The same functional location cannot occur more than once in the system, but functional locations can be copied (the copy must have a different number/identifier).

Although functional locations can be defined as equipment or machines, it is most often convenient to think of a functional location, particularly a lower level functional location, as a place where a piece of equipment can be located, placed or installed.

One or more functional locations may be assigned to a "superior" functional location.

One or more pieces of equipment may be assigned to a functional location (unless the functional location is set to prohibit or restrict such assignment).

One or more pieces of equipment may be assigned to a "superior" piece of equipment (which means that those assigned pieces of equipment would become *sub-equipment*).

One or more materials can be assigned to a piece of equipment, in effect becoming an *equipment bill of materials*. Bills of materials will be discussed further.

One or more materials can be assigned to a "superior" material, in effect becoming a *material bill of materials* (or an *assembly*). Bills of materials will be discussed further.

The above potential assignments allow for the functional locations, equipment and materials to be structured as required. The most simple method of displaying a structure or part of a structure is to use transaction code IH01, found in the menu path **Logistics → Plant Maintenance → Management of Technical Objects → Functional Location → Structural Display**. See *Figure 12* for the *Functional Location Structure: Selection* screen. The structure will be displayed from the functional location entered, upwards and/or downwards, depending on the numbers entered in the fields "Display Levels Above" and "Display Levels Below." The higher the number(s) entered, the longer the results will take to be displayed. Keep the number(s) low, even at 1, initially. Additional levels can be displayed on the resulting screen. The checkboxes on the screen determine what will be displayed. For the display of equipment, sub-equipment and bills of material, check the boxes *Equipment installed, Equipment hierarchy* and *BOM explosion* respectively.

If a display of the hierarchy is not necessary, a list of functional locations can be obtained through transaction code IH06 (menu path **Logistics →Plant**

Maintenance → Management of Technical Objects →Functional Location → List Editing → Display. A single functional location can be displayed with transaction code IL03 (Logistics → Plant Maintenance → Management of Technical Objects → Functional Location → Display). This transaction is best used if the functional location code is known.

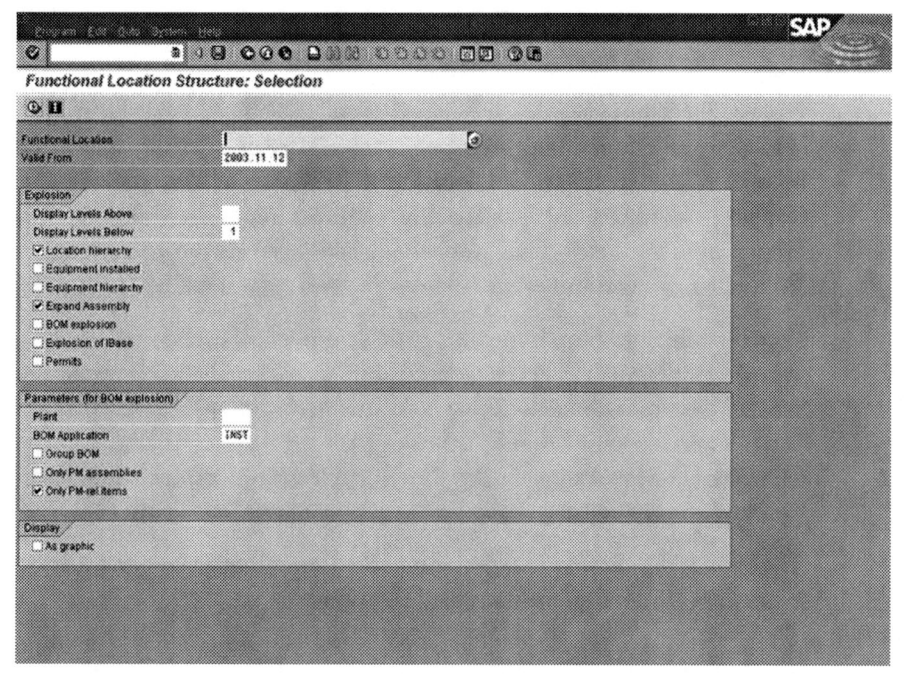

Figure 12. Transaction IH01, "Functional Location Structure: Selection" screen.
© SAP AG

Functional location numbers are not assigned by the system. Functional location numbers/identifiers must be provided manually according to the appropriate structure indicator.

When testing an initial data load of functional locations into a test system, be aware that functional locations can only be loaded once. Since the system will prevent duplicate records, the functional locations in the data load file will need to be altered (perhaps by changing the first number/identifier character of every record) before a second test load is attempted. It is a good idea to alter the records from the very first load test and then, when the data load works without fail, alter the data records to reflect their "real" state. When the final test load works without fail and the data records are in their "real" state, there should be no problem with the data load into the productive system.

Reference Functional Locations

Reference functional locations are not "real" functional locations and do not actually represent a specific location. They are best used when multiple similar functional locations need to be defined and maintained as a group.

When a functional location is being created, it is possible to copy its definition from a functional location ("FunctLocation" on the screen) or from a reference functional location ("RefLocation" on the screen). Copying the functional location from another functional location will simply copy the field values from the functional location being copied. No further relationship exists between the two functional locations.

Copying the functional location from a reference functional location appears similar. However, a relationship is maintained automatically between the functional location being created and the reference functional location being copied. Whenever a field value is changed in the reference functional location, all functional locations copied from it will "inherit" the change.

A reference functional location can save time when changes must be made to multiple similar functional locations.

Equipment

Equipment is most often the central object on which maintenance is performed. A piece of equipment may or may not be installed at a functional location, but its installation at a functional location allows it to inherit field values, such as cost center, from the functional location.

Maintenance costs incurred to maintain a specific piece of equipment may be settled to the functional location's cost center at which the equipment is installed at that time. As the piece of equipment moves from functional location to functional location, its maintenance costs are settled to the appropriate cost center. In addition, cost records can be viewed from the perspective of the piece of equipment or from a functional location.

For example, the total cost of maintaining a piece of equipment, regardless of how many places that equipment has been installed, can be obtained from the equipment records. In addition, the total cost of maintenance at a particular functional location can be obtained from that functional location, regardless of which pieces of equipment have been installed at that functional location.

So, by installing and dismantling pieces of equipment to and from functional locations, it is possible to not only review the maintenance cost of a piece of equipment regardless of the functional locations at which it has been installed, but also to review the maintenance cost at a functional location regardless of which pieces of equipment have been installed there.

While more than one piece of equipment may be installed at a functional location, it is sometimes preferable to define a functional location for each piece of equipment to be installed. By defining a "one-to-one" relationship between functional locations and equipment, it is possible to analyze the performance and maintenance cost of an individual equipment location.

Functional locations may be defined as pieces of equipment and the R/3 system supports such definition as much as possible, but it is somewhat more awkward to remove a functional location from a superior functional location and "install" it at a different functional location. The most common implementations of SAP R/3 Plant Maintenance where only functional locations are used (no equipment) or only equipment is used (no functional locations) are in cases where the objects never move and there is never a need to keep track of equipment that moves.

It is possible for the same piece of equipment to be defined more than once in the system, particularly with internal (system assigned) equipment numbering, so care should be taken to ensure that the same specific piece of equipment is not defined twice.

Each distinct piece of equipment must have its own equipment number. Two pieces of equipment cannot share the same number. The most common field used to store an equipment number from a previous system is the *Technical ID* field.

A piece of equipment, as defined in the Plant Maintenance module, can also be defined as a material, particularly for purchasing reasons, in the Materials Management module. The material master record only exists once, although there may be a quantity of more than one of that material. Regardless of the quantity of that material shown in the Materials Management module, each piece of equipment reflected by each unit of that quantity must have its own equipment master record. This is often accommodated by defining the material as a *serialized material*. Each serial number of the material is associated with an equipment number. This relationship allows each piece of equipment to be individually identified while still allowing quantities of the material to be manipulated (ordered, issued, etc.) in the Materials Management module.

Of course, in many cases, smaller, less important materials such as nuts and bolts would not be serialized or defined as pieces of equipment, with the possible exception of such parts that play a critical role in an important process.

Equipment can also have a hierarchy, as with functional locations, but an equipment hierarchy, when used, tends to be of less levels and of more limited use than a functional location hierarchy.

For initial data loading into the system, if internal numbering is used, there is no mechanism to prevent the same equipment from being loaded more than once (although each will have its own equipment number). Ensure that an initial equipment data load has been tested without fail before loading the data into the "real" productive system. The data file must only be loaded once into the productive system.

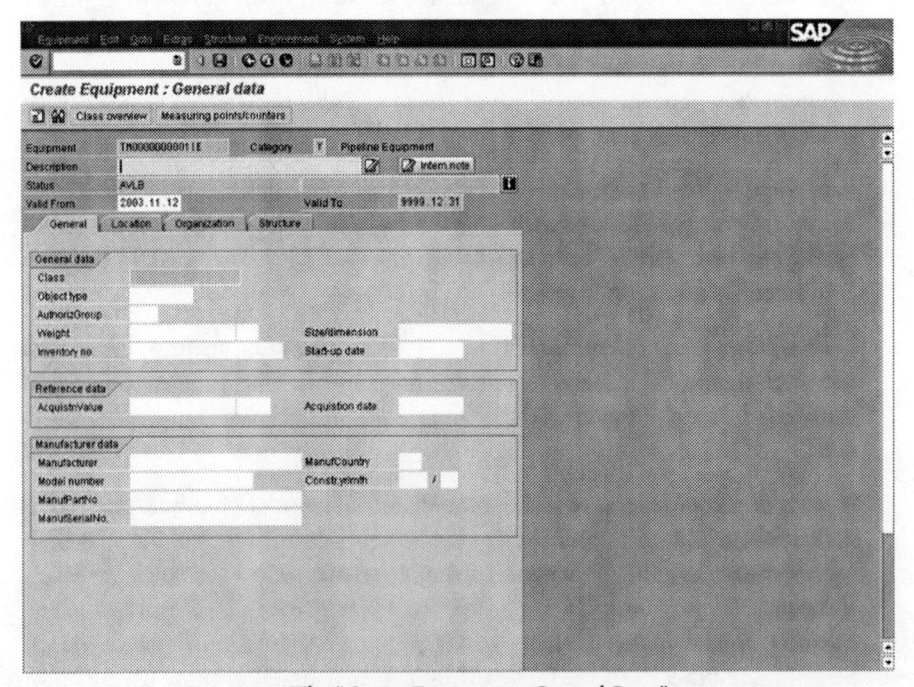

Figure 13. The "Create Equipment: General Data" screen.
© *SAP AG*

Notice on the *"Create Equipment: General Data" screen* shown in *Figure 13*, there are four tabs, *General, Location, Organization* and *Structure*. Each of these tabs contains fields that can be used to store information related to the piece of equipment. The more data is entered and maintained in the fields on a consistent basis, the more reporting capability the system will be able to deliver. However, the more data entered and maintained, the more time will be spent performing those tasks. Determine the data that is important and enter and maintain that data consistently. It is possible, through configuration in the Implementation Guide, to make entries for selected fields to be "required, " thereby ensuring that the field contents are entered and maintained consistently.

Note that, depending on the configuration of the SAP R/3 system, there may be additional, or even fewer, tabs than those displayed in *Figure 13*. Using view profiles in the Implementation Guide for equipment or other technical objects will affect the tabs displayed as well as the groups of fields each tab contains.

If the fields available are insufficient, the use of the classification system in SAP R/3 is recommended. Through the use of classes and characteristics, many additional attributes of equipment can be stored. Classification cannot be adequately covered here, but SAP training is available. For example, on the web page www.sap.com/usa/education in the "Find a Course" section, enter the course code PLM130.

Also note in *Figure 13* that the number displayed in the *Equipment* field is not the actual number of the equipment. If internal (system assigned) numbering is used, the actual number of the equipment will not be assigned until the equipment master record is saved.

Object Links

While functional locations tend to be associated with each other by their hierarchies, and with equipment by its installation at a functional location, it is possible to link functional locations to other functional locations or equipment to other equipment. This is desirable particularly when perhaps a gas line, water line, or other "medium" connects pieces of equipment, regardless of their installation location.

If a piece of equipment, such as a pump, fails, other equipment may be affected that depend on water to flow from the failed pump. The relationship between those two pieces of equipment (or between two functional locations) may be defined with an Object Link.

Object links are optional. The management of object links may outweigh the benefit to be gained from it, or it may be critical functionality.

Equipment cannot be linked to functional locations by using object link functionality. Object link functionality can be found in the Functional Location and Equipment menu paths.

Materials

Materials are typically defined by Materials Management personnel, but the option to create materials is available from the Plant Maintenance menus. If there are people dedicated to materials management, it is likely that the definition of material master records should be performed by them.

Before bills of materials can be defined for Plant Maintenance (or other) use, the materials to be contained in the BOM must already be defined in the system.

Unlike equipment, the same materials share the same material number. The stocks of that material may increase or decrease, but they share the same material number. If it is important to identify a specific occurrence of a material, that material can be serialized. That is, each occurrence of the material will have a material/serial number combination.

When a material master record is created, it will contain only the "views" that were defined for it. Each material master "view" contains data specific to a purpose. For example, there is a view that contains purchasing information, while there are several views containing MRP (Material Requirements Planning) information.

A material master record can be defined for a specific plant. Ideally, the same material should have the same material number at each plant. However, if the material master record is not initially created for more than one plant, the material master record must be "extended" to the additional plants. To extend a material master record, it must be "created" for the additional plant (i.e. use the "Create" transaction, not the "Change" transaction).

To be useful for Plant Maintenance purposes, materials must have a value. That is, they must be defined as "valuated" materials. If they are not, it will be impossible to determine planned or actual material costs.

Bills of Material

A bill of materials is, at its simplest form, a list of materials of which a piece of equipment consists. However, an entire material hierarchy, including assemblies, can be created.

In SAP R/3 Plant Maintenance, there are three types of bills of materials. A functional location bill of materials and an equipment bill of materials are practically the same, so when an *equipment BOM* is discussed, the same principles apply to a *functional location BOM*. The third type of BOM is the *material BOM* (yes, a material bill of materials).

An *equipment BOM* is, at its simplest, a list of materials that make up the piece of equipment and/or are used in its maintenance. An equipment bill-of-materials can contain one or more material bills of materials, as described below.

A *material BOM* is simply a material that is made up of other materials. Typically, a material BOM can be procured in its entirety by ordering the material that is the "header" of the BOM. Alternatively, the components of the material BOM can be procured individually, if desired. Assemblies can be defined in this way.

By assigning materials and material BOMs to other materials BOMs, a bill-of-materials hierarchy can be constructed.

It is common to see both equipment BOMs that consist of many materials as well as equipment BOMS that consist of one or more material BOMs instead of, or in addition to, individual materials.

One primary advantage to defining bills of material is that, when materials are required for a work order, the materials can be selected from the appropriate BOM, rather than being searched and entered manually. This reduces both the time required to create the work order and the chance for errors.

Work Centers

Since SAP's Plant Maintenance work centers are based on the same functionality as Production Planning work centers, there is an opportunity for confusion. Production Planning work centers typically (but not always) depict a machine that has an operating capacity. Since a person also has a capacity, eight hours per day, for example, Plant Maintenance work centers are treated the same as Production Planning work centers.

A Plant Maintenance work center can also sometimes depict one or more machines, but more typically a Plant Maintenance work center represents one or more people. Each work center has a capacity. In simple terms, two people who work eight hours per day would have a total capacity for work of 16 hours per day. So, if those two people comprised a work center, that work center would have a capacity of 16 hours per day.

For more than one person to be included in the same work center, they should possess similar enough qualifications that, should one of them be required to perform a task, it would not matter which one was assigned.

Each work center is assigned a cost center. This is not a cost center to which work order costs will be settled. Rather, this cost center will have one or more activity types and activity rates defined for it. Usually, setting up such cost centers, activity types and activity rates is performed by those responsible for managing the CO (Controlling) module. There may only be one activity rate defined, which would represent the normal labor rate for that work center. If there is more than one activity rate defined, one rate might represent regular working hours, while another might represent overtime hours, if work center overtime labor is charged to the work order. This allows for the planned labor on the work order to be at the regular rate, for example, while the actual labor might be charged at an overtime rate. Many other possibilities exist by using different activity types and rates, including allowances for different shifts.

Depending on the cost reporting requirements of the Plant Maintenance department as well as the cost reporting requirements of management, a decision will likely be required whether to assign "standard" rates or "actual" rates to activity types. Standard rates are often used to charge time for a work center on a work order regardless of the type of work performed or whether the work was during regular hours or overtime. Actual rates are usually more accurate, but require more attention when defining and using those activity types. In any case, the rates probably need to be reviewed on a yearly basis, or as often as may be appropriate.

One important screen/tab when defining a work center is the "Capacity Header" screen/tab, found on the "Capacities" tab by clicking the "Capacity" button ![Capacity] near the bottom of the screen.

It is on this screen that the work center is associated with a factory calendar. Presumably, those people represented by the work center do not work 365 days per year, so their work days are defined by the factory calendar that is identified on this screen. The factory calendar that is used must accurately reflect the actual days on which members of the work center will work.

Factory calendars are not defined within Plant Maintenance configuration and representatives for the Plant Maintenance module often are not responsible for the maintenance of factory calendars. Determine who is responsible for maintenance of factory calendars before creating or attempting to change a factory calendar. For reference, maintenance of factory calendars is performed within the Implementation Guide under the menu path **General Settings → Maintain Calendar.**

Also on the Capacity Header screen/tab for the work center is the basic definition of a shift for the work center. A start time, an end time, and a total number of hours and minutes for breaks can be specified.

The "Capacity utilization" depicts the percentage of a work center's remaining time, after specified breaks, that a work center could realistically be expected to work. Allowing time for travel to and from a work site, additional unaccounted breaks, time to retrieve tools, and so on, the actual capacity utilization of a work center might vary from work center to work center. The purpose of reflecting actual work time enables the system to better schedule work, not overloading a work center with work that the work center cannot realistically be expected to perform in a given time.

The "Number of individual capacities" simply reflects the number of people included in the work center.

When creating a work center, some of the more important fields are as follows:

Basic Data Tab

- The *Usage* must be set to maintenance task lists or (less recommended) all task list types.
- The *Standard value key* should be set to "SAP0" unless there is a valid reason for it to be set to a different value. Other values are more often used for the Production Planning module.

Default Values Tab

- The *Control key* can be set to "PM01" (Plant maintenance—internal) presuming it hasn't been changed or superseded in the

Implementation Guide. This simply provides a default value for each work order operation to which this work center is assigned. If the work center actually defines an external (contract) resource, it would likely be more appropriate to set this value to "PM02."

Capacities Tab

- The *Capacity Category* should be set to reflect labor (usually 002) unless the capacity for an actual machine is being defined.

- The *Other formula* can be set to SAP008 (unless the formulas have been reconfigured for the implemented system). The other formulas—Setup, Processing and Teardown—can be ignored for the vast majority of Plant Maintenance purposes.

Capacity Header Screen

On the Capacity Header subscreen, found by clicking the "Capacity" button near the bottom of the "Capacities" tab, the following fields should be entered:

- *Factory calendar ID*—An appropriate factory calendar, a calendar that specifies working and non-working days of the year, should have already been defined in the Implementation Guide. The factory calendar specified here determines when the work center can and cannot be scheduled.

- *Base unit of meas.*—This specifies the unit of measure on which the work center is normally scheduled—hours, for example. In many SAP R/3 systems, the abbreviations H and HR are both active and both represent hours. If this is the case, determine which of the two to use and try to always use that one. Using both, if both are available, will lead to confusion and may affect reporting.

- *Start*—This indicates the "normal" daily start time of the work center. 8 a.m. will be entered as 08:00:00, while 6 p.m. will be entered as 18:00:00, for example.

- *Finish*—This indicates the "normal" daily finish time of the work center. The same 24-hour clock standards apply, as in the example above.

- *Length of breaks*—This field should contain the total amount of time included in "official" breaks for the work center during a normal day. A one-hour lunch break only would be specified as 01:00:00, while a one-hour lunch and two 15-minute breaks would be specified as 01:30:00.

- *Capacity utilization*—This field should contain a percentage, which indicates how much of the work center's remaining time (after deducting the "official" break time) can realistically be used to schedule the work center. For example, if the people included in a work center spend about 10 percent of the day in transit to or from the actual work, a capacity utilization of 90% might be realistic.

- *No. of indiv. cap.*—This field should contain the number of people that the work center represents (how many people are "in" the work center).

- Upon pressing the "Enter" key, the system will calculate the resulting daily capacity of the work center. The number of hours between the start and finish times will be used as a starting point. The length of breaks will be deducted, the capacity utilization will be factored in, and the result will be multiplied by the number of capacities (people, in most cases). The resulting figure can be used by the system in capacity checking to determine whether enough capacity exists in a work center to perform work as scheduled. This capacity is also used as a basis for capacity leveling, should that option be desired.

- *Relevant to finite scheduling*—Capacity checking will only be enabled if this checkbox is checked.

- *Can be used by several operations*—This checkbox, when checked, permits the work center's time to be split between work order operations. In other words, a work center can be assigned to two operations at the same time. One operation does not have to be completed prior to the start of another operation, for example.

- *Overload*—This field allows the specification of a percentage above a work center's normal capacity at which the work center is actually considered overloaded, or the scheduled work exceeds the work center's capacity. An overload of 10% indicates that the work center load must exceed 110% before a capacity overload is indicated.

The green arrow (Back) button must be clicked to return from the "Capacity Header" subscreen.

Scheduling Tab

On the "Scheduling" tab, pay particular attention to these fields:

- *Capacity Category*—This should be set, in most cases, to indicate "Labor," usually 002.

- *Other formula*—This should be set to SAP004 (unless the formulas have been reconfigured in the Implementation Guide).

- *Work dimension*—This is normally set to "TIME," which indicates the unit of measure dimension that includes the time-based units of measure.

- *Work unit*—This should be set to the normal unit of measure on which this work center's time will be scheduled, often H or HR for hours (again, determine whether to use H or HR and try to always use that unit).

Costing Tab

On the "Costing" tab, the following fields are important:

- *Cost Center*—This field should contain the cost center, usually defined by a person responsible for maintaining the CO (Controlling) module, that reflects this work center's activities.

- *ActType Int.Proc.*—The Activity Type Internal Processing field should contain the activity type, also defined by a person responsible for maintaining the CO (Controlling) module. An activity rate, which determines the rate at which the work center is "charged" to a work order operation, is assigned to the activity type. By specifying more than one activity type to a cost center, and then assigning that cost center to a work center, the work center can be "charged" at different rates to reflect regular time, overtime, holiday time, etc. if desired. In many cases, however, a "standard rate" is determined and assigned to a single activity type, which is then assigned to all work performed by the work center, regardless of the amounts of regular time, overtime, etc. Standard rates can be easier to set up and manage, especially initially, but are often a rough estimate and must be reviewed on a regular basis to ensure their relative accuracy. A combination of standard rates and actual rates is quite difficult to manage and should only be considered after serious discussions with those responsible for the CO (Controlling) module.

- Unlabeled field to the right of the previous field (*Formula key for costing*)—This field should contain SAP008 (unless the formulas have been reconfigured in the Implementation Guide).

If any additional tabs appear on the work center screen, ignore them for Plant Maintenance purposes. Depending on how work center configuration has been defined, there may be a required field on such a tab (for other purposes, such as Production Planning). If there is no valid value to provide for the required field, it will be difficult/impossible to save the values entered on the previous tabs.

Tabs on the work center screens are controlled in the Implementation Guide in the configuration step "Configure Screen Sequence for Work Center."

The Work Order Process

In the SAP R/3 system, the work order process typically consists of the following steps:

1. Notification creation
2. Work order creation
   - Planned operations
   - Planned labor
   - Planned materials
3. Work order release
4. Work is performed
   - Actual labor is confirmed

5. Materials are used
   - Goods issues are posted
6. Operations are completed
7. Findings (catalog entries) are recorded in the notification
8. Work order is technically completed (labor is complete, materials all issued)
   - Notification is completed
9. Work order is settled to a cost center or other settlement object
10. Work order is closed

With configuration changes and individual requirements, the process actually implemented may differ somewhat from the process as listed above. The list above, however, provides a good overview.

The SAP system tends to split work order processing into two paths. One is preventive maintenance, which is known as planned maintenance in many SAP documents. SAP also sometimes refers to preventive maintenance work orders as scheduled orders. The other work order processing path, which is often referred to as breakdown maintenance, includes all non-preventive work orders.

The distinctive difference between the two different types of work order processes is how the processes begin. Preventive maintenance work orders are typically created from maintenance plans and scheduled at regular intervals. Non-preventive maintenance work orders are typically created for specific purposes and are generally not repeated. In many instances, in addition to preventive maintenance work orders, there are two other distinct types of work, scheduled and unscheduled, the work order process for both types of work in SAP R/3 is similar.

To clarify the previous statements, preventive maintenance orders are scheduled, while non-preventive maintenance orders can be scheduled or unscheduled.

In some SAP documentation, reference has been made to planned and unplanned orders. Historically, those terms meant preventive and non-preventive, respectively, causing some confusion. When those terms appear in SAP documentation, be aware of the context in which they are used.

Notification Creation

The non-preventive work order process typically begins with the creation of a notification. The notification is intended for someone (often an operator) to communicate that there may be a problem or a breakdown. It is often the responsibility of a different person to determine whether the problem warrants the creation of a work order.

The notification has no real integration points with other SAP R/3 modules and, while it is possible to plan and perform work solely based on a notification without a work order, costs will not be considered.

Three default Plant Maintenance notification types are provided with the R/3 system:

- *Malfunction Report*—This notification type is most suited for reporting breakdowns.

- *Activity Report*—This notification type is most suited for recording information on work that may already have been completed. In the case of an emergency or rush order, where the work order may be created first, this type of notification can be created with the work order and used to record the work that was performed, particularly if catalogs are being used for later analysis.

- *Maintenance Request*—This notification type is similar to the Malfunction Report, but is more used to request maintenance for objects that have not necessarily broken down.

If necessary, it is possible to define additional notification types, or even delete the default notification types provided, in the R/3 Implementation Guide.

As mentioned previously, it is technically possible to operate the Plant Maintenance module with notifications and no work orders or with work orders and no notifications, however some functionality will be lost without both components of the module.

Notifications, in addition to providing a problem reporting tool, serve as a standard record of problems and the actions that were taken to correct the problems. Through the use of the catalog system and subsequent analysis, it is possible to recognize patterns and trends. Action can then be taken to prevent recurring or growing problems.

The "Breakdown" checkbox, found on two of the previously mentioned notifications (the exception is the Activity Report), is used to trigger mean-time-to-repair and mean-time-between-failure statistics. If those statistics are important, it is also important for the "Breakdown" checkbox to be checked consistently in the case of actual breakdowns.

In its most simple state, the only absolute requirements for a notification are:

- A description of the problem or requirement
- The location of the problem or requirement

Some other field values, such as dates and the person reporting the problem or requirement, are usually provided by default. Of course, additional requirements for a notification will differ among implementations.

Once a notification has been created, it is often the responsibility of a planner, scheduler or some other type of approver to determine whether the "request" warrants the creation of a work order.

Work Order Creation

Work orders are the Plant Maintenance objects that provide the primary integration with other SAP modules. Some of the basic integration points are:

- The Controlling (CO) module provides cost integration.
- The Financial (FI) module provides accounting integration.
- The Materials Management (MM) module provides "real-time" access to inventories, purchasing, contracts, and so on.
- The Human Resources (HR) module can provide the available labor as well as a method of entering actual time worked.
- The Project Systems (PS) module can use work orders as part of projects.
- The Production Planning (PP) module can reflect the requirements for equipment maintenance work orders in its reports.

When a work order is created, the following information is typical of that included in the work order:

- A short, and possibly a longer, description of the overall work required.
- The equipment or functional location at which the work is required.
- The work center that will be responsible for the completion of the overall work order.
- The maintenance activity type.
- Start and finish dates. Depending on the configuration of the system, these dates may be set automatically on exiting the work order, regardless of whether they have been changed manually. It is necessary to display/change the work order again to determine whether the dates have been automatically changed from a manual setting (or click the "Schedule" button before saving and exiting). This automatic scheduling can be removed for an individual order by clicking the "Show further scheduling data" button 🗓 to the right of the date fields on the work order screen, and then removing the check mark from the "Automat. sched." checkbox. This button also reveals additional scheduling fields and options. The default settings for automatic scheduling and other scheduling-related fields are made in the Implementation Guide.
- One or more operations, each of which may contain:
    - A description of work required for that operation.
    - The work center responsible for performing that operation.
    - The amount of labor required to perform that operation.
    - The number of people required to perform that operation.
    - The CO activity type/rate at which the labor should be charged to the work order.
    - Materials required to perform that operation.

The "Components" tab can be used to enter or display the materials required for the work order, regardless of the specific operation in which they are required.

The "Costs" tab can be used to display the planned and actual costs associated with the work order. The breakdown of costs displayed here is dependent on the value categories defined in configuration.

The "Objects" tab can be used to enter or display one or more functional locations, equipment, notifications, etc. that are associated with the work order. For example, more than one notification can be associated with the work order by entering them on this screen.

The "Location" tab contains information regarding the physical location of the work. In a system where the master data has been properly defined, some of the fields will contain default values.

The "Planning" tab contains information regarding the maintenance plan and task list from which the work order was generated, in cases where the work order was actually generated as such.

The "Control" tab contains miscellaneous fields related to the creation and change of the work order, costing and profile parameters, planning, and the timing of the creation of purchase requisitions and material reservations for the work order.

Depending on the configuration of the system, there may be one or more additional tabs available. It may also be the case that not all of the tabs described above are displayed.

Although there are many more fields contained in the various work order tabs, the list above contains some of the more central tabs and fields. Depending on a particular implementation of the SAP R/3 Plant Maintenance module, other fields may be of more importance than those listed above.

If the work order is created from a notification, some of the field values from the notification will be copied into the work order. Review these field values to ensure that they are accurate from the work order perspective. For example, the notification description may not be an adequate description of the work to be performed.

As of R/3 Enterprise (version 4.7), the notification long text can be copied into the work order automatically, on the condition that the work order has been configured in the Implementation Guide to allow the long text copying. This configuration is defined for each order type independently.

If task lists have been previously created, a task list may be copied into a work order, bringing with it all of the labor and materials required to perform the work. Despite the initial work that is required to define the task list, time is saved each time the task list is copied into a work order, not to mention the additional advantages of the work order inheriting the operations, labor and materials required to perform the work. In addition, there is little chance for error, since the entire work order is not re-entered from the beginning. In most cases, taking the time to create task lists for repetitive work, whether preventive or not, will save time in the long term in addition to reducing the chance for errors.

Work Order Release

Once all of the planned information has been entered on the work order, the work order can be released. This can also be referred to as putting the work order in process. The subtle difference between the two buttons, "Release" and "Put in process," on the work order screen is that the "Put in process" button provides some print options, releases the work order (gives it the "REL" status), saves any changes, and exits from the work order screen. The "Release" button provides no print options, although they are still available from the "Order" menu, and the actual release and the assigning of the "REL" status are only performed after the "Save" button has also been clicked.

Until a work order is released, time confirmations cannot be made to the work order, materials cannot be issued to the work order, and no print options are usually available. Once the work order has been released, those functions become available. In addition, depending on configuration settings, reservations for stock materials are issued and purchase requisitions for non-stock materials are issued.

Work is Performed

As work is performed, the actual work is recorded on the work order as "confirmations." Depending on the other SAP R/3 modules or other external systems that may be in use, the confirmations may be entered directly in the Plant Maintenance module, through the Cross Application Time Sheet

(CATS), which is usually set up with the SAP R/3 Human Resources module, or through another method and transferred into the PM module. Regardless of the method of entering actual time worked, it is important that the time eventually exists in the PM module in order to determine planned vs. actual time as well as costs.

Although it is possible to have time entered into the Plant Maintenance module and then transferred to the Human Resources module, it is more common for data to be transferred from the HR module to the PM module, presuming both modules are in use.

If CATS is not available for time entry, the "Set Screen Templates for Completion Confirmation" step in the Implementation Guide can be used to modify the "Overall Completion Confirmation" screen found with transaction code IW42. Depending on the configuration, this screen can be used to enter actual time, goods issues, catalog codes for the notification, as well as measurement readings.

The most simple method of entering confirmations, if CATS will not be used and without configuring the overall completion confirmation transaction, is "Individual Time Confirmation, " transaction code IW41.

When entering time confirmations, it is possible to use a different "activity type" than was used in the planning of the work order. Where appropriate, if the two activity types carry different activity rates, this can be used to determine differences between the planned labor and the actual labor, along with any difference between planned time and actual time.

Note that Plant Maintenance confirmations, once saved, cannot be changed or deleted. If a mistake is made, the "Cancel" (transaction code IW45) function can be used to reverse the confirmation. This function simply created another confirmation record containing negative time to offset the record being reversed. The correct information must then be entered in another confirmation. This provides an audit trail to determine when information was entered, and by whom, as well as to determine the details of cancelled entries.

Be aware that when viewing a list of confirmations, the cancelled confirmations may also be displayed with negative numbers.

Materials are Used

As materials are used as part of the work being performed, it is important for materials to be issued to the work order as "goods issues," a function often performed by those responsible for the Materials Management (MM) module, although not always.

Goods issues ensure that the actual cost of materials are assigned to the work order and, in addition, maintain proper inventory levels and values. If Material Requirements Planning (MRP) is being used as part of the Materials Management implementation, proper inventory levels help to ensure that reordering of materials is performed on a timely basis.

For non-stock materials, those are received (and issued) directly to the work order, not to stores. Note that, even though a material can be defined in the Materials Management module as a stock material, that material can still be specified as a non-stock material on a Plant Maintenance work order. That means that, even if there may be a quantity of that material in stores, the quantity of that material required for the work order should be purchased independently of the stock on hand. This is not normally advisable, but it is possible should the need arise.

There are some settings, both in and outside of the Implementation Guide, that allow for materials to be issued to work order operations automatically upon completion of the operations, but for the most part, materials are issued to work orders manually or through other means.

It is advisable to create material master records for materials that are, or will be, used repetitively, whether the materials are stock or non-stock. This is another area where time spent now will save more time in the future. Referring to an existing material master record will save time entering the same information each time the material is required, again in addition to reducing the chance of data entry errors. Proper reference to existing material master records in addition to the proper use of MRP will help ensure that appropriate stocks are maintained and ordered.

In addition, if bills of materials are assigned to equipment, the selection of the required materials on a work order can be made from the BOM, further reducing the risk of an incorrect part being used.

Operations are Completed

As operations are confirmed (actual time is entered), the operations can individually be marked as completed by checking the "Final confirmation" checkbox. This means that no further work is expected to be performed on that operation of the work order and, consequently, no further material consumption is expected.

As operations are marked with the "Final confirmation" check mark, the work order itself adopts a "Partially confirmed" (PCNF) status. If all of the operations on a work order are marked with the "Final confirmation" check mark, the work order adopts the status of "Confirmed" (CNF). If work order operations are managed in this way and are current, the CNF status can be used to identify work orders that are ready for "Technical completion."

The process of completing operations will vary somewhat, mainly depending on whether CATS (Cross Application Time Sheet) and the HR (Human Resources) module are in use.

Findings (Catalog Entries) are Recorded in the Notification

As previously discussed, catalogs can provide a method of entering a variety of information in a standard format that can easily be reported at a later date. If catalogs are used for such data gathering, the ideal time to record the type of damage, the cause of damage, and other catalog codes as required is as the operations are completed.

After the notification has been updated, it can then be closed automatically when the work order is technically completed (it can also be closed independently of the work order, if desired).

Some of the most common catalogs that are used for data gathering and later analysis for Plant Maintenance are described in the "Notification Content" section found on page 114.

Also as previously discussed, some catalog fields can be merged into the work order screen, which may save some time by the user not having to go to the notification screen to enter the catalog codes. In addition, if the Plant Maintenance "Overall Completion Confirmation" screen is used (in the absence of CATS), the screen can be configured for the entry of catalog codes.

Defining catalogs and recording the appropriate information on the notification is strictly an optional process, depending on whether there is perceived value in using the functionality. It is often one of the first building blocks towards implementing reliability centered maintenance. However, once the decision has been made to use the functionality, it is important that it be used consistently. Otherwise, later analysis of the data will be unreliable.

Work Order is Technically Completed

A work order can be technically completed when all of the actual labor has been recorded and all of the required materials have been issued to the work order. The technically complete status (TECO) can indicate that a work order is ready to be settled to a cost center or other settlement object.

The most simple method of technically completing a work order is by using the "checkered flag" button on the work order screen. Incidentally, the checkered flag button also appears on order lists in change mode, but not in display mode, to provide an easy method of technically completing multiple work orders.

During technical completion of a work order, there are several decisions that can be made. The reference date and time can reflect the date and time that the work was actually completed, although they usually default to the current date and time.

The "Complete notifications" checkbox will, unless unchecked, cause the associated notification to be completed with the work order.

If the notification shows that this work order is in response to an actual breakdown by having the "Breakdown" checkbox checked, or if the "Breakdown" checkbox will be checked upon technical completion, an actual malfunction end date and time must be entered. In the case of an actual malfunction or breakdown, the failure to check this checkbox and provide realistic dates and times will adversely affect mean-time-between-failure and mean-time-to-repair statistics.

When the above decisions have been made, the work order can be technically completed.

If necessary, the technical completion of a work order can usually be reversed. This function can be found, from the work order screen, in the menu **Order → Functions → Complete**.

Work Order is Settled

Often, the task of settling a work order or groups of work orders falls outside the responsibility of those responsible for the Plant Maintenance module, in which case the financial (FI) or controlling (CO) personnel usually accept responsibility for settlement. Discuss the responsibility to ensure that it will be performed by someone.

The work order acts as a temporary container for costs. All costs associated with a work order are attributed to that work order until the work has been completed. Sometime after that point, an entity is usually "charged" for the cost of the work order. The entity may be a cost center, a project, or numerous other settlement objects. Work orders can even be settled to other orders. The available settlement objects for any order type are defined in the Implementation Guide. In any case, the costs cannot remain with the work order indefinitely and must be settled somewhere. There are some configuration settings that require a work order to have a settlement "rule" before being released, for example. If a work order is created for a piece of equipment that has a cost center assigned to it, that cost center may be provided as the settlement object in the settlement rule by default (depending on configuration settings).

In the case of a refurbishment work order, the cost of performing the work can optionally be settled to the materials being refurbished.

Often, settlement takes place on a "periodic" basis. That means, for example, that if a work order spans two accounting periods (two months), the costs that have been accumulated in the work order by the end of the first period are settled at the end of that period. Subsequent costs are settled at the end of the periods in which they were incurred. Although "full" settlement can be imposed, where the entire cost of the work order is settled at the completion, it is common to see periodic settlement. Note that where the settlement rule on a work order contains a full settlement and a periodic settlement, the periodic settlement will take precedence.

Since settlement takes place on a regular basis, it is also common for "background" or "batch jobs" to be scheduled to perform settlement automatically.

The methods of settling work orders should be thoroughly discussed with financial and controlling personnel to ensure that the methods are agreed upon.

Work Order is Closed

After a work order has been completely settled, the work order can be closed. The system will prevent the closing of a work order that has not been completely settled.

The closing of a work order is also referred to as "business completion" or "complete complete, " since the menu steps to perform that function include the steps "Complete → Complete."

In some cases, the concept of closing a work order after its settlement is so automatic that the step of closing the work order is simply added to the automatic program that settles the work orders. If not automated, work orders can be closed individually or through a list of orders in change mode.

Refurbishment Work Orders

The primary difference between a "normal" work order and a refurbishment work order is that a "normal" work order may have goods (material) issued towards the repair or maintenance of a piece of equipment, while a refurbishment order has material issued, the material itself is repaired (refurbished) and returned to stock or stores.

While it is possible to use refurbishment orders for materials that have the same value, whether new, used or refurbished, it makes more sense to use the refurbishment order functionality for materials that have different values.

For example, if a part has a new value of $100, it may be assigned a value of $1 after use, when worn. If the part is refurbished, it can be used again, but may not necessarily have the same value as if it was a new part. In addition, there may need to be an incentive to use a refurbished part before a new part. If the refurbished part is valued at $25 or $50, it may be more economical to issue to a work order than a new part would be at $100.

So, in order to gain an economic advantage from refurbishment orders, a material might have three "valuations," referred to as "split valuation," new, used and refurbished. The material master number would be identical for all three valuations of the material, so the overall quantity on hand of the material could be tracked. There can be more than three valuations defined for a material, but three valuations are good for demonstration purposes.

When viewing stock quantities, if no valuation type is entered, the entire stock for that material, regardless of valuation, is displayed. If, when prompted, a valuation type is entered, then only the stock at that valuation is displayed.

Each individual valuation of the material is considered a standard price, while the overall value of the stock is regarded as a moving average price.

Although a refurbishment order will, by default, manage the "movement types" required to issue the materials from stock the work order and back into stock again, the material must be in stock before the refurbishment work order process can begin. Consult with those responsible for managing the Materials Management (MM) module and possibly the Controlling (CO) module as to the proper procedure and movement type to be used to return a "used" material back into stock at its "used" value.

All materials of the same material number issued to a refurbishment order must be at the same valuation, and all materials of the same material number returned to stock must also be at the same valuation, although it is quite possible to return materials to a different storage location than the storage location from which they were issued.

A work order type suitable for refurbishment is provided with the default SAP R/3 Plant Maintenance module.

The Preventive Maintenance Process

In the SAP R/3 system, the preventive maintenance process resembles most of the work order process previously discussed. The major differences are at the beginning of the process.

1. Task list creation
   - Planned operations
   - Planned labor
   - Planned materials

2. Maintenance plan creation
3. Maintenance plan scheduling
4. Work order (and/or notification) creation
5. Work order release
6. Work is performed
    - Actual labor is confirmed
    - Materials are used
    - Goods issues are posted
7. Operations are completed
8. Findings (catalog entries) are recorded in the notification
9. Work order is technically completed (labor is complete, materials all issued)
    - Notification is completed
10. Work order is settled to a cost center or other settlement object
11. Work order is closed

With configuration changes and individual requirements, the process actually implemented may differ somewhat from the process as listed above. In the list above, for preventive maintenance only, steps one through three are performed once, while the remaining steps are typically performed repeatedly.

Task List Creation

A task list is typically a standard list of maintenance tasks, or operations, that must be performed to accomplish a goal, whether the goal is to restore a machine to its full operating capacity, to simply take some measurements, or any other preventive function. A task list can be used in one or more maintenance plans, for one or more pieces of equipment or functional locations, and it can be copied directly into one or more work orders. The more a task list is used, the more time it saves.

The creation of a task list is very similar to the creation of a work order. Operations are defined and planned labor and materials are assigned to the operations (tasks) of the task list.

Task lists are typically created for a plant and, although task lists can be copied, it is awkward to try to maintain standard task lists centrally. Even if it results in some duplication, it is easier if each plant maintains its own task lists.

One consideration when creating task lists is the earliest date on which the task list must be available for use. The "Key date" field, found on the initial screen when creating a task list, often defaults to the current date. However, if the task list must be used retroactively (for a past start date) in a maintenance plan, the key date must be back-dated to the earliest required date (or even earlier) during the creation of the task list. The key date cannot be changed later.

Another consideration during the creation of a task list is whether the task list should be based on a strategy or not. As previously discussed, a strategy consists of a group of "packages," or cycles. Basing a task list on a strategy enables the operations within the task list to be performed in different cycles than other operations in the same task list. When defining a strategy-based task list, each operation must be assigned a package (cycle) from the associated strategy.

If all of the operations in the task list are to be performed on exactly the same schedule, however, consider leaving the "Strategy" field blank and using the task list in a "Single cycle plan." With a single cycle maintenance plan, the cycle is determined by the plan, so the task list need not be associated with a maintenance strategy.

In short, task lists with no strategy are used in single cycle plans. Task lists with a strategy must be used in maintenance plans that are based on the same strategy.

Maintenance Plan Creation

There are essentially four different types of plans that can be created in the SAP R/3 system:

- *Strategy-based plan*—This type of maintenance plan is scheduled based on a maintenance strategy, which may contain more than one cycle (package). A task list that is assigned to a strategy-based plan must also be based on the same strategy. The operations in the task list need not all be scheduled according to the same cycle, but they all must be scheduled according to cycles in the assigned strategy. See the additional notes on page 176 regarding strategies.

- *Single cycle plan*—This type of plan must not have a strategy assigned to it. Neither can a task list contained in the plan have a strategy assigned to it. All operations in the task list must be performed on the same cycle, which is designated in the single cycle maintenance plan. This is the simplest plan and task list combination that can be created.

- *Performance-based plan*—Although this is not strictly a separate type of plan, it uses measurements instead of dates to schedule the next work order in the cycle. Typically, to use a performance-based maintenance plan, a piece of equipment must have a measuring point defined on it (an odometer, for example). An annual estimate is entered for the measuring point. Measurement readings (odometer readings) are taken from time to time and, based on the initial estimate as well as ongoing readings, the system predicts the date on which the next work order will be required. A performance-based plan can be defined as a strategy-based plan or a single cycle plan.

Before defining a measuring point on a piece of equipment, for example, a characteristic must be created that provides some of the definition for the measuring point. For the odometer example, a characteristic would be created that defines the corresponding measuring points as numeric based with six digits and no decimal places, along with some additional settings.

Then, the same characteristics can be used on which to base any measuring point with the same attributes.

The menu paths for creating characteristics and measuring points can be found in Plant Maintenance → Management of Technical Objects → Environment → Measuring Points

It is not necessary for a characteristic used in this manner to be assigned to a class.

- *Multiple counter-based plan*—A multiple counter-based plan is used to schedule maintenance based on a combination of factors. For example, maintenance on a vehicle may need to be scheduled based on 20, 000 kilometers or 12 months, whichever happens first. The parameters are first defined in a "cycle set, " which is then used in the maintenance plan. The system then uses a combination of dates and measurement readings to determine the scheduling of upcoming work orders.

The maintenance plan provides the link between a task list, the object, such as a piece of equipment, to be maintained, and the start date of the schedule.

Although it is possible to assign the task list to more than one object within a plan by using a "maintenance item, " the maintenance item has been merged into the plan for ease of use. While the maintenance item was previously separate from the plan, the maintenance item now appears as a tab on the maintenance plan screen. If additional items are required, that is if the task list must be assigned to additional objects within the same plan, there is a button to create additional maintenance items on the maintenance item tab.

Keep in mind that, if assigning a plan to multiple objects (equipment, etc.) by adding maintenance items, the same single task list must be relevant to all of the objects. Each maintenance item will create a work order according to its scheduling. If even one work order is completed late, it will affect the scheduling of all subsequent orders in the plan.

If the intent is to simply assign a single task list to a single object, the existence of the maintenance item may, for the most part, be disregarded. The data on the maintenance item tab can be considered part of the maintenance plan.

Once the type of plan has been determined, the appropriate piece of equipment or other object must be provided. Some of the additional required data may default from the equipment once the "Enter" key has been pressed or the "Enter" button clicked.

After the remaining required information has been entered, the appropriate task list must be assigned to the maintenance plan. Use the binocular icon to the right of the task list field to select the task list.

Pay particular attention to the "Maintenance plan scheduling parameters" tab on the maintenance plan screen. These parameters determine when subsequent work orders will be scheduled and created and are often a source of confusion. The fields on the "Maintenance plan scheduling parameters" tab are described below:

- *Shift factor late completion*—This parameter affects the scheduling of the next work order. If the current work order is completed late, the next work order will be scheduled later based on this percentage of the lateness. On a four week cycle, if the current order is completed two weeks late and this shift factor is set to 50%, the schedule for the next work order will be delayed by one week (50% of two weeks late). This factor is only applied when the lateness of the current work order falls outside of the tolerance contained in the next field, "Tolerance (+)."

- *Tolerance (+)*—This tolerance, a percentage of the cycle length, indicates that the scheduling of the next work order should not be affected if the lateness of the current work order falls within this tolerance.

- *Shift factor early completion*—This parameter has a similar effect as the "Shift factor late completion" field, except that it affects the scheduling of the next work order based on the current work order being completed early.

- *Tolerance (-)*—This tolerance, a percentage of the cycle length, indicates that the scheduling of the next work order should not be affected if the early completion of the current work order falls within this tolerance.

- *Cycle modification factor*—This field provides a relatively easy method of adjusting the length of a cycle, and is particularly useful for seasonal adjustments where maintenance might be performed more often in summer, for example. Any value of more than 1 in this field will cause the cycle length to increase. A value of 2 will result in maintenance being scheduled half as frequently, while a value of 0.5 will result in maintenance being scheduled twice as frequently.

- *Factory calendar*—This field, which is only active if the "Scheduling indicator" (discussed later) is set to "Time—key date" or "Time—factory calendar," determines the factory calendar on which maintenance scheduling will be based. If factory calendar scheduling is used and the factory calendar contained in this field has weekends defined as non-working days, then no maintenance will be scheduled for weekend days. This is particularly useful when a plant is shut down each weekend and maintenance is not usually performed on those days. For plants that operate seven days a week and at least some maintenance work is usually performed on all seven days, consider not using factory calendar-based scheduling. For those work centers that do not work on weekends, the work centers themselves will be based on such a factory calendar.

- *Call horizon*—This indicates, as a percentage, the point through the cycle at which the next work order will be created. For a four week cycle, a call horizon of 75% would cause the creation of the next work order three weeks through the cycle, or in other words, one week before its due date. The next work order will not be rescheduled with this setting. A call horizon of 0% will cause the creation of the next work order immediately upon the completion of the current work order, disregarding all other parameters. A call horizon of 100% will cause the creation of the next work order on the date on which it is due. In many cases, longer cycles will have a higher call horizon, while shorter cycles will have a lower call horizon, so that the next work order will be created within a reasonable margin prior to its due date.

- *Scheduling period*—The total length of time that the system will predict scheduling for the plan. For long term planning, it may be beneficial to set this parameter depending on how far into the future there is a desire to view upcoming scheduling. If this parameter is not used, the system will create the next "call" only. In previous versions, this field was limited to 999 days, however there is a unit of measure field to the right, enabling the use of units besides "days."

It is not normally advisable to set a very high scheduling period for a task list or plan that will be performed frequently. Doing so can cause the system to predict a great many calls into the future, as well as creating an unnecessary load on system resources. Attempting to schedule calls beyond the calendars defined in the system will cause an error. If it is necessary to schedule further into the future than the current calendar allows, determine who is responsible for maintaining factory calendars (this responsibility is normally limited to a very few individuals) and determine whether the calendar(s) can be extended as far into the future as required. Attempting to extend a calendar far into the future will cause the system to issue a warning, since doing so can allow further unnecessary loads on system resources.

- *Completion requirement*—Also absent from some previous versions, this checkbox, when checked, prevents the creation of the next work order if the current work order has not yet been completed. If this checkbox is not checked, it is possible for the next work order to be created before the current work order has been completed, if the current work order is late enough.

- *Scheduling indicator*—The three options are described below. Only one can be selected:
    - **Time**—Work orders can be scheduled for every day of the year. This would be the preferable option for plants that operate continuously. Although not all maintenance personnel will work on weekends and holidays, as long as some do, then maintenance scheduling should be permitted for weekends and holidays.
    - **Time—key date**—Particularly useful for monthly schedules where work will be scheduled for the same date of each month. This is not the same as every four weeks. It is possible, with this scheduling option, to schedule maintenance for the 15th of each month.
    - **Time—factory calendar**—As previously discussed, this setting is particularly useful for plants that close on particular days and no maintenance should be scheduled for those days. Maintenance will not be scheduled for days that are marked as non-working days in the selected factory calendar (in the "Factory calendar" field).

- *Start of cycle*—If a date is provided here, it serves as a default date during the initial scheduling of the maintenance plan.

Maintenance Plan Scheduling

Note that, until scheduling has been performed, no work orders or notifications (call objects) will be generated from a maintenance plan, even though it may be possible to see "scheduled" calls in the maintenance plan.

After the maintenance plan has been created and saved, it must be scheduled. Scheduling the maintenance plan involves little more than clicking the "Start" button on the scheduling screen and providing a start date for the plan, although there are some additional functions on the scheduling screen.

The primary consideration for a start date for the plan is when the first work order should be due. If the cycle is every four weeks, but the next work order should be due in one week, the plan should have a start date of three weeks ago. Keep in mind that, in this case, the task list should also have a key date of at least three weeks ago (of course, if it doesn't already, it's too late to change it now).

The intention of the "key date" functionality is to allow more than one version of a task list to exist. For example, it may be valid to perform a specific set of operations up to a certain date, but the set of operations used must change on that date. Although the same task list is used, its contents (operations) differ, depending on whether the task list is viewed with a key date prior to the change date or after. The key date can also be used to prevent the use of a task list prior to it being valid.

The default start date for the maintenance plan suggested by the system will either be the "Start of cycle" date that was entered in the maintenance plan or, if a "Start of cycle date" was not entered in the maintenance plan, the current date.

Once the date has been accepted or changed, a tentative schedule will be displayed. At this point, the plan has not been scheduled. Consider the displayed schedule a preview based on the scheduling parameters. The scheduling parameters can be viewed from here on the "Maintenance plan scheduling parameters" tab, but cannot be changed from here.

If the scheduling is not acceptable, it is still possible (if the "Save" button has not been used) to either click the "Undo scheduling" button or exit from the scheduling screen altogether, and then make any necessary changes to the maintenance plan.

Once scheduling has been performed, the first "call" will indicate "New start, " usually also with either "Save to call" or "Hold." Based on the scheduling parameters, "Save to call" indicates that the date on which the first work order should be created has already arrived or has passed. That work order will be created upon saving the scheduling. "Hold" indicates that the work order for that "call" will not be created after saving, since the call date has not yet arrived.

On the "Scheduled calls" tab, the "Plan date" indicates the scheduled start date for that "call, " or work order. The "Call date" indicates the date on which the work order will be created for that call.

When satisfied that the scheduling is as intended, the scheduling can be saved.

Note that, unless the appropriate work order type has been configured in the IMG as "immediate release, " any work orders created from a maintenance plan must still be released appropriately.

At this point, the work order process for preventive maintenance work orders is similar to the work order process for non-preventive work orders, with one possible exception. Notifications are commonly, but not always, used to accumulate information regarding breakdowns and malfunctions. This information can be analyzed over time, so that preventive maintenance plans can be created and adjusted to reduce the breakdowns and malfunctions. If this is the case, then notification information may not be maintained with preventive work orders. It is possible to prevent notifications from being created with preventive maintenance orders.

On the other hand, it is also possible to configure maintenance plans so that only notifications are created, rather than work orders, by the maintenance plan, if so desired. Determine and implement the configuration of notifications, work orders and maintenance plans that is the most appropriate.

An Additional Note on Maintenance Strategies

When defining a strategy-based task list, it is possible to indicate that some operations in the task list should be performed on a different cycle than other operations. For example, the same task list could include the operations required to perform an overhaul as well as an oil change. The overhaul operations, of course, should be performed less frequently than the oil change operations.

Let's assume that the oil change must occur every four weeks, while the overhaul must occur every 16 weeks. Operations 0010 through 0030 (the first three operations) define the steps required to perform the oil change, and operations 0040 through 0080 (the next five operations) define the steps required to perform the overhaul. The first three times that this task list is scheduled (as part of a maintenance plan), on weeks 4, 8 and 12, only operations 0010 through 0030 will be performed. However, on week 16, all of the operations should be performed.

Operations 0010 through 0030 are assigned the package (cycle) defined as 4 weeks. Operations 0040 through 0080 are assigned the package defined as 16 weeks.

In this case, the packages for 4 weeks and 16 weeks in the strategy must both use the same hierarchy level. That means that when both packages coincide, as they will on week 16 (and 32 and so on), the operations assigned both packages will be performed.

If the 16 week package had been defined with a higher hierarchy level than the 4 week package, on week 16 only those operations assigned the package with the higher hierarchy level will be scheduled.

To avoid the possible confusion of multiple hierarchy levels, many people find it more convenient to define the 4 week operations in one task list and the 16 week operations in a separate task list. They can then be scheduled to coincide with each other, although each has its own schedule. The primary disadvantage to this approach is that, on week 16, two separate work orders will be due, one for the oil change operations and the other for the overhaul operations. Even though the work may need to be performed at the same time by the same people, it will be listed on two separate work orders.

The system provides the flexibility to define maintenance scheduling based on a variety of requirements. Become familiar with the various methods of defining task lists and plans and, when properly defined, a substantial amount of time can be saved by the system generating and scheduling work orders as required.

Performance-based Maintenance

Performance-based maintenance is required when maintenance should be scheduled according to parameters that are not time-related. For example, if maintenance should be performed on a truck according to the number of kilometers it has traveled, performance-based maintenance scheduling is required.

The first step in setting up performance-based maintenance is to define a "measuring point" on the appropriate piece of equipment. This is a place where a measurement can be taken. For this example, the truck odometer can be defined as a measuring point. Note that before the measuring point can be created, a suitable "characteristic" must be defined in the classification area of SAP R/3. The characteristic will simply provide a definition for the type of data that the measuring point requires, such as the number of digits, the number of decimal places, etc.

The definition of the measuring point will include the current reading of the odometer as well as an annual estimate of the number of kilometers the truck will travel. The system uses these values to estimate a date on which the next maintenance will be required, even if the maintenance is based on the number of kilometers.

As "measurement readings" are taken on the odometer, preventive maintenance work orders may be created based on whether or not the reading is above the threshold defined for maintenance. In the SAP R/3 system, the recording of a measurement reading in the system creates a measurement document.

The basic SAP R/3 system assumes that, for the purposes of preventive maintenance, the measurement readings taken from a measuring point will either always increase or always decrease. Maintenance work can be scheduled in increments of the increase or on increments of the decrease. For readings that fluctuate, where maintenance should be performed when a reading falls outside, above or below set thresholds, the standard system cannot accommodate the generation of maintenance orders or notifications, although that functionality could be provided through the use of a "business add-in" or customer (user) exit.

Work Order (and/or Notification) Creation

In the Implementation Guide, the configuration for maintenance plan categories determines the "call object" that will be created on schedule from a maintenance plan, based on the category of the maintenance plan.

Although service entry sheets or inspection lots can be created from a maintenance plan, service entry sheets are used more in conjunction with a Materials Management external services requirements and inspection lots are use more in conjunction with Quality Assurance, so this description will focus more on the mainstream creation of work orders and/or notifications from maintenance plans.

A maintenance plan category can be configured to create either a notification or a work order. In older versions of R/3 Plant Maintenance, a notification could not be created directly from a maintenance plan.

If a maintenance plan category is configured to create a notification from a maintenance plan, of course a work order can then be manually created from the notification, if appropriate. If a maintenance plan category is configured to create a work order from a maintenance plan, a notification can then be manually created from the work order. Note that in R/3 Enterprise, the configuration step "Define Notification and Order Integration" can be used in part to have a notification created automatically when a work order is created.

Originally, the purpose of a notification was to provide notice that a breakdown or incident had happened, or that maintenance was otherwise required. Any statistical data captured in the notification, such as through the catalog codes for damage, cause, etc. was intended to support the reduction of "reactive" (breakdown, incident) work through the adoption of more preventive and predictive maintenance measures. However, many R/3 Plant Maintenance implementations determined that the catalog codes used in the notifications could also be used to perform analyses on preventive maintenance.

In addition, it is not always preferable for a work order to be produced automatically by a maintenance plan. It may, in some cases, be more beneficial for a notification to be produced on a regular basis for someone to determine whether the work is actually required prior to the creation of the work order.

If a work order is created directly from a maintenance plan, it is optional to then create a notification from such a work order. In fact, it may be prevented through configuration settings (or even vice-versa).

Assuming that a work order is produced from the maintenance plan, the remainder of the process is similar to that of the work order process, beginning with the release of the work order, described on page 203. The work order is released, work is performed, actual time is entered, either through the Cross-Application Time Sheet (CATS) or completion confirmations, goods are issued, the work order/operations are completed, the work order is settled, and finally closed.

Depending on the definition of a maintenance plan, the date and time of completion of a preventive maintenance work order may be critical to the scheduling of the subsequent work order(s) in the plan. Scheduling parameters may be set that require the current work order to be completed prior to the creation of a work order for the next call in the plan.

Also, additional scheduling parameters can be set that affect the scheduling of the next work order, depending on how early or how late the current work order is completed.

Reporting

The approach to reporting in the SAP R/3 system may be somewhat different than many people have experienced. Many legacy systems provided a finite quantity of predetermined, "canned" reports. Additional reports would require programming effort.

SAP's approach, from a Plant Maintenance module perspective, is to provide a method of reporting that allows the people using the system to easily define and lay out many different types of "list" reports without depending on programming requests. The reporting of lists, often referred to as "list editing," can be easily accomplished. In addition, lists can be exported in formats such as spreadsheets to enable further formatting and printing.

In addition to list editing, the Plant Maintenance module provides the "Plant Maintenance Information System" (PMIS), which is a subset of the Logistics Information System (LIS). The PMIS allows analysis based on predefined catalog codes in order to determine patterns identified during the accumulation of data. The PMIS also provides functionality such as the ability to automatically send a message if a specified threshold is reached, such as exceeding a specific figure for maintenance on a piece of equipment.

List Editing

List editing is actually comprised of "list change," "list display" and "list entry." "List entry," will not be discussed here, since it pertains to the entry of multiple records rather than reporting. The only difference between "list change" and "list display" is that, even though both will provide a list of work orders, for example, "list change" will allow changes to any of the work orders listed, while "list display" will not allow changes. List editing functionality can be found throughout the Plant Maintenance menus under "List Editing" menus, with the notable exception of list editing for work orders, which can be found under the menu "Order List" ("List of Orders" in previous versions).

There is a sequence of two screens involved with list editing and displaying a list of objects. The first screen is the selection screen. On the selection screen, entries can be made in numerous fields. When the "Execute" button is clicked on the selection screen, an object must match the entries made (or meet other criteria) on the selection screen in order to appear in the resulting list. A range of values can be entered by using "From" and "To" entries for each field, if desired. A list of individual values can be entered by using the "Multiple selection" button to the far right of the various fields.

The "Multiple selection" button can also be used to enter conditions such as "> $5000" (greater than five thousand dollars) for actual costs for work orders, for example.

Whatever the search criteria specified on the selection screen, an object must match the criteria in order to be displayed in the resulting list. If no objects meet the search criteria, a message will appear to that effect. If only one object matches the search criteria, then that single object will be displayed and no list will appear.

If numerous search criteria have been entered and it is expected that the same search criteria will be used repeatedly in the future, the criteria can be saved in a "selection variant." From the selection screen, before clicking the "Execute" button, follow the menu path **Goto → Variants → Save as Variant,** provide a variant name and a description and save the variant. Although there are numerous additional functions available on the variant definition screen, it is unnecessary to use any other functions in order to save your own entries for later use. To use the selection variant the next time it is required, follow the menu path **Goto → Variants → Get.**

As mentioned before, there is a sequence of two screens involved with list editing. The first screen was the selection screen. The second screen in the sequence is the display screen, which usually displays a list of the objects that match the search criteria as entered on the selection screen.

When the display screen first appears, it will contain the fields that were configured as default fields for that type of list display. Unwanted fields/columns can be removed and additional fields that may be available can be added to the display by clicking on the "Current…" button .

In the resulting "Change layout" window, there are two lists of fields. The list on the left shows the fields that are currently displayed in the report list display, while the list on the right shows fields that are not currently displayed but are available for display. The fields can be moved from one side to the other by selecting the field(s) and clicking on the appropriate direction button found between the two lists.

While still in the "Change layout" window, if the layout is one that will be used again, the layout can be saved in order to save time in the future by clicking on the "Save" button. A name and description have to be provided, along with checkboxes indicating whether the saved layout is user-specific (recommended, unless being created for all users) and/or whether this layout should be the default layout (recommended if this layout should always be displayed by default for this list of objects). Setting the default layout as user-specific is highly recommended unless purposely setting the default layout for all users.

Functions such as sorting, filtering, changing column widths, graphing, and downloading to applications such as spreadsheet applications are available from the list editing screens. Once the data has been downloaded to another application, of course all the functionality of that application is then available to manipulate, display and print the data.

The real benefit to reporting through list editing is the scope and variety of up-to-date information that is available in a variety of formats without having to involve others in developing custom reports. Of course, not every report requirement can be satisfied with a relatively simple list, so it is likely that some custom reports still must be developed, but the cost involved will likely be much less than it would have been without the availability of list editing.

The Plant Maintenance Information System (PMIS)

In order for meaningful information to be produced from the PMIS, the definition and use of catalog codes should be performed, although some information will still be available even without the use of catalogs.

Start with the information and data structures that are available within "Standard Analyses." If the structures and information available through

Standard Analyses seems limited, consider using Business Information Warehouse (BW) functionality.

While list editing can be considered a great method of obtaining "real time" information, the PMIS should be considered as a great view of longer term, historical information, excellent for comparing data month to month, for example.

A major benefit to the standard analysis (and flexible analysis) section of the PMIS is that it is possible to "drill down" on data. As with list editing, there is a two screen sequence involved with the PMIS. The first screen serves to restrict the data selection and the second screen is the display, or results screen.

Initially, the list displayed on the results screen may appear to contain a limited selection of data. However, an item on the list, usually in the leftmost column and usually colored blue, can be double-clicked in order to "drill-down" on that item. The item that was selected will then appear at the top of the display as a heading, and further information relevant to the heading will appear in a list. "Drilling down" on the information can continue until the preset drill down options have all been used.

It is possible, through menu selections and buttons on the screen, to change the drill down order, to sort the columns, to change the fields displayed, to download the data to a spreadsheet, and so on.

Within a drill down path in the PMIS, clicking the green "Back" arrow button will cause the display to "back up" one level in the drill down, while clicking the yellow "Exit" button will cause the display to return to the top level selection screen.

The Early Warning System

Another function found in the Plant Maintenance Information System menu that is worth mentioning is the "Early Warning System." This function can be set to provide an alert when a predefined threshold has been reached or exceeded.

There are two basic steps (and an additional note) required for the Early Warning System:

1. An "exception" must be created. This defines the data that the system will consider and the threshold at which exceptions will be reported.

a. An "info structure" must be entered, which corresponds to the info structures used in standard analysis in the PMIS.

b. "Characteristics" must be selected, which define the basic data for the reporting. As with the PMIS, these are the fields on which a user can "drill down."

c. "Requirements" must also be defined. The "requirements" include the number of previous periods to analyze, whether to include the current period and whether the conditions will be linked with an "and" or an "or."

d. "Key figures" must be selected. This is the actual data that will be reported.

e. Selecting one of the "key figures, " a "requirement" must be defined. For example, if the key figure "Actual breakdowns" is selected, a requirement could be defined, based on "threshold value analysis, " that reporting be performed when more than three actual breakdowns occur. During the definition of the "requirement, " specify whether the "requirement" be considered over the full range of periods selected, or in any one of the periods. For example, should three or more breakdowns in total in the last four periods be reported, or three or more breakdowns in any one of the last four periods?

f. "Follow-up processing" can then be defined. If a threshold, in our example, has been reached or exceeded, what action should be performed? The selection of follow-up processing options may be somewhat limited, depending on additional functionality that may or may not be installed with a specific SAP R/3 implementation. For example, it may be possible for the system to send mail to other SAP system users through the SAP R/3 system, but not to send email to an internet email address. Workflow and faxing are two of the other options that may be restricted, depending on whether that functionality has been enabled.

During the set up for follow-up processing, there is a checkbox to make the exception "active for periodic analysis." It is not necessary to check this box if the analysis is always to be performed on demand. However, if the analysis is intended to be run on a predetermined schedule, this box must be checked.

2. The exception must be run either on demand or on schedule, called *periodic analysis.*

   a. To run the exception on demand, the "Exception Analysis" menu item can be performed. This allows the user to restrict the selection based on the "characteristics" defined in step 1b, above.

   b. To schedule the exception, once or repeatedly, a "Periodic Analysis" must first be created. This step provides default selection values for the system to use when scheduling and running the analysis. Since periodic analysis enables the system to automate the analysis, there is no opportunity to prompt a user for selection values. If no restriction is desired, simply save the blank selection screen and name it.

   c. The "Dispatch" menu item can be used to schedule the analysis based on the "periodic analysis" previously created. Select one of the scheduling options and, if the analysis should be performed repeatedly automatically, check the "Periodic job" checkbox and provide a "Period value," which defines for the system the frequency on which the analysis should be performed.

An additional word on periodic analysis: Confirm with the SAP "Basis" personnel or system administrators the proper use of "background" or "batch" jobs before scheduling a periodic analysis. Although rare, from time to time something may go wrong with a scheduled job, such as a periodic analysis or many other types of programs, and the administrators must then determine who is responsible for a particular job. They may require naming or other standards in order to better manage the system. In an extreme case, a periodic analysis job may be simply cancelled, if required, by a system administrator. If that happens, and the administrator cannot determine who to contact, the periodic analysis may not run again in the future without being resubmitted.

Of course there are many additional options for configuring and administering SAP R/3 Plant Maintenance than can be covered in any text. The concepts, instructions, hints, tips, and suggestions contained in this text are a means of familiarizing the reader with how SAP R/3 can be used to manage Plant Maintenance.

The primary focus of this book is the configuration of SAP R/3 Plant Maintenance. The section regarding the administration of the Plant Maintenance module discusses the use of the module, but not in great detail, since the use of the module is determined somewhat by the way that it has been configured.

For more detailed information regarding the use and management of the R/3 Plant Maintenance module, an excellent resource is the book *SAP R/3 Plant Maintenance,* by Britta Stengl and Reinhard Ematinger (ISBN 0-201-67532-3).

ADDITIONAL RESOURCES

Google ™ directory's SAP categories and web pages:
http://directory.google.com/Top/Computers/Software/ERP/SAP/

SAP ™ web site:

http://www.sap.com

SAP ™ online help documentation:

http://help.sap.com

Americas' SAP User Group (ASUG®) web site:

http://www.asug.com

SAP ™ Education web site:

http://www.sap.com/education/

APPENDIX A: TOPICS NOT COVERED

Classification

Classification is a cross-application function in SAP R/3, which means that the functionality can be used by more than one module.

Within a Plant Maintenance context, equipment, for example, can be assigned to a "class." Each class has one or more "characteristics."

A class for electric motors may include characteristics such as "Voltage, " "Frequency, " and "Speed Rating." A characteristic, in turn, has a value (it can, in fact, have multiple values if defined as such).

The value for the "Voltage" characteristic could be 575 (volts), the value for "Frequency" could be 60 (Hertz), and the value for "Speed Rating" could be 3, 600 (R.P.M.). By using classification functionality, it is quite simple to determine what other 575 volt, 60 Hz., 3, 600 RPM motors are available.

CATS (Cross Application Time Sheet)

Cross Application Time Sheet functionality is often implemented from a Human Resources (HR) perspective. It enables employees to enter the time they spend doing work, but in a central point of entry. If implemented, from a Human Resources and Plant Maintenance perspective, it enables the employee to enter his or her time once and the time is properly attributed to the employee's HR record, ensuring payment for the services. In addition, where relevant, the time is also attributed to the Plant Maintenance work order on which the employee worked, ensuring that the work order is properly charged for that employee's (work center's) activity rate.

Document Management

Document management functionality can be used with the Plant Maintenance module, as well as other modules. While limited Document Management functionality can be implemented to accommodate simply linking a document to a piece of equipment, for example, the Document Management module consists of much more functionality for the complete management of documents. In addition, web-based interfaces can be used to take advantage of some existing external document management systems.

Archiving

While master data, such as functional locations and equipment, as well as transactional data, such as work orders, can be "marked" for deletion by authorized users of the system, those records are not actually physically deleted from the system until "archiving and deletion" have been performed.

Usually, the archiving process is not performed by users of the system, nor even those responsible for managing a particular module. Often, the process falls within the scope of those responsible for Basis and the management of the system, but not always.

Archiving is a function that is often overlooked during the initial implementation of an SAP R/3 system, since its function is not strictly necessary for work in the system to begin. However, over time, data is created by accident and even data that is meaningful accumulates, requiring more and more storage (disk) space as well as impacting system response times. It takes longer for any system to find a specific record among 500, 000 records than it does for the system to find a specific record among 10, 000 records, for example. Archiving can be used to reduce the number of "active" records within the R/3 system.

Proper archiving, however, requires some thought. What types of records in which modules are candidates for archiving? How long must records be retained in order to satisfy external, perhaps legal, requirements as well as internal requirements? How often should records that are marked for deletion be physically deleted through the archiving process? Arriving at a good archiving plan requires the cooperation of the individuals responsible for managing each module as well as that of the Basis individuals.

Customer Service (Formerly Service Management)

While the Customer Service module relies largely on Plant Maintenance functionality, it also relies on Sales and Distribution (SD) functionality. For that reason alone, not enough attention can be given to the subject in a Plant Maintenance context.

One reason for using Customer Service functionality is when a maintenance contract is "sold" to a customer, requiring SD functionality, for which the maintenance must then be performed, requiring PM functionality. There are variations on that process as well as additional processes that may require Customer Service functionality.

Work Clearance Management (WCM)

Work Clearance, which includes the ability to manage lockout/tag-out functionality, particularly as required by nuclear facilities, does not appear in the Plant Maintenance menus by default as of the R/3 Enterprise (4.7) version of R/3.

If Work Clearance Management is required, the appropriate R/3 Enterprise Extension Set must be activated as described below.

In the Implementation Guide (transaction code SPRO), find the step named "Activation Switch for SAP R/3 Enterprise Extension Set." Click the Execute button to its left. Check the checkbox beside "PLM Extension" and save the change. Do not activate other extension sets without understanding the implications. Activating an extension set will change Implementation Guide structures and menu structures. It may not be possible to deactivate an extension if configuration is changed or data is saved within those structures (menus).

For many maintenance shops, the overhead required to maintain Work Clearance Management may not be worth the benefits delivered, but if lockout/tag-out functionality is critical and must be meticulously managed and recorded, WCM may be an essential add-on.

Appendix B: PM Transaction Codes

Functional Location-related Transaction Codes:

IL01	Functional Location Create	IL10	Alternative Labeling Reusability
IL02	Functional Location Change	IL11	Reference Location Create
IL03	Functional Location Display	IL12	Reference Location Change
IL04	F.L. List Editing Create	IL13	Reference Location Display
IL05	F.L. List Editing Change	IL14	Ref. Location List Editing Create
IL06	F.L. List Editing Display	IL15	Ref. Location List Editing Change
IL07	F.L. List Editing Display Multi-level	IH07	Ref. Location List Editing Display
IL08	F.L. Create (Customer Service)	IH01	Functional Location Structural Display
IL09	Alternative Labeling User Profile	IH02	Ref. Location Structural Display

Equipment-related Transaction Codes:

IE01	Equipment Create (General)	IE10	Equipment List Editing Create
IE02	Equipment Change	IE20	Find Replacement Equipment Using Classification
IE03	Equipment Display	IE25	Equipment Create (PRT)
IE05	Equipment List Editing Change	IE31	Equipment Create (Fleet Object)
IE06	Equipment List Editing Change (Customer Service)	IE36	Equipment List Editing Display (Vehicles)
IE07	Equipment List Editing Display (Multi-level)	IE37	Equipment List Editing Change (Vehicles)
IE08	Equipment Create (Customer Service)	IE4N	Remove Equipment, Place in Storage

Material-related Transaction Codes (this is not a complete listing of material-related transaction codes):

MM01	Material Create (General)	IH09	Material List Editing Display
MM02	Material Change	MMP1	Material Create (Special) Maintenance Assembly
MM03	Material Display	MMS1	Material Create (Special) Services
MMBE	Stock Overview		

Bill-of-material-related Transaction Codes:

IB11	Functional Location BOM Create
IB12	Functional Location BOM Change
IB13	Functional Location BOM Display
IB17	Functional Location BOM Plant Assignment Create
IB18	Functional Location BOM Plant Assignment Display
IB19	Functional Location BOM Plant Assignment Change

Miscellaneous Transaction Codes:

IBIP	PM Batch Input Utility	SU51	Maintain User Profile/Address
SMX	Display Own Jobs	SU52	Maintain User Profile/Parameters
SU50	Maintain User Profile/Defaults	SU53	Authorizations Required for Transaction

INDEX

A

Alternative Labeling, 45, 54-55
Archiving, 130, 234
Assets, 49

B

Bills of Material, 9, 44, 50-52, 69, 72, 74-76, 184, 191
    Control Data, 72, 169-170
        BOM Status, 72
        Default Values, 39, 69, 71-73, 91-92, 106, 113, 128, 135, 139, 148, 152, 158, 163-164, 193, 202
        Modification Parameters, 72
    Copy Default Values, 73
    Default Values for Item Status, 73
    Equipment BOM, 191
    Functional Location BOM, 191
    History Requirements, 74
    Item Data, 74-75, 85
        Item Categories, 74, 148
        Material Provision Indicators, 75
        Material Types, 73-74
        Object Types, 8, 25, 29, 41, 59, 66-69, 74
        Spare Part Indicators, 75
    Material BOM, 73, 191
    Usage, 51, 59, 61-62, 67, 72-73, 75, 89-90, 95, 193
    Valid Material Types for BOM Header, 73

C

Catalogs, 97-99, 108, 114-115, 117-119, 199, 206-207, 225
    Activities, 72, 85, 98, 108, 114-118, 165, 196
    Causes, 29, 57-58, 99, 115, 117, 165, 168, 170
    Change for Notification Type, 109
    Directory, 117, 231
    Field Selection for List Display of Partner Data, 119
    Maintaining, 73, 78, 81-82, 100, 116, 141, 186, 196, 217
    Object Parts, 115-116
    Overview of Damage, 115-116
    Partner Determination, 39, 56, 63, 108, 119, 152
    Profile, 63, 66-67, 92, 98, 103, 109, 115, 118, 120, 122-124, 134-135, 147, 202
        Code Groups, 98, 115, 117-118
        Codes, 14-15, 23-24, 34, 39, 98-99, 115-118, 123, 204, 206-207, 222-223, 225, 237-238
    Profiles, 23-24, 31, 43, 59-60, 63, 66, 70, 91-92, 103, 108, 118-119, 122-124, 130, 134-135, 147, 171, 189
    Tasks, 18-20, 48, 53, 77-79, 86, 89, 92, 98-99, 109, 115-116, 118, 120, 123, 136, 189, 211-212
CATS *See* Cross Application Time Sheet
Classification, 25, 33, 39, 44, 52, 127, 160, 189, 221, 233
Client, 2, 5-7, 15-17, 20-21, 34, 61
    Client-dependent, 7

239

Client-independent, 7
Condition Indicator, 127
  Operation Effects, 128
  System Conditions, 127, 151
Configuration Data, 7-8, 19, 182
Cost Centers, 6, 8-9, 85, 96-97, 192
Cost Elements, 8, 105-106, 172
Cross Application Time Sheet, 163, 169, 203, 206, 233
Customer Service, 30, 40-41, 65, 69-70, 96-97, 105-106, 109-110, 112, 114, 118, 120, 127, 129, 131-132, 150, 160, 162, 172, 234-235

D

Data
  Inheritance, 46-47, 49, 183
  Transfer, 46, 71, 101, 104, 137, 142, 165, 169, 174-175
Document Management, 26, 233-234

E

Early Warning System, 226
  Periodic Analysis, 227-228
Engineering Change Management, 25, 74
  Engineering Change Orders, 25
  Engineering Change Requests, 25
  Revision Levels, 25
Equipment, 2, 8, 24-29, 31-35, 37-39, 41-53, 58-71, 76, 78-80, 83, 91, 95-98, 101, 107, 110, 114-118, 121, 124-125, 127-128, 131, 134, 151, 156, 158-159, 172, 175-178, 182-184, 186-191, 200-202, 205, 208-209, 211, 213-214, 221, 223, 233-234
  Equipment Category, 28-29, 37, 59-63, 67, 70
    Additional Business Views, 60

Field Selection for Multi-Level List Displays, 58, 65, 128, 163
Installation, 48, 59, 62, 186, 189
List Editing, 33, 37-38, 58, 64-65, 69, 71, 85, 93, 96, 128, 143, 163, 171, 185, 223-226
List Structure, 64, 69
Master Record Field Selection, 63
Multilingual Text, 63
Number Ranges, 25, 27-29, 34-35, 38, 59-61, 68-70, 83-84, 91, 100, 105, 112, 132-133
Partner Determination Procedure, 39, 63, 108, 119, 152
Usage History, 59, 61
Usage List, 62
User Status Profile, 63, 122-123

F

Field Selection, 35-37, 40, 57-58, 62-63, 65, 68, 71, 84-88, 90, 92, 111, 119, 128, 140, 161-163, 171
  Disp., 36
  Hide, 35-36, 57, 161
  HiLi, 37
  Input, 36-37, 88, 161, 175-177
  Req., 36, 141
Fleet Management, 66, 68, 174
  Assign View Profile, 66
  Calculation Method, 67
  Consumable Types, 67
  Engine Types, 67
  Equipment Categories, 27-28, 37, 41, 59-60, 62-63, 66, 70
  Field Selection, 35-37, 40, 57-58, 62-63, 65, 68, 71, 84-88, 90, 92, 111, 119, 128, 140, 161-163, 171
  Object Types, 8, 25, 29, 41, 59, 66-69, 74

Special Measurement Positions, 67
Units of Measurement, 67
Usage Types, 67
Functional Location, 32-33, 39, 41, 44-51, 53-59, 62, 68, 76, 91, 107, 124, 131, 134, 159, 175, 177, 182-191, 201
   Category, 27-29, 33-35, 37-38, 56, 59-63, 67, 70, 83, 86-88, 105-106, 148-149, 158, 172-173, 194, 196, 221-222
   Field Selection, 35-37, 40, 57-58, 62-63, 65, 68, 71, 84-88, 90, 92, 111, 119, 128, 140, 161-163, 171
   Field Selection for Multi-Level List Displays, 58, 65, 128, 163
   Labeling Systems, 55
   List Editing, 33, 37-38, 58, 64-65, 69, 71, 85, 93, 96, 128, 143, 163, 171, 185, 223-226
   Numbers/Identifiers, 184
   Reference Functional Location, 45-46, 48-49, 56-57, 186
   Structural Display, 44, 56-57, 64, 69, 184
   Structure Indicator, 46, 53-55, 185
   Subordinate Functional Location, 183
   Superior Functional Location, 49, 183-184, 187

I

Implementation Guide, 6, 8, 12-14, 21, 30-32, 35, 37, 42, 44, 46, 49, 53, 76-77, 82, 86-87, 89, 100, 103, 108-109, 113, 115, 117, 125, 148, 174, 179, 183, 189, 193-194, 196-197, 199, 201, 203-205, 208, 221, 235
   Enterprise IMG, 13
   Project IMG, 13, 15, 30

SAP Reference IMG, 12-13
Instance, 4-8, 16, 18, 20-21, 28, 35, 102, 119, 152, 182

L

List Display, 33, 37, 40, 57-59, 65, 71, 90, 93, 119, 124, 143, 223-225
List Editing, 33, 37-38, 58, 64-65, 69, 71, 85, 93, 96, 128, 143, 163, 171, 185, 223-226
   Field Selection for Multi Level List Displays, 53, 74, 81, 144, 179
List Variants, 128, 163

M

Maintenance Activity Types, 139-140
Maintenance and Service Notifications, 107
Maintenance and Service Orders, 129, 140
   Completion Confirmations, 163-164, 168, 171, 222
      Causes for Variances, 170
      Control Parameters, 81, 164
         Checks, 131, 144, 165
      Control Data, 72, 169-170
      Default Values, 39, 69, 71-73, 91-92, 106, 113, 128, 135, 139, 148, 152, 158, 163-164, 193, 202
      HR Update, 168-169
      Logs/Error Handling, 167
      Material Movements, 168
      Selection, 26, 33, 35-38, 40, 43-44, 51-52, 57-58, 62-65, 68-69, 71, 75-76, 84-88, 90, 92-93, 111, 118-119, 124, 126-128, 136-137, 140, 143, 160-163,

168, 171, 184-185, 205, 224, 226-228
  Execution Time for Confirmation Processes, 169-170
  Field Selection, 35-37, 40, 57-58, 62-63, 65, 68, 71, 84-88, 90, 92, 111, 119, 128, 140, 161-163, 171
  List Editing, 33, 37-38, 58, 64-65, 69, 71, 85, 93, 96, 128, 143, 163, 171, 185, 223-226
  Parallelized Confirmation Processes, 170
  Schedule Background Jobs, 170
  Screen Templates, 110, 171, 204
Control Keys, 89, 92, 95, 139, 156, 169
Control Keys for Order Types, 139
Costing Data, 140
General Data, 41, 72-74, 148, 188-189
  Accounting Indicators, 149, 174
  Basic Date, 151
  Component Item Categories, 148
  Movement Types, 70, 148, 210
  Operating Conditions, 151
  Priorities, 75, 108, 120, 150
Goods Movements, 71, 143, 167
Inspection Control, 145
  Batch Assignment, 147
  Capacity Availability, 147
  Material Availability, 146
  PRT Availability, 146
Inspection Types, 134
List Editing, 33, 37-38, 58, 64-65, 69, 71, 85, 93, 96, 128, 143, 163, 171, 185, 223-226
  List Variants, 128, 163
Notification and Order Integration, 138, 222

Number Ranges, 25, 27-29, 34-35, 38, 59-61, 68-70, 83-84, 91, 100, 105, 112, 132-133
Object Information, 41, 43-44, 124-127, 131, 159-161
  Information Keys to Order Types, 161
  Keys, 31, 41, 43, 88-89, 92, 95, 124, 126-127, 139, 156, 159, 161, 169-170
Order Types, 100, 113-114, 129-135, 137-140, 143, 148, 151-153, 157-158, 161, 170, 182
Print Control, 103, 120-121, 157
  Message Control, 158
  Settlement Areas, 158
  Shop Papers Forms and Output, 102, 120, 157
  Control Keys, 89, 92, 95, 139, 156, 169
  Formulas, 75, 95-96, 156, 194, 196-197
Profile Assignments, 135
Scheduling, 77, 79-82, 84-85, 88-89, 92, 95, 150-151, 153-156, 170, 195-196, 201, 211, 214-221, 223, 228
  External Scheduling, 155
  Parameters, 72, 79-81, 88, 93, 95, 101, 114, 130, 150, 153-154, 156, 164, 171, 202, 214-216, 218-219, 221, 223
  Revisions, 155
  Types, 6, 8, 15, 25, 27-29, 38, 41-42, 50, 52, 54, 59, 66-70, 73-74, 86-87, 89-91, 93, 95, 97-98, 100, 104, 108-114, 118-121, 123, 126-127, 129-135, 137-140, 143, 147-148, 150-154, 157-159, 161, 170, 182, 191-193, 198-199, 204, 210, 212, 223, 228, 234

Settlement Rule, 136, 208
Standard Texts, 113, 148
Task List Data, 135
User Status, 24, 31, 63, 121-124, 152
    Partner Determination, 39, 56, 63, 108, 119, 152
    Workflow, 109, 120, 129, 142-143, 145, 227
Maintenance and Service Processing, 82-83, 100
    ABC Indicators, 42, 83, 101
    Activate Printing in Online Processing, 102
    Allocation Structures, 104
    Authorizations, 6, 22-25, 30-31, 82, 100, 123-124
    Background Jobs for PDC, 100
    Consistency of Value Category Assignment, 106
    Cost Elements to Value Categories, 105
    Default Values for Value Categories, 106
    Download, 101, 103, 226
    Download Parameters for PDC, 101
    General Order Settlement, 103
    Number Ranges for Settlement Documents, 105
    PA Transfer Structure, 104
    Planner Groups, 24, 42, 83, 91, 101
    Plant Sections, 42, 82, 101
    Print Diversion, 102, 121, 157-158
    Printer, 102, 121, 157-158
    Quotation Creation and Billing for Service Orders, 106
    Settings for Display of Costs, 105, 172
    Settlement Profiles, 103
    Value Categories, 105-106, 172-174, 202
    Value Fields, 104

    Version for Cost Estimates for Orders, 106
Maintenance Plans, 77-78, 82-84, 101, 138, 198, 211-212, 219, 222
    ABC Indicators, 42, 83, 101
    Authorizations, 6, 22-25, 30-31, 82, 100, 123-124
    Field Selection, 35-37, 40, 57-58, 62-63, 65, 68, 71, 84-88, 90, 92, 111, 119, 128, 140, 161-163, 171
    Field Selection for Operation Data, 85
    List Editing, 33, 37-38, 58, 64-65, 69, 71, 85, 93, 96, 128, 143, 163, 171, 185, 223-226
    Maintenance Planner Groups, 42, 83
    Number Ranges, 25, 27-29, 34-35, 38, 59-61, 68-70, 83-84, 91, 100, 105, 112, 132-133
    Number Ranges for Maintenance Items, 84
    Plan Categories, 83, 221
    Plant Sections, 42, 82, 101
    Sort Fields, 84
Master Data, 7-8, 12, 30, 32, 53, 58, 88, 151, 181-182, 202, 234
    Authorization Keys, 31, 124
    Authorizations, 6, 22-25, 30-31, 82, 100, 123-124
    Currency, 32, 172
    User Status, 24, 31, 63, 121-124, 152
Matchcode, 8
Materials, 2, 6, 8-9, 22, 25, 44, 50-52, 67, 69-71, 73-75, 79, 92, 95-96, 99, 131, 134, 141-148, 155-157, 162, 165, 168, 182, 184, 187-188, 190-191, 197-198, 200-203, 205, 207-212, 222
Measurement Documents, 34-35, 38, 174
    List Editing, 33, 37-38, 58, 64-65, 69, 71, 85, 93, 96, 128, 143, 163, 171, 185, 223-226

244 • Enterprise Asset Management

Number Ranges, 25, 27-29, 34-35, 38, 59-61, 68-70, 83-84, 91, 100, 105, 112, 132-133
Measuring Points, 34-35, 38, 52, 67, 174, 213
  Categories, 27-28, 32-34, 37-38, 41, 56, 59-60, 62-63, 66, 68, 70, 74, 83, 105-106, 148, 172-174, 202, 221, 231
  Field Selection, 35-37, 40, 57-58, 62-63, 65, 68, 71, 84-88, 90, 92, 111, 119, 128, 140, 161-163, 171
  List Editing, 33, 37-38, 58, 64-65, 69, 71, 85, 93, 96, 128, 143, 163, 171, 185, 223-226
  Number Ranges, 25, 27-29, 34-35, 38, 59-61, 68-70, 83-84, 91, 100, 105, 112, 132-133
mySAP, 2-3

N

Notifications, 31, 39, 41, 43-44, 83, 96-100, 102-103, 107-109, 111-115, 119-125, 127-129, 138, 150, 152, 159-160, 163, 182, 199-200, 202, 207, 218-219, 221-222
  Activity Report, 97, 110, 199-200
  Additional Functions, 23, 120, 169, 218, 224
  Allow Change, 158, 224
  Assign to Order Types, 113
  Authorization Keys, 31, 124
  Creating, 6, 13, 20, 24, 28, 34-35, 43, 46, 48-49, 52, 59, 70, 78, 86-87, 89, 92, 95, 112, 114-115, 117, 129-130, 175, 193, 212-213, 216
  Define Printer, 102, 121, 157
  Field Selection, 35-37, 40, 57-58, 62-63, 65, 68, 71, 84-88, 90, 92, 111, 119, 128, 140, 161-163, 171
  Maintenance Request, 97, 110, 199
  Malfunction Report, 97, 199
  Number Ranges, 25, 27-29, 34-35, 38, 59-61, 68-70, 83-84, 91, 100, 105, 112, 132-133
  Print Control, 103, 120-121, 157
  Response Time Monitoring, 109, 120
  Selection Profiles, 124
  Standard Texts for Short Messages, 113, 148
  Status Profile, 63, 109, 122-123
  Transaction Start Value, 107, 113
  Types, 6, 8, 15, 25, 27-29, 38, 41-42, 50, 52, 54, 59, 66-70, 73-74, 86-87, 89-91, 93, 95, 97-98, 100, 104, 108-114, 118-121, 123, 126-127, 129-135, 137-140, 143, 147-148, 150-154, 157-159, 161, 170, 182, 191-193, 198-199, 204, 210, 212, 223, 228, 234
    Long Text Control, 108, 111
    Screen Templates, 110, 171, 204
  User Status, 24, 31, 63, 121-124, 152
  Workflow, 109, 120, 129, 142-143, 145, 227
Number Ranges, 25, 27-29, 34-35, 38, 59-61, 68-70, 83-84, 91, 100, 105, 112, 132-133
  Buffering, 29
  Defining, 23, 27-29, 33, 44, 47-48, 52, 54, 73, 85-86, 105, 112, 122, 132, 150, 152, 172, 187, 191-192, 207, 212-213, 219-220
  External Number Range, 26, 132-133
  Internal Number Range, 26, 28
  Mixed Number Range, 26

O

Object Information, 41, 43-44, 124-127, 131, 159-161
Object Information Keys, 41, 43, 126-127, 159, 161
Object Links, 68-69, 189-190
   List Editing, 33, 37-38, 58, 64-65, 69, 71, 85, 93, 96, 128, 143, 163, 171, 185, 223-226
   List Editing for Material Data, 69
   Media, 68
   Number Ranges, 25, 27-29, 34-35, 38, 59-61, 68-70, 83-84, 91, 100, 105, 112, 132-133
   Object Types, 8, 25, 29, 41, 59, 66-69, 74
   Structural Display, 44, 56-57, 64, 69, 184
   Transaction Based Default Values, 69

P

Partners, 39, 63, 119, 155
   Copy Partners, 39
   Partner Determination, 39, 56, 63, 108, 119, 152
PDC *See* Plant Data Collection
Permits, 26, 32-34, 51, 74, 156, 195
   Categories, 27-28, 32-34, 37-38, 41, 56, 59-60, 62-63, 66, 68, 70, 74, 83, 105-106, 148, 172-174, 202, 221, 231
   Groups, 6, 21, 24, 28, 32-33, 42-43, 47, 60, 83, 91, 94-95, 98, 101, 106-107, 111-112, 115, 117-119, 133, 136, 144, 189, 208
   List Editing, 33, 37-38, 58, 64-65, 69, 71, 85, 93, 96, 128, 143, 163, 171, 185, 223-226
Plant Data Collection, 100-101, 142
Plant Maintenance Information System, 49, 99, 105, 114, 172-173, 179, 223, 225-226
   Currency for Maintenance Statistics, 32, 172
   Customer-Specific Key Figures, 173
      Measurement Document Update, 174
      Value Categories, 105-106, 172-174, 202
   Early Warning System, 226
   Updating, 82, 169, 172, 174, 179
   Value Categories, 105-106, 172-174, 202
Plants, 8, 21-22, 24, 28, 44, 47, 53, 112, 130, 133, 170, 190, 216-217
Planning Plants, 22
PMIS *See* Plant Maintenance Information System
Preventive Maintenance, 2, 76-77, 81-82, 96, 138, 181, 198, 210-211, 219, 221-223
   Maintenance Calls, 81-82
      Deadline Monitoring, 81-82
      Releasing Calls Manually, 81
      Skipping Calls, 81
   Maintenance Items, 78-79, 84, 138, 214
   Maintenance Package, 77-78
   Maintenance Plans, 77-78, 82-84, 101, 138, 198, 211-212, 219, 222
      Maintaining, 73, 78, 81-82, 100, 116, 141, 186, 196, 217
      Scheduling, 77, 79-82, 84-85, 88-89, 92, 95, 150-151, 153-156, 170, 195-196, 201, 211, 214-221, 223, 228
      Initial Start, 79-80
      Start In Cycle, 80

Maintenance Strategies, 77, 219
Performance-Based Maintenance, 213, 221
Task Lists, 25, 48, 77, 84, 89-95, 136, 193, 203, 212, 220
Preventive Maintenance Process, 181, 210
　Maintenance Plan Creation, 211-212
　Maintenance Plan Scheduling, 79, 211, 215, 218
　Task List Creation, 210-211
Production Resources/Tools, 94
　Authorization Group, 23, 42-43, 94
　Control Keys, 89, 92, 95, 139, 156, 169
　Formulas, 75, 95-96, 156, 194, 196-197
　Group Keys, 95
　Status, 15, 23-24, 31, 61, 63, 72-73, 90, 94, 103, 109, 121-124, 141, 146-147, 152, 161, 203, 206-207
　Task List Usage Keys, 89, 95
PRT *See* Production Resources/Tools

R

Reference Functional Location, 45-46, 48-49, 56-57, 186
　Category, 27-29, 33-35, 37-38, 56, 59-63, 67, 70, 83, 86-88, 105-106, 148-149, 158, 172-173, 194, 196, 221-222
　Field Selection, 35-37, 40, 57-58, 62-63, 65, 68, 71, 84-88, 90, 92, 111, 119, 128, 140, 161-163, 171
　List Editing, 33, 37-38, 58, 64-65, 69, 71, 85, 93, 96, 128, 143, 163, 171, 185, 223-226
　Structural Display, 44, 56-57, 64, 69, 184

Reporting, 32, 49, 74, 114, 117, 126, 129-130, 159, 172-173, 179, 181, 189, 192, 194, 199-200, 223, 225, 227
　List Editing, 33, 37-38, 58, 64-65, 69, 71, 85, 93, 96, 128, 143, 163, 171, 185, 223-226

S

Search Helps, 40
Security, 6, 18, 22-24, 30-31, 43, 61, 81-82, 94, 100, 123-124
　Authorization, 19-20, 23-25, 31, 42-43, 71, 94, 123-124, 170, 182
　Roles, 6, 22-25, 30-31, 82, 94, 100
Serial Number Management, 70
　Deactivate Lock for Internal Assignment, 70
　Default Equipment Categories, 59, 62, 70
　Field Selection, 35-37, 40, 57-58, 62-63, 65, 68, 71, 84-88, 90, 92, 111, 119, 128, 140, 161-163, 171
　List Editing, 33, 37-38, 58, 64-65, 69, 71, 85, 93, 96, 128, 143, 163, 171, 185, 223-226
　Serial Number Profiles, 70
　Serialization Attributes, 70
　Transfer of Stock Check Indicator, 71
Service Contracts, 96
　List Editing, 33, 37-38, 58, 64-65, 69, 71, 85, 93, 96, 128, 143, 163, 171, 185, 223-226
Service Management *See* Customer Service
Structural Displays and BOMs, 44
System Enhancements and Data Transfer, 174
　Business Add-Ins, 174
　Execute Data Transfer, 175

T

Task Lists, 25, 48, 77, 84, 89-95, 136, 193, 203, 212, 220
  Control Keys, 89, 92, 95, 139, 156, 169
  Field Selection, 35-37, 40, 57-58, 62-63, 65, 68, 71, 84-88, 90, 92, 111, 119, 128, 140, 161-163, 171
  List Editing, 33, 37-38, 58, 64-65, 69, 71, 85, 93, 96, 128, 143, 163, 171, 185, 223-226
  Number Ranges for Equipment, 29, 91
  Number Ranges for General Maintenance, 91
  Planner Group, 24, 42, 82-83, 91, 101-102, 138
  Presetting for Free Assignment of Material, 92
  Profiles, 23-24, 31, 43, 59-60, 63, 66, 70, 91-92, 103, 108, 118-119, 122-124, 130, 134-135, 147, 171, 189
  Status, 15, 23-24, 31, 61, 63, 72-73, 90, 94, 103, 109, 121-124, 141, 146-147, 152, 161, 203, 206-207
  Suitabilities, 89-90, 93
  Usage, 51, 59, 61-62, 67, 72-73, 75, 89-90, 95, 193
  User Fields, 93
Technical Objects, 33-34, 41-44, 59, 66, 79, 82-83, 101, 182, 184-185, 189, 213
  ABC Indicators, 42, 83, 101
  Authorization Groups, 42, 94
  Equipment type, 41, 59, 116
  Object Hierarchy, 44-45
    Equipment, 2, 8, 24-29, 31-35, 37-39, 41-53, 58-71, 76, 78-80, 83, 91, 95-98, 101, 107, 110, 114-118, 121, 124-125, 127-128, 131, 134, 151, 156, 158-159, 172, 175-178, 182-184, 186-191, 200-202, 205, 208-209, 211, 213-214, 221, 223, 233-234
    Bills of material, 9, 44, 50-52, 69, 72, 74-76, 184, 191
    Materials, 2, 6, 8-9, 22, 25, 44, 50-52, 67, 69-71, 73-75, 79, 92, 95-96, 99, 131, 134, 141-148, 155-157, 162, 165, 168, 182, 184, 187-188, 190-191, 197-198, 200-203, 205, 207-212, 222
    sub-equipment, 34, 44, 49, 184
    Functional Location, 32-33, 39, 41, 44-51, 53-59, 62, 68, 76, 91, 107, 124, 131, 134, 159, 175, 177, 182-191, 201
  Object Information Keys, 41, 43, 126-127, 159, 161
  Planner Groups, 24, 42, 83, 91, 101
  Plant Sections, 42, 82, 101
  View Profiles, 43, 59-60, 66, 189
Transaction Codes, 14, 23-24, 39, 237-238
Transactional Data, 7-8, 16, 182, 234
Transporting, 4, 6, 16, 20, 28, 61, 115
Transports, 11, 15, 20-21
  Change Requests, 11, 15-18, 20, 25

U

Unit Testing, 5-6

V

ValueSAP, 4

W

Warranty, 38-39, 43

Categories, 27-28, 32-34, 37-38, 41, 56, 59-60, 62-63, 66, 68, 70, 74, 83, 105-106, 148, 172-174, 202, 221, 231

Counters, 39

Transaction Start Default, 39

Types, 6, 8, 15, 25, 27-29, 38, 41-42, 50, 52, 54, 59, 66-70, 73-74, 86-87, 89-91, 93, 95, 97-98, 100, 104, 108-114, 118-121, 123, 126-127, 129-135, 137-140, 143, 147-148, 150-154, 157-159, 161, 170, 182, 191-193, 198-199, 204, 210, 212, 223, 228, 234

    Number Ranges, 25, 27-29, 34-35, 38, 59-61, 68-70, 83-84, 91, 100, 105, 112, 132-133

WCM *See* Work Clearance Management

Work Centers, 9-10, 79, 85-89, 93, 136, 152, 182, 191, 216

    Control Keys, 89, 92, 95, 139, 156, 169

    Default Work Center, 89

    Employees Responsible, 88

    Field Selection, 35-37, 40, 57-58, 62-63, 65, 68, 71, 84-88, 90, 92, 111, 119, 128, 140, 161-163, 171

    Parameters, 72, 79-81, 88, 93, 95, 101, 114, 130, 150, 153-154, 156, 164, 171, 202, 214-216, 218-219, 221, 223

    Screen Sequence, 86-87, 90, 197, 226

    Standard Value Key, 88, 193

    Suitabilities, 89-90, 93

    Task List Usage Key, 89, 95

Types, 6, 8, 15, 25, 27-29, 38, 41-42, 50, 52, 54, 59, 66-70, 73-74, 86-87, 89-91, 93, 95, 97-98, 100, 104, 108-114, 118-121, 123, 126-127, 129-135, 137-140, 143, 147-148, 150-154, 157-159, 161, 170, 182, 191-193, 198-199, 204, 210, 212, 223, 228, 234

Work Clearance Management, 235

Work Order Cycle, 77, 96, 136

Work Order Process, 6, 181, 197-199, 210, 219, 222

    Findings (Catalog Entries) are Recorded in the Notification, 198, 206, 211

    Materials are Used, 198, 205, 211

    Notification Creation, 107, 109, 197, 199, 211, 221

    Operations are Completed, 198, 206, 211, 223

    Work is Performed, 85, 139, 197, 203, 211, 222

    Work Order Creation, 197, 200

    Work Order is Closed, 198, 209, 211

    Work Order is Settled, 198, 208, 211, 223

    Work Order is Technically Completed, 198, 206-207, 211

    Work Order Release, 197, 203, 211

Work Orders, 129, 140 *See* Maintenance and Service Orders

    Completion, 32, 93, 96, 99, 136-137, 163-168, 171, 176-177, 201, 204-209, 215-217, 222-223

    Refurbishment Work Orders, 131, 209

0-595-32575-0

Printed in the United States
81641LV00003B/269